Aristotle, Robert Williams

The Nicomachean Ethics of Aristotle

Aristotle, Robert Williams

The Nicomachean Ethics of Aristotle

ISBN/EAN: 9783741179600

Manufactured in Europe, USA, Canada, Australia, Japa

Cover: Foto ©Andreas Hilbeck / pixelio.de

Manufactured and distributed by brebook publishing software (www.brebook.com)

Aristotle, Robert Williams

The Nicomachean Ethics of Aristotle

THE NICOMACHEAN ETHICS
OF
ARISTOTLE.

LONDON: PRINTED BY
SPOTTISWOODE AND CO., NEW-STREET SQUARE
AND PARLIAMENT STREET

THE
NICOMACHEAN ETHICS
OF
ARISTOTLE

NEWLY TRANSLATED INTO ENGLISH

BY

ROBERT WILLIAMS, B.A.

FELLOW AND LATE LECTURER OF MERTON COLLEGE, AND SOMETIME
STUDENT OF CHRIST CHURCH, OXFORD.

LONDON:
LONGMANS, GREEN, AND CO.
1869.

'Nos hoc liquido affirmare possumus, minus esse obscuritatis in Aristotele, quam optarent prolixissimi interpretes, quorum interest ne plus sapiat juventus quam ipsi, aut ne cito eum intelligat, sine quibus ipsi nomen philosophi et existimationem tueri non possent. Longe alia veterum ac praecipue Graecorum mens fuit: qui cum genus dicendi Aristotelicum recte perceipissent et mentem, utramque breviter et sine ambitione ulla proponebant. Inter quos principem illi locum obtinere videntur, qui fusius paulo summam illam viri divini brevitatem, non interrupto sermonis ordine, illustrarunt: et ubi necesse esset, quae a minus rerum harum peritis desiderari possent, interjunxerunt. Quod jam olim in urbe De physica auscultatione libros, tres De anima, et alios nonnullos a Themistio admirabili quadam ratione factum esse, omnes fatentur.'—HEINSIUS, *Praef. in Andronici Rhodii Paraphrasin.*

DEDICATED

TO

THE REV. B. JOWETT, M.A.

REGIUS PROFESSOR OF GREEK IN THE

UNIVERSITY OF OXFORD.

PREFACE.

Not only do the Nicomachean Ethics lie almost at the threshold of Moral Philosophy, but they have, perhaps, more in common with modern thought than any other among the treatises of Aristotle of equal length and importance. The whole of the eighth and ninth books, and, with them, the fourth, the last half of the third, and a considerable portion of the first, may be read without any previous knowledge of Greek Philosophy, and will be found intelligible. The discussion of the physical basis of certain forms of depravity apparently moral, the casuistical determination of the degrees of responsibility, and the treatment of the question of education, are by no means the only points that occur which have in the present day a great interest of their own, and on which it is as well to hear what any great thinker has advanced. And, lastly, the Nicomachean Ethics are of especial value as being a brief and methodical system of Moral Philosophy, instead of a desultory and unconnected discussion of some one question in a great subject. Indeed, from this point of view, there is no work extant at once of equal brevity and worth.

Now that the thoughtful study of Greek Philosophy is beginning to take its proper place, a translation of the Nicomachean Ethics, intended not so much to aid the tyro in grappling with the difficulties of the Greek text, as to reproduce the original in an intelligible and connected form for the benefit of the general reader, needs no apology, except on the especial ground of its own demerits. In this respect I hope I have done my best to avoid all serious errors. But a translation is always a wearisome task, and one that requires most minute attention to render it as little as possible obnoxious to those differences of opinion which must always exist as to the exact meaning of any given combination of words in a dead language. I shall be more than content if I have done a little to promote that general acquaintance with Greek Philosophy for which so much is already due to the labours of others.

My best thanks are due to the accomplished scholarship and kind care of R. Dear, Esq., of Merton College—who, in a final revision of the proofs, has made several important suggestions, of which I have most gladly availed myself.

The text followed is that of Bekker, as given in the small Oxford Edition of 1867, published by Messrs. Parker. The paging of this edition has, to facilitate reference, been given in the margin, and all deviations from the text have been noticed at the foot of the page.

OXFORD: *June* 30, 1869.

CONTENTS.

BOOK I.

All action presupposes an end.—This end is the object of Political Science.—Ethical generalisations are only approximate.—Ethics requires for its study a mind properly trained.—Happiness is the one end of all our actions.—Ethics consists of generalisations from experience.—Erroneous conceptions of Happiness.—The Idea of Good as conceived by Plato.—The Chief Good must be final, all-adequate, and *sui generis*.—Happiness consists in the consciousness of a life in which the highest Virtue is actively manifested, and which must be of adequate length.—How far is Ethics matter of demonstration?—Our definition of Happiness is confirmed by popular opinion, and by recognised theories.—Happiness is in our own power.—Discussion of the *dictum* of Solon.—The evil fortune of the living in no way affects the dead.—Happiness is a thing which calls for honour rather than for praise.—The Soul may be divided into two parts, the Rational and the Irrational . Page 1.

BOOK II.

Moral Virtue does not come by nature.—It is acquired by the practice of virtuous acts.—Both excess and defect are alike prejudicial to Moral Virtue.—Moral Virtue is concerned with pleasure and pain. —The analogy between the Arts and the Virtues is faulty.—Moral Virtue is a Habit or Formed State.—It differs from other habits in that it observes the mean between excess and defect.—This can be confirmed by a detailed examination of the various moral virtues.—Relation of the mean to the two extremes.—Practical rules for the acquisition of Moral Virtue . . . Page 35.

BOOK III.

Involuntary acts are either done under compulsion, or from Ignorance.—Mixed actions.—Distinction between involuntary and non-voluntary acts.—Ignorance of details.—Acts of anger and of desire are not involuntary.—Definition of Purpose.—Definition of Deliberation.—What is the object of Wish?—Bad acts are as much in our own power as are good.—We are responsible for our character.—Discussion of the Platonic *thesis* that vice is involuntary.—Bravery.—Spurious forms of Bravery.—Temperance . Page 59.

BOOK IV.

Liberality.—Magnificence.—High-mindedness.—Ambition.—Gentleness.—Friendliness.—Truthfulness.—Wittiness.—Shame. Page 99.

BOOK V.

Various meanings of the terms "Justice" and "Injustice."—Justice considered as co-extensive with Virtue.—Particular Justice, and its various kinds.—Distributive Justice.—Corrective Justice.—Catallactic Justice.—Theory of exchange.—In what sense it is that Justice is a mean.—The field of Justice proper is civil society.—Justice is either natural or conventional.—All wrong-doing must be voluntary.—Various kinds of wrong-doing.—A man cannot suffer wrong against his own will.—Casuistical questions concerning Justice and Injustice.—Equity.—A man cannot wrong himself . . . . Page 138.

BOOK VI.

The rational part of the Soul may be subdivided into two parts—the Speculative and the Deliberative.—The office of the speculative part is pure thought; that of the deliberative part, moral action.—Science.—Art.—Prudence.—Induction.—Philosophy.—Philosophy is higher and nobler than is any form of Prudence.—Prudence is concerned with singulars, Philosophy with universals.—Moral Perception.—Good Deliberation.—Appreciation.—Consideration.—Mutual inter-dependence of the Moral Faculties.—Problems with regard to Philosophy and Prudence.—Relation of Prudence to Cleverness, and of true Virtue to instinctive.—Prudence and Virtue are reciprocally connected . . Page 181.

BOOK VII.

Degrees of Virtue and of Vice.—Problems with regard to Incontinence.—Partial solution of these problems.—Discussion of the *thesis* of Socrates, that a man cannot know what is right and do what is wrong.—Distinction between Incontinence proper and quasi-Incontinence.—Brutality.—Incontinence of desire is worse than is Incontinence of anger.—Effeminacy and Endurance.—Strength of character.—Prudence and Incontinence are incompatible.—Various arguments of the detractors of Pleasure.—These arguments are inconclusive.—Bodily Pleasure is only bad when pursued to excess.—It has not been shown that the Chief Good is not identical with some particular kind of Pleasure . . . . Page 209.

BOOK VIII.

Various theories concerning Friendship.—The three objects of affection are the Good, the Pleasant, and the Useful.—Upon each of these three a friendship may be based.—Friendships of pleasure or of utility are accidental or imperfect.—Friendships of virtue are essential, complete, perfect, and lasting.—Friendship is kept alive by intercourse.—One cannot have many real friends at one and the same time.—Friendships of inequality.—Connection between Justice and Friendship.—The essence of Friendship is to love rather than to be loved.—The field of all Friendship is some form or other of community.—Friendship in the various forms of political community.—Friendship between relations.—Settlement of disputes in friendships of utility.—Settlement of disputes in friendships of inequality . . . . . . Page 259.

BOOK IX.

The return to be made for a kindness received must be fixed by its value to the recipient.—Rules for the settlement of diverse and conflicting obligations.—Causes that justify a discontinuance of Friendship.—We love our friends in the same way as we love ourselves.—Kindly feeling.—Unanimity.—Why does the doer of a kindness love the recipient more than he is loved by him?—Ought we to love ourselves or others most?—Distinction between Selfishness and Love of Self.—The happy man will stand in need of friends.—How many friends is it well to have?—Is it in prosperity or in adversity that friends are most necessary?—Friendship commences and grows with intercourse . . . Page 307.

BOOK X.

A discussion with regard to Pleasure is a necessary part of an Ethical treatise.—Dialectical discussion of the *thesis* of Eudoxus, that Pleasure is the Chief Good.—Discussion and refutation of the contrary *thesis*, that no Pleasure whatever is a good.—Pleasure is in itself an absolute whole, and complete at any moment.—Pleasure is the inseparable accompaniment of a perfect act.—Pleasures differ from one another in kind.—Happiness consists in the exercise of pure thought.—Praises of the Life Philosophic.—To educate others successfully we require a knowledge of Political Philosophy.—The condition of Political Philosophy is at present unsatisfactory.—Sketch of the Politics . . . Page 349.

THE NICOMACHEAN ETHICS OF ARISTOTLE.

I.

1. (1.) ALL MORAL ACTION, that is to say all purpose, no less than all art and all science, would seem to aim at some good result, from which has come a not inapt definition of the chief good as that end to which all human action whatever is directed. Now ends clearly differ from one another. For, firstly, in some cases the end is an act, while in others it is a material result beyond and beside that act. And, where the action involves any such end beyond itself, this end is of necessity better than is the act by which it was produced. And, secondly, since there are many kinds of moral action, and many arts, and many sciences, the ends of these are also many; medicine, for example, giving us health, boat-building a boat, tactics victory, and economics wealth. And, where many such arts are subordinated to some one,—as to riding is subordinated bridle making, and all other arts concerned with the production of accoutrements for horses, while riding itself, and with it all other martial service, is subordinated to the science of military

tactics, and in many other arts the same scale of subordination is to be found,—in all such cases the end of the supreme art or science is higher than are the ends of the arts subordinate to it; for it is only for the sake of the former that the latter are sought. And herein it matters not, as can be seen from the instances above given, whether the end of the supreme act be the act itself, or a something beyond that act.

2. If then there be some one end of all that we do, for which we wish for its own sake, while for other things we wish only in so far as they are means to this,—that is to say, if every object of choice be not a

(2.) means to something further, | in which case the chain of means would be infinite, and our desires empty and objectless,—it is evident that this end will be the chief and the supreme good. Surely then a scientific knowledge of it will have a critical influence upon our lives, and will make us, like bowmen who have a mark at which to aim, all the more likely to hit upon that which is our good. And, if this be so, we must endeavour to describe it at least in outline, and to say of what science or of what art it is the province. It would seem to be the object of that art which is the master art, and so the most supreme. And such, manifestly, is the art political. For this it is that determines what branches of knowledge ought to be pursued in States, and which are to be studied by the individual citizens, and up to what point. And to this art moreover we see subordinated all those arts that are held in most esteem, such as are the arts strategic, economic, and rhetoric. And so, since this art uses as its instruments all the other practical branches of knowledge, and further lays down general principles as to what must be done and what avoided, its end will comprehend the end of all these other arts, and will consequently be the supreme human good. For, although the end of the individual and of the State may perhaps be identical, yet that of the State is evidently a grander and more complete object both to win and to preserve. Choiceworthy as perfection may be even for the individual, far more noble and divine is it for Nations and for States. Such then is the object of our treatise, which may consequently be described as political.

3. Our statements will be adequate if made with as much clearness as the matter allows. Abstract accuracy is no more to be expected in all philosophic treatises than in all products of art, and noble and just acts with which the art political is concerned admit of such great variation and of so many differences that they have been held to depend upon conventional rather than upon real distinctions. And much the same variation is to be found in things good, in that by them many are injured; for men have often, ere now, been brought to ruin by wealth, and in some cases again by courage. We must consequently rest well satisfied if in treating of such matter, and with premisses thus uncertain, we can (4.) exhibit a rough | outline of the truth, and if, since our premisses are mere generalities, and our matter akin to them, we can derive from them conclusions of a like generality.

And it is in this same spirit that all our statements ought to be received. A man who has been well trained will not in any case look for more accuracy than the nature of the matter allows; for to expect exact demonstration from a rhetorician is as absurd as to accept from a mathematician a statement only probable. Now each man can give a good judgment upon matters with which he is acquainted, and is in such cases a good judge. In each particular case, therefore, he judges best who has been taught the matter in question, and on all matters he whose education has been universal. And hence it is that a young man is not a fit student of the art political; for he has had no experience in matters of daily life, with which matters our premisses are concerned, and of which our conclusions treat. And since, moreover, he is prone to follow his desires, he will listen without purpose, and so without benefit. For the true object of ethical study is not merely the knowledge of what is good, but the application of that knowledge. And this is true of him who is young in character equally with him who is young in years, since the defect is not so much because his years have been few as because his life as a whole, and consequently his every action, is guided by the passion of the moment. And so knowledge of what is right is as profitless to such men as it is to the incontinent; whereas, if a man controls his desires and his actions as reason orders, knowledge of ethical science cannot but aid him much. And this is sufficient preface as to the fit student of ethics, the modality of the matter, and the end which we propose.

4. And now again, to resume, since all our acts, whether intellectual or moral, aim at some good end, what is the end at which we assert that the art political aims,—that is to say, what is the highest of all goods attainable by human action? Upon its name almost all men are agreed. For both the untaught many and the educated few call it Happiness, and understand this same happiness to consist in a good and a prosperous life. But as to what this happiness
(4.) exactly is they disagree, so that hereupon | popular and philosophic views conflict. Some say that it is a something tangible and conspicuous, such as is pleasure, or wealth, or honour,—some, in short, give one account of it, and some another; and often the same man's views will vary, and when seized by sickness he will assert that happiness is health, and when pressed for money that it is wealth; while those, again, who are conscious of their own ignorance, marvel at him who converses upon matters which are great, and too high for them. And some, again, have held that, beyond and beside these many particular goods, there is an absolute and universal good, from which is derived the goodness of these many singulars. To sift so many views were perhaps a purposeless task. It will be sufficient if we examine those which are most widely spread, or which seem to have some foundation upon which to rest. We must further bear in mind the difference between the synthetical method, which

proceeds from the universal to the singular, and the analytical, which proceeds from the particular to the universal. And, indeed, Plato did well in investigating, and in attempting to solve the question whether method is to be synthetic or analytic,—either being conceivably possible, exactly as in a race-course one can run from the stewards to the goal, or from the goal to the stewards. In either case, however, we must begin with truths taken upon their own evidence. Of these there are two kinds—the universal, which is first in the order of nature; and the particular, which is first for man, or in the order of experience. We then had, perhaps, best begin with those principles which are first for man. And hence he who is to be a competent student of what is noble, and of what is just, or, in a word, of the art political, ought previously to have been trained in good habits. For the first principle from which ethics start is the particular fact of experience, of which if we are perfectly convinced that it is such or such, our conviction is in no way strengthened by knowledge of the why and wherefore. He who has been thus trained will either already know the most general principles of the science, or will with ease acquire them. But he who knows neither the universal rule, nor the particular fact, had best bear in mind the proverb of Hesiod—

> Wisest is he who of himself hath knowledge,
> And wise is he who lists to prudent counsel;
> But whoso nor hath knowledge, nor to others
> Lendeth his ear, is but an idle dullard.

5. But, to return to the point from which we commenced our digression, the many and baser sort give by their lives a fair presumption that their conception of the chief good and of happiness is that it consists (5.) in | material pleasure: for their only delight is in a life of gross enjoyment. There are, indeed, but three noteworthy modes of life, the one just mentioned, the life of the statesman, and the third, the life of the philosopher. Now the many are clearly in no way better than slaves, in that they deliberately choose the life of brute beasts. Nor would their view call for consideration, were it not that many of those who are high in power are of like passions with Sardanapalus. On the other hand, the better and educated class, who devote themselves to active life, identify the chief good with honour. Honour, indeed, seems upon the whole to be the end of the statesman's life. Yet this is clearly too purely external and superficial a thing to be the good of which we are in quest. For honour would seem to rest rather with those who give than with those who receive it, whereas we divine that the chief good is a something that rests with a man's self, and that is hard to be alienated. Moreover, it would seem that statesmen only pursue honour as a self-convincing proof of virtue: certain at least is it that they seek to be held in honour by the prudent and among those by whom they are known, and for their virtue. And hence it is clear that in their view at least, if not in that of others, virtue must rank the higher. And hence one may perhaps be led to suppose that it is virtue that is the end of the statesman's

life. Yet even virtue itself would seem to fall short of being an absolute end. For it is possible that the possessor of virtue should for the whole of his life either sleep, or be otherwise inactive, or, yet more than this, that the greatest evil and misfortune should befall him. And no one, save from pure love of paradox, can maintain that he is happy whose life is such as this. Of these two modes, then, of life enough has now been said: they have, indeed, been adequately discussed in popular treatises. There remains only the third life, the life philosophic, which we shall consider hereafter. As for the money-getting life, it violates the natural fitness of things. Wealth is clearly not the absolute good of which we are in search, for it is a utility, and only desirable as a means. Hence one would be better justified in adopting as the chief good any of the ends mentioned above; for they are choiceworthy in and for themselves. And yet it is evident that the chief good is none of these, although in their behalf many arguments have been constructed.

6. Thus much, then, for these views. And next we had best, perhaps, consider what is the exact meaning to be attached to the conception of the one absolute good;

(6.) although such a discussion cannot but be | repugnant, in that the doctrine of transcendental ideas was introduced by those whom we hold dear. And yet, where the interests of truth are at actual stake, we ought, perhaps, to sacrifice even that which is our own—if, at least, we are to lay any claim to a philosophic spirit. Both are dear to us alike, but truth must be religiously preferred. In the first place, then, even they who were the first to introduce this notion did not form universal ideas embracing individual conceptions essentially prior and posterior to one another, and hence did not frame any one universal idea comprehending all numbers. Now good can be conceived as substance, and as quality, and as relation. But essence, that is to say substance, is of necessity prior to relation, which would seem to be so purely an outgrowth of essence, and hence accidental to it, that there cannot be any one common universal idea which embraces the two. Secondly, good can be conceived in as many modes as can being: it can be conceived as substance, as God, for example, or as intellect; and as quality, as the various excellencies; and as quantity, as the exact mean; and as relation, as that which subserves to a given end; and as time, as the exact moment; and as place, as a healthy abode; and in many other like ways. And it is therefore plain that there cannot be any one and indivisible common universal of goods; for, if so, good would not fall under all possible categories, but under only one. Thirdly, since of those things that fall under one universal idea the science is one and the same, it would follow that there ought to be but one science of all possible goods. But, as it is, there are many different sciences, even of those goods that fall under one category. Take, for example, time, and in war we have tactics, and in disease medicine; or take the mean, and we have in diet medicine again, and in exercise gymnastics. And, again, it is difficult to determine what it is that is meant by the phrase "absolute," since only one and the same account can be given of the humanity of the absolute man and of that of the individual man. In so far as each is man there can be no difference between them; and so, in so far as each is good, there can be no difference between the absolute and the individual good. Nor will its eternity make the former any the more good, just as that which has been white for centuries is none the more white than is that which is white only for a day. A more reasonable account of the whole matter (7.) is that of the Pythagoreans. They make | unity only one of their file of goods: and even Speusippus would seem inclined to follow their view. Of these matters, however, we will treat elsewhere. But against the arguments above alleged it would seem that the objection may be urged that the conception of an absolute good is not intended to apply indiscriminately to all concrete goods whatever; for that of such there are two distinct kinds, firstly, those that are sought and are held precious for their own sake, and, secondly, those that produce, or in some way tend to preserve these former, or to counteract their contraries; and that these latter are called good in only a secondary sense, as being means to the former. Now it is clear that this double division of concrete goods, namely, into ends and into means, is justifiable; let us then consider, quite apart from all means, those goods that are ends in themselves, and see if these can be embraced in any one generic conception. Now what are these goods that are ends in themselves?

Are they all the several ultimate and independent objects of human pursuit, such as reason, and sight, and certain kinds of pleasures and of honours; all of which are undeniably ends in themselves, although, perhaps, capable of being pursued as means? Or is there no such good at all save and except the one absolute good itself? In this latter case we shall have framed an abstract universal without any concrete intent. In the former case we ought to be able to show of all such goods that one and the same account can be given of their goodness, as can of the whiteness in snow and in ceruse. But of honour, and of reason, and of pleasure, entirely distinct and different accounts must be given, even in so far as each of them is a good. And so the goodness of these goods cannot be brought under any one generic conception. Why, then, is it that they are all called good? For it hardly seems to be a case of accidental equivocation. Is it that they all have one common origin, or that they all tend to one and the same end? Or is it not rather that they all stand in an analogous relation to their various objects; much as the relation of sight to the body is analogous to the relation of reason to the soul, and to certain other relations between various objects? And here, perhaps, we had best close these questions about good in the abstract (an accurate investigation of which is the province of other branches of philosophy rather than the present), and with them all questions concerning the one absolute and transcendental good. For, even if there were some one such unity of all good, either essentially predicable of all

possible concrete goods, or transcendent and separable from them, it is clear that man could not make it the end of his action, or in any way gain possession of it; whereas the good of which we are in quest must be of this nature. And yet it may, perhaps, seem that in our search for such goods as can be acquired by man, or be gained by human action, a theoretic know-
(8.) ledge of | such an absolute good would be of great avail. For it would serve us as a type by reference to which we should be more likely to know, and so, consequently, to obtain all such concrete things as are good for our particular selves. And, indeed, this argument is not devoid of plausibility, although it would seem to find its refutation in the actual practice of the various arts. For, although all the arts aim at some concrete good, with respect to which they seek to supply all our defects, yet they altogether ignore all knowledge of this one absolute good. And yet, were it really so great an aid, one would hardly expect that all those who practise the various arts should not only be ignorant of it, but should never even inquire into it. And it is, indeed, hard to see wherein a weaver or a carpenter will, in so far as regards his own particular craft, gain anything from a knowledge of the one absolute good; or how any speculation upon transcendental health, or transcendental victory, will make a man a better physician, or a better general. It is indeed evident that the physician is not concerned with health in the abstract, but with the health of man ; or rather perhaps with

the health of individuals, since it is the individual, after all, whom he has to heal.

7. And here we will close this digression, and return to the question of what is that highest human good of which we are in quest. It is clear that every course of action and every art has its own peculiar good; for the good sought by medicine is one, and the good sought by tactics is another; and of all other arts the same holds good. What, then, is in each case the chief good? Surely it will be that to which all else that is done is but a means. And this in medicine will be health, and in tactics victory, and in architecture a house, and so forth in other cases; and in all free action, that is to say in all purpose or conscious choice of means to a desired end, it will be that end; for it is with this in view that we always take all the other steps in the particular action. And so, if there be but one end of all things that we do, this will be in all human action the chief good; while, if there be more than one, it will be their sum. Our argument, therefore, has now returned to the question from which it originally digressed, and which we must now endeavour yet more thoroughly to clear up. Now since there are clearly many and divers ends, some of which we occasionally choose as means, such as wealth, or pipes, or instruments generally, it is clear that all these ends are not final; whereas the chief good is clearly a something absolutely final. So that, if there be but one thing that is final, this will (9.) be the good of which we are in quest; and, | if there

be more than one, then the most final among them.
Now we call that which is pursued for its own sake
more final than that which is pursued as a means to
something further, and that which is never chosen as
a means more final than any such things as are choiceworthy both as ends in themselves and as means to
this; while, to sum up, we call that alone absolutely
final which is in all cases to be chosen as an end, and
never as a means. And happiness would seem to be
pre-eminently such; for happiness we always choose
as an end, and never as a means; while honour, and
pleasure, and intelligence, and all excellence we do
indeed choose as ends (for we should choose each
one of them even if they bore no good fruit), but we
choose them also for the sake of happiness, thinking
that by their means we shall be happy. But happiness
itself no man ever chooses for the sake of these things,
or indeed as a means to aught beyond itself. And the
all-sufficiency of happiness clearly leads to the same
conclusion; for the final human good is always held
to be all-sufficient. Nor do we understand that the
range of this all-sufficiency is to be restricted to the
individual in a life of isolation, but we hold that it
also includes his parents, and his children, and his
wife, and indeed his friends and his fellow-citizens,
since man's nature is to be citizen of a free state.
But herein some limit must be fixed; for were one
so to extend this as to take in a man's ancestors, and
his descendants, and the friends of his friends, the
circle would become infinite. Of this question, however, we will hereafter treat, and for the present will

define as all-sufficient that which alone and by itself can make our life desirable, and supply all our needs. And we are of opinion that happiness is such. And, moreover, happiness is the most desirable of all things, in that there is nothing else which is on a par with it, and so capable of being added to it. Were not this so, then the addition of any such other good, no matter how small, would evidently render it more desirable. For any such addition would constitute an excess of good; and of any two goods the greater is always the more choiceworthy. Happiness, then, is clearly a something complete in itself, and all-sufficient, forming the one end of all things done by man.

But still to say nothing more about happiness than that it is the greatest of all goods is clearly but little better than a truism, and one seems to yearn for a yet more definite account. This we shall most prob-
(10.) ably obtain from the consideration of what it is that man as such has to do. For, as in the case of flute players, and of sculptors, and of all craftsmen, and indeed of all those who have any work of their own to do, or who can originate any peculiar train of action, it is in this their especial work that their chief good and greatest welfare lie, so too ought it to be in the case of man as man, if as man he has any special functions of his own. Are we then to believe that man as carpenter, or that man as cobbler, has a function of his own, and so can originate a course of action; while as man he lacks this, and has no task assigned him by nature? Shall we not rather say

that as the eye, and the hand, and the foot, and each of the various members, evidently has its office, so too, beyond and beside all these, must be assigned an office to man as such? And, if so, what are we to say that this office is? Life he has in common even with plants, whereas what we seek is a something peculiar to himself. The life of mere nutrition and growth must therefore be dismissed. Next to this in order is what may be called the life of the senses. But even this is shared by horses, and by oxen, and by all beasts. There is only left what may be described as a life of free moral action, belonging to that part of us which possesses reason, and which may possess it, either as being obedient to its commands, or as properly possessing and exercising it in consecutive thought. And, as this life can be conceived in two aspects, we will take it in its active state, for then more properly is it called life. If, then, the function or office of man as such be an active life or activity of the soul in accordance with reason, or at least not without reason, and if we say that the work of such an one and that of such an one who is good of his sort differ not in kind, as in the case of a harper and of a good harper,—and if we are to say this in every case, our conception of the work itself remaining unaltered by any additional excess of excellence; so that a harper's work is to play the harp, and the work of a good harper is to play it well,—if all this be so, and if we are to take as the function of man a certain kind of life, and to make this life consist in an activity of the soul, that is to say in moral action consciously accompanied by reason; and to take as the function of the good man the doing all this well and perfectly, remembering that it is its own excellence alone that causes each thing to be done well,—then, if all this be so, we shall find that the chief good of man consists in an activity of the soul in accordance with its own excellence (or, in other words, such that the essential conditions of its excellence are fulfilled), and, if there be many such, in accordance with the best and the most perfect among them. And we must further add the condition of a perfect life; for a single day, or even a short period of happiness, no more makes a blessed and a happy man than one sunny day or (11.) one swallow | makes a spring.

Such then in outline is our conception of the chief good; for it is perhaps best first to sketch out our idea, and then afterwards to fill it in. And it would indeed seem that, when such an outline has once been correctly traced, anyone can add to it the necessary boldness of relief, and distinctness of connection in its details; and that it is time that discovers such improvements, or that is at least a good helper in the quest. And in this way it is that the arts have grown, since what is in each case deficient any man can supply. And we must further remember what we have said before, and must not require abstract exactness in all cases alike, but only so far in each as is allowed by the matter, and as suits the investigation. That which a carpenter requires in a straight line is one thing, and that which a geometrician requires is another. The one is concerned with it only in so far as it is of actual use for the work which he has in hand; the other regards it in its generic and essential aspects, since abstract truth is the object of his speculations. And in other matters also we must be guided by the same rule, lest the details should outgrow and so obscure the main conception. Nor must we in all cases alike require demonstration by causes, but must sometimes rest content with a clear statement of fact. All first principles, for example, must be taken upon their own evidence; and each fact of experience is a first principle, being an ultimate truth, upon which further arguments can be based. Some first principles are given us by induction, others by the senses, while others again require a special habituation,—in short, various principles are gained in various ways. And we must do our best to acquire each kind as suits its nature, and must use all zeal to apprehend them clearly and distinctly, for they have a great and a critical influence upon our conclusions. Indeed it would seem that

The principal is more than half the sum,

and that a clear statement of premisses makes many problems self-evident.

8. But, to resume, we must investigate the nature of happiness, not only from the point of view afforded us by our conclusion, and by our premisses, but also from that of the statements made by others. For with a true theory all facts agree, while with what is false truth is quickly found to conflict. Now there is an old triple division of goods into goods external, | goods of the soul, and goods of the body;

of which it is held that those of the soul are the highest and the chief. But moral action, inasmuch as we make it an activity of the soul, belongs to the soul; so that our statements hold good by the test of this view, which has been sanctioned by time, and by the assent of philosophers. And we are right, moreover, in that we make the end of life to consist in an activity, that is to say in moral action. For happiness thus becomes a good of the soul, and not a good external. And, again, the proverb that the happy man lives well and fares well is in harmony with our definition. For what we have described is but a sort of fair-living and prosperity.

And, again, all the scientific determinations of happiness are clearly contained in our definition. For some hold that happiness lies in virtue, others that it is prudence, or some kind of philosophic knowledge, or that it is all of these together, or some one of them, accompanied by pleasure, or at least not without pleasure; while others again hold that material prosperity is in it an essential element. And of these views some depend on common experience and old authorities, and others on the authority of a few, but those men of high repute. Nor is it likely that either side are entirely wrong, but rather that in some one point at least they are right, if not in most. Now with those who say that happiness is either virtue as a whole, or some one particular form of virtue, our definition concords. For an activity in accordance with virtue will itself involve such virtue. And it matters perhaps no little whether the chief good be conceived as a mere possession, or as a something of which use is to be made—that is to say as a mere formed habit, or as an activity. For such a habit may possibly exist in a man, and yet bear no good fruit, as when he is asleep, or otherwise inactive. But with the activity it cannot possibly be thus. He who displays this cannot possibly but act, and, what is more, act well. For as at the Olympic games it is not the fairest and the strongest who are crowned, but they that run—for some of these it is that win the victory—so too, among the noble and good in life, it is they that act rightly who become masters of life's prize. And the life of such men has in itself a pleasure of its own. Activities of the soul, no less than those of the body, have their own pleasure; and, since each man takes pleasure in that which he is said to love—as a (13.) lover of horses | in horses, and a lover of shows in shows—it follows that, in the same way, the lover of justice will take pleasure in justice; and the lover of virtue as a whole, in virtue. Now, for the many, the objects that yield them pleasure are discordant, inasmuch as they are not really pleasant in themselves; but, to those who love what is noble, those things give pleasure that are intrinsically pleasant. And all virtuous acts are such; so that to such men they give a pleasure—and that a pleasure intrinsic to themselves. Such a life then needs no pleasure to deck it like an amulet, for it has in itself a pleasure of its own. And, indeed, we may add that the man who takes no pleasure in noble acts cannot be a good man. For surely no one would call him just who took no pleasure in fair dealing; or him liberal who took no pleasure in liberal acts; and so forth in every virtue. And, if this be so, then virtuous acts cannot but be intrinsically pleasant. Aye, and, more than this, they are also both good and noble; and are moreover preeminently each of these, if the judgment of the upright man about them be true: and his judgment is as ours. Happiness then is the best, and the noblest, and the most pleasant of all goods; nor are these things distinct, as said the inscription at Delos,

> Justice is noblest; best of goods is health;
> Sweetest to win the object of desire;

for in our best acts all these characteristics are to be found. And it is in these acts, or in that one among them that is the best, that we say that happiness consists. And yet, as we have said, it obviously wants the addition of external goods; for, if not impossible, it is at least difficult to do noble deeds, if bared of all such equipments. Friends, and wealth, and power in the State, serve as instruments by which to win many fair ends. And some things there are to be bereft of which casts a shadow over our happiness—such as are noble birth, fair offspring, or beauty of person. For he surely will not find happiness
(14.) easy to win who is of utterly mean appearance, [or of ignoble birth, or who is childless, and alone in life; and perhaps still less so, should his sons or his friends be utterly depraved, or should they have been noble only to die. As, then, we have said, happiness would seem to need external aids such as these. And hence

it is that some have made it identical with mere good fortune,—I say some, for others make it virtue.

9. Hence, too, arises the doubt whether happiness is to be taught, or to be gained by habituation, or by any other kind of practice, or whether it comes to us by some divine lot, or even perhaps by chance. Most certainly, if there be aught that is a free gift of God to men, it were well to suppose that happiness is such, and the more so as it is the best of all human goods. But still this question would perhaps be more in place in another treatise than the present. Happiness, at all events, even if it be not sent by the Gods, but is acquired by virtuous action, and by a course of teaching, or of some such other practice, is clearly an object most divine. For the prize of all virtue cannot but be the chief and final good, and consequently a something divine and full of joy. And it ought to be widely shared, since it may be won through a course of pupilage and of good practice by all those who are not of their own nature absolutely incapable of virtue. For, if it be better that happiness should come to us thus rather than by chance, it is but reasonable to hold that it does so come; since the works of nature, as a whole, are ordered in the fairest possible way, exactly as are the results of art, and indeed of all causation, and especially those of virtue, the noblest of all causes. So that to intrust to chance the greatest and fairest of all goods would be too sore a discord in Nature's harmony. And, moreover, our own definition of happiness, as an activity of the soul in accordance

with virtue, makes the question clear. For, of all other goods, some—those of the body—are necessary for happiness; while others—those external—are fitted by their very nature to be means and instruments for its acquisition. And this, moreover, agrees with what we said at first, when we stated that the end of the art political was the chief good; for this art spares no trouble to inspire the citizens with a definitely virtuous character—such that they may (15.) be disposed towards noble deeds. | And thus it is with good reason that we never call happy either ox, or horse, or any other beast; for to brute beasts nature has given no share in action such as this. And hence, too, is it that not even a boy is held happy, since his youth puts such acts, as yet, out of his power; so that to call him happy is but a fond expression of hope. For happiness presupposes, as we have said, perfect virtue and a life in all respects complete. But many are the changes and divers the chances in life; and it is possible that he who now flourishes most should, as is fabled of Priam in the epic, stumble in his old age upon great mishaps. And him whose fortunes have been such as this, and his end wretched, no man can call happy.

10. Are we then to call no man happy while he yet lives, but to wait, as Solon advises, until we have seen the end of his life? And, if we are to adopt this view, are we then to say that the man is actually happy after his death? Or is not this an altogether untenable position, especially for us who have defined happiness as an activity? And if, on the other hand,

we do not mean that the man when dead is actually
happy, nor must Solon be understood to say this,
but rather that it is only when he is dead that we can
with safety assert that a man is happy, since then only
is he beyond the range of all evil and mishap,—with
this view also issue can be joined. For it is held
that things good and evil can happen to him who is
dead, exactly as they can to him who is alive but not
aware of them, such as are the honour or dishonour,
and indeed all other good or evil fortune, of his
children, and of his descendants generally. And
herein arises a fresh difficulty. For, however happy
may have been a man's life up to his old age, and
however fitting thereunto his death, it is none the
less possible that many changes should befall his
descendants, and that some among them should be
upright, and should meet with a life according to their
deserts, while with others of them it should be far
otherwise; and it is also clear that in successive generations every possible degree of relationship may arise
between descendants and their ancestors. So that,
(:6.) while on the one hand it is absurd to conceive | the
dead man as sharing all their vicissitudes, and as
becoming happy one moment and wretched the next,
it is on the other hand equally absurd to suppose that
the fortunes of descendants never, for however short
a time, reach to their ancestors. Perhaps, however,
the solution of the present question will present itself
if we return to our original problem. For, if we are
to wait that we may see how a man's life ends, and
are then, and then only, to call him happy, not as

being now actually happy, but as having been such; then surely it is absurd that when a man is actually happy we should hold it premature to predicate of him that which he actually enjoys, merely because the changes of life are such that we are unwilling to call men happy who are still alive; our conception of happiness being that it is abiding and in no way likely to change, while fortune's wheel often rolls many cycles in the same man's lifetime. For it is clear that, if fortune be our test, we shall over and over again have to call a man first happy and then wretched, thus making the happy man

> Chameleon-hued; his house upon the sand.

Is it not rather true that fortune must in no way be our guide? For, although man's life needs good fortune, as we have said, yet it is not in fortune that good and evil lie, but it is virtuous acts that determine life for happiness, acts evil for misery. So that our present problem but serves to testify to the accuracy of our definition of happiness. For there is nothing human so surely lasting as are virtuous acts. More lasting are they than even scientific knowledge, and the most precious among them are the most lasting, in that those whose lot is blessed most earnestly and most continuously pass their life in the pursuit of them. And this would seem to be the reason why their practice cannot be forgotten. Thus, then, the happy man will enjoy that security of which we are in quest, and will continue happy throughout his whole life. For most continuously, or at least more continuously than for any other man, will all his acts and all his thoughts be most excellent, and his treatment of fortune most noble and most consistently harmonious, who is

(17.)   Truly good,
    Square-finished, free from every flaw | of blame.

But, since the results of fortune are manifold, both great and small, small changes of luck, whether for good or for the reverse, clearly cannot turn the scale of life. But Fortune, if she come for our good in many and in great shapes, will make our life more blessed (for it is in the nature of her gifts thus to add a lustre to our happiness, and to use them well is fair and upright); while, if she come thus for our harm, she crushes and mars our blessedness, bringing with her a sore burden of pains, and hindering many noble acts. But nevertheless even here true nobility shines out, when a man bears calmly many and great mishaps, not through dulness of feeling, but from true high-breeding, and greatness of spirit. And, since, as we have said, it is our own acts that determine our life, no one of the really blessed can ever become wretched, for he will never do hateful and disgraceful deeds. For we hold that the really good and prudent man will bear all changes of fortune with good grace, and will always, as the case may allow, act most nobly; exactly as a good general will use such forces as are at his disposal most skilfully, and even a good cobbler will, out of such leather as he may have, make the most perfect shoe ; and of all those who practise any other art the same rule will hold good. And, if this be so, then never will he who is once happy become wretched, though, if he become entangled in a lot such as that of Priam, he can hardly be called blessed. Nor will his life have many shades and changes. For no light thing will move him from his happiness, nor any chance mishap, but only misfortunes great and many: and after such he will not again become happy in a moment, but only in a long and all-adequate time, sufficient to make him master of prizes great and noble. Why, then, should we not call him happy whose acts have been those of consistent and perfect virtue, and whose equipment of external goods has been sufficient, and (18.) that not for any chance period, | but for a lifetime of fair length? Or must we add that he is to continue so to live, and that his death is to match his life? Since for us the future lies in obscurity, while we hold that happiness is the perfect crown of life, and a thing in all ways absolutely complete. And, since all this is so, we will call those among the living happy whose lot is and will be such as we have said, but happy only in so far as man can be so.

I I.   Thus far then let us hold this question as settled. But, as regards the misfortunes that befall a man's descendants, and indeed all those whom he holds dear,—to suppose that they in no degree contribute to the fortune of the dead is a view far too cold, and too opposed to all that men love to believe. But, since the misfortunes that affect us are many and of every shade, and some come more home to us and some less, to treat of each separate case would clearly be a long and indeed an infinite task, and we shall perhaps do best to rest content with a roughly-sketched and general statement. If then it be true that the mishaps which befall all those whom we love are like the mishaps that affect ourselves, so that some of them have great weight, and turn the scale of life, while others by comparison seem but light; and if also it in each case matters much more whether such evil befall them during our own lifetime or after our death, than it matters whether lawless and dread deeds be put before us in a tragedy, or form an integral portion of our actual life;—then from all this we cannot but conclude that the difference in question is as great as we have said; or rather perhaps that it is, after all, a doubtful point whether the dead are sharers in human good or ill of any kind. For it would seem from what we have said that, even if any such impression reach them, it will be a something but shadowy and trifling, either intrinsically or in its effects upon them, or at any rate that it will only be such and of such extent as neither to make happy those who are not so already, nor to rob the happy of their blessedness. The good fortune, then, no less than the bad fortune of their friends upon earth clearly contributes to the lot of the dead; but its effect is only such, and of such extent, as neither to make unhappy those who are already happy, nor to produce any other change of equal importance.

I 2.(19.) And, now that this question is settled, let us consider whether happiness belongs to the class of things that deserve praise, or rather of those that are held

in honour; for it evidently is not a mere faculty, to
be used indifferently for evil or for good. Now it is
clear that all such things as deserve praise are praised
in that they have certain definite qualities, and so
stand in a certain relation to a something else. The
just man, for example, and the brave man, and indeed
the good man generally, and his goodness, we praise
because of his actions and of their results; and the
strong wrestler, and the quick runner, and so all
others, we praise for a certain definite gift of nature
which they possess, and in virtue of which they stand
in a certain relation to some good and worthy end.
And this is clear from the fact that praise given to the
Gods makes them appear ridiculous, in that it refers
them to a human standard. Nor could this be otherwise, since all praise, as we have said, involves a
reference to some standard of excellence. And, since
it is only in cases such as this that praise is given, it
is evident that to the best things praise must not be
given, but a something greater and higher. And
this is clear from the fact that we attribute to the
Gods perfect blessedness and happiness, and call
those men who come nearest to the Gods blessed.
And so, too, is it with things that are good. No
one praises happiness, as he praises just acts, but,
as being a something more divine and better, calls
it blessed. Eudoxus, moreover, seems to have well
pleaded the cause of pleasure for the first prize. For
the fact that it is a good thing, and yet is not praised,
he held to be a proof that it is higher and better than
are all such things as deserve praise; as is God, and

us is the chief good, with reference to which it is that praise is bestowed upon all things else. Now praise is given to virtue, for virtue it is that disposes us to noble deeds; while panegyrics are awarded to external results whether of bodily or of intellectual activity. An accurate treatment of this question is, however, rather their task whose business is panegyrics. We are content if from what has been said we can clearly see that happiness has honour for its meed, being a something absolutely perfect. And this would indeed be evident, were we to reflect that it is an ultimate motive, for the sake of which we all of us go through (10.) all the various acts of life; and that | the ultimate motive and cause of all other things good we cannot but suppose to be a something deserving of honour and divine.

1 3. And now, since happiness is an activity of the soul in accordance with perfect virtue, we must inquire what is virtue; for thus perhaps we shall be in a better position to consider the nature of happiness. He who is a political philosopher in the true sense of the word will give virtue his most thorough attention, his object being to make the citizens good, and so obedient to the laws. And, as instances of this, we have the lawgivers of Crete and of Lacedæmon, and all such others as are upon record like to these. And so, since the discussion of virtue is the province of political science, it is clear that the present investigation will harmonise with our original purpose. We have therefore to consider virtue, that is to say, of course, the virtue of man; for it was man's highest

good, and man's happiness, of which we were in quest.
And by man's virtue we understand not the virtue
of the body but the virtue of the soul, since we have
defined happiness as an activity of the soul. And, if
this be so, it is clear that the politician must no less
know about the soul than he who is to heal the eye
must know about the body as a whole, and all the
more so in that the art political is higher and nobler
than is medicine. And indeed physicians of the
higher and better sort interest themselves no little in
the knowledge of the body as a whole. And hence
it follows that the politician must consider about the
soul, and must consider it with this end in view, that
is to say so far only as is sufficient for our present
object; for further minuteness of discussion would
only entail more labour than is needed for our purpose.
Now concerning the soul even ordinary language lays
down certain sufficient distinctions, of which we will
make use; as, for example, that the soul has two
parts, the one irrational, the other possessed of reason.
But whether these parts be distinct in the same sense
as are the members of the body, and all else that is
capable of physical division, or rather be only distinct
in thought, being in their own nature absolutely inseparable, exactly as are concavity and convexity in
(21.) an are, is a question | immaterial to our purpose. And,
again, of the irrational part there is yet a further part
that would seem to be common to man with other living
things, and to form the soul of plants. I speak of that
principle which is the cause of all nutrition and growth.
For a vital faculty of this nature one assigns to all

things that assimilate nutriment, as even to the fœtus; and this self-same faculty one also assigns to the full-grown being, since such a supposition is more reasonable than it is to hold that any substitution has taken place. Any excellence or virtue that this part of our soul may possess is clearly not peculiar to man, but is shared by him with animals and with plants. It is in sleep, indeed, that this part or faculty of our soul is most active, and it is in sleep that the good man and the bad are least distinguishable from one another; whence has come the proverb, that for one half their lives the happy in no way differ from the wretched. Nor could we expect it to be otherwise. For sleep is a torpor of our soul, in so far as it can be called morally good or bad, save only where to some slight extent certain of the movements of active life carry themselves on into our slumber, and so render the dreams of the good better than are those of ordinary men. But on these matters we have now said enough, and here we will close our discussion of the nutritive soul, since nature has given it no part in that virtue which is peculiarly human. And, again, there would seem to be another element in the soul, which also is irrational, and which yet to some extent partakes of reason. For, in the self-restrained, and also in the incontinent man, we give praise to their reason, that is to say to the rational portion of their soul, for that it exhorts them as is right, and to the best course. But there is clearly, in each of them, a something else, of its own nature opposed to reason, which conflicts with reason, and strives to counteract

it. For, exactly as a palsied limb, when a man purposes to move it to the right, swings round on the contrary to the left, so too is it with the soul of the incontinent man; for his impulses run counter to his reason. Only, whereas in the body we can see the part that so moves, in the soul we cannot see it. And yet, perhaps, we must none the less on this account hold that there is in the soul an element contradistinguished from reason, which sets itself in opposition to reason, and goes its way against it; although wherein precisely it is distinct from reason
(22.) concerns us not. And yet even this part too has clearly, as we have said, some share in reason, for in the self-restrained man it certainly obeys his reason. And, in the man who is thoroughly temperate and brave, it is perhaps yet more amenable; for in him all his members are in harmony with reason. Hence, then, it clearly appears that the irrational part of our soul has two members, of which one, the nutritive, is in no way concerned with reason; while the other, the concupiscent, or, more generally, the appetitive part, in a certain sense partakes of reason, in so far as it listens to reason, and obeys its commands. It is in this sense that we speak of showing a rational obedience to one's father or to one's friends, and not in that in which we speak of a rational understanding of mathematical truths. And, that the irrational part of our souls is to some extent amenable to reason, all admonition, all rebuke, all exhortation, is a proof. And hence, since even this part of our soul is in a certain sense to be called rational, it fol-

lows that the rational element in us will also have two parts, the one in its own right possessing reason in itself, while the other is obedient to reason, as is a son to his father. And, in accordance with this division, we can classify the virtues, and call some of them intellectual and others moral,—philosophy, appreciation, and prudence being excellences or virtues of the intellect, while liberality and temperance are moral virtues, or virtues of the character. For, when speaking of a man's character, we do not say that he is a philosopher, or a man of quick appreciation, but that he is gentle or temperate. And yet we none the less praise the wise man also for his state of mind, and understand by virtue a praiseworthy state of mind.

II.

1. THERE are, then, two kinds of virtue, the intellectual and the moral, of which the intellectual owes, for the most part, its birth and growth to a course of inference, so that for its perfection it needs experience, and consequently length of time; while moral virtue, on the other hand, is acquired by habit; the very word "moral," indeed, varying but little etymo-
(23.) logically from its root, "habit." | And hence too it is clear that no one of the moral virtues is an innate law of our nature. For no law of nature can be altered by habit. A stone, which of its own nature moves downwards, no force of habit will ever accustom to move upwards, nor would one ever habituate it to such a motion by hurling it upwards any number of times. Neither could fire be thus brought to move downwards; nor, in short, can the action of any natural law whatever be altered by habituation. Neither, then, are the moral virtues an innate law of our nature, nor is their acquisition a contravention of any such law; but nature has given us a capability for them, and we become perfected in them by habituation. And, again, in the case of all things innate or connate in us we first have the faculty, and then afterwards we manifest its acts. Of this the senses are a clear instance, for we did not acquire them by

repeated acts of sight, or of hearing; we did not, that
is to say, acquire these faculties by practising their
acts; but, on the contrary, we had the faculty in
question before we practised its acts. But the virtues
we acquire by previous practice of their acts, exactly
as we acquire our knowledge of the various arts.
For, in the case of the arts, that which we have to be
taught to do, that we learn to do by doing it. We
become masons, for instance, by building; and harpers
by playing upon the harp. And so, in like manner,
we become just by doing what is just, temperate by
doing what is temperate, and brave by doing what is
brave. And to this the practice of States bears witness; for lawgivers make the citizens virtuous by a
course of habituation. It is this that every lawgiver
has in view; all want of success in this respect argues
defective legislation; and it is herein that a good
State differs from a bad. And, moreover, it is from
and by acts of the same kind that all virtue has both
its development and its decay, exactly as has all
artistic skill. For it is by playing upon the harp that
men become either good harpers, or else bad; and of
masons, and indeed of all other craftsmen, the same
rule holds good. For if men build well they will
become good masons, and if badly bad. Were not

(24.) this | so, no art would have needed an apprenticeship,
but men would have been either good craftsmen or
else bad from the very first. And so, too, is it with
the virtues. For, accordingly as we bear ourselves in
our transactions with other men, so do we become
either just or unjust; and, accordingly as we bear

ourselves in dangers, and accustom ourselves to act
as cowards or as brave, so do we become either
cowards or brave. And of all lust, and of all anger,
the same rule holds good. For men become either
temperate and gentle, or intemperate and hasty, accordingly as they bear themselves in such matters either
one way or the other. And, indeed, in a word, all
habits are formed by acts of like nature to themselves.
And hence it becomes our duty to see that our acts
are of a right character. For, as our acts vary, our
habits will follow in their course. It makes no little
difference, then, to what kind of habituation we are
subjected from our youth up; but it is, on the contrary, a matter that is important to us, or rather
all-important.

Since, then, the present treatise is not intended like
certain others to give mere abstract knowledge,—for
our investigations are not undertaken merely that we
may know what virtue is (else wherein would they
benefit us?), but rather that we may ourselves become
virtuous,—we must therefore now consider after
what fashion we are to mould our acts. For it is our
acts, as we have said, that determine the character of
our habits. That they must be in accordance with
right reason is an element common to them with
other things, and which may with safety be assumed
of them; and what this right reason is, and what is
its relation to the virtues, we will hereinafter explain.
And here again, before proceeding further, it must be
understood that all statements concerning human
action are to be taken as being true only in rough

outline, and not as being abstractedly exact; as indeed we said at first when we showed that only such proof is to be expected as the matter allows. Men's actions and men's interests are no more a matter of fixed rule than are the conditions of health. And, since the general principles of morality are of this nature, still less accurate will be their application to
(25.) | particular cases. Such application falls under no known art or traditional system of rules, so that we must, on the occasion of each separate action, be to a great extent guided by the circumstances of the time, exactly as we are in the practice of medicine and of navigation. But, albeit that the difficulties of the present subject are such, we must none the less do our best to aid in its elucidation. First of all, then, we must observe that in all human matters excess and defect are alike prejudicial; as we can see (to take things seen for our evidence of things unseen) in the case of strength and of health. For too much and too little exercise both alike destroy our strength; and in like manner too much meat and drink, and too little, both alike destroy our health; while to eat and to drink in moderation, or to take exercise in moderation, both produce, and increase, and preserve health and strength. And so, too, is it with temperance, and with bravery, and with the other virtues. For he who shuns all dangers, and who is frightened at everything, and who never bears a bold front, becomes a coward; while he who never fears anything at all, and who enters upon every venture, becomes foolhardy. And so, too, he who takes his fill of every

pleasure, and who refrains from none, becomes depraved; while he who avoids all pleasures alike, as do the churlish, becomes insensible. For both temperance and bravery are destroyed by excess and by defect, and are preserved in perfection by moderation. And not only is it from and by the same kind of acts that all virtue has its birth, and its increase, and its decay, but it is also in this same class of acts that the energies in which it manifests itself will lie. And in more obvious matters, such as strength for example, the same rule holds good. For strength is produced by eating much food, and by undergoing much severe labour, and no one can do this so well as he who is strong. And so, too, is it with the virtues. For by abstaining from pleasures we become temperate, and when temperate we are best able so to abstain. And (26.) the same rule holds good of bravery. For by accustoming ourselves to bear our soul above all terrors, and to confront them boldly, we become brave. And it is when we are brave that we shall best be able to

3. meet dangers with a bold front. And as the test of our habits we must take the pleasure or the pain that results from our acts. For he who abstains from the pleasures of the body, and who takes delight in such abstinence, is a temperate man, while he to whom such abstinence gives pain is depraved. And he who faces danger, and does so with delight, or at any rate without pain, he is brave; while he who feels pain in acting thus is a coward. It is with pleasure and with pain, indeed, that moral virtue is concerned ; for it is pleasure that leads us into

disgraceful acts, pain that forces us to abstain from acts noble. So that, as Plato says, we ought to have been trained from our youth up to feel pleasure and pain in fitting objects; for this, and this alone, is good education. Moreover, since it is our actions, that is to say our emotions, that are the field of moral virtue, and since either pleasure or pain follows upon every emotion, and upon every action, it becomes clear that virtue is concerned with pleasure and with pain. And punishment, which is inflicted in the shape of pain, is a proof of this. For punishment is intended as a moral medicine, and the nature of all medicines is to act as the contraries of the diseases which they cure. And moreover, as we have said before, all mental habits are of their very nature directed towards and concerned with those same things by which they are made either better or worse. And it is through the action of pleasures and of pains that they become bad,- in that we pursue, or, as the case may be, avoid these pleasures or pains either when they are such that we ought not to do so, or upon wrong occasions, or in a wrong manner; or fall into some other of the various forms of error that are logically conceivable. And hence it is that virtue has been defined as a state of tranquillity and of freedom from emotion,—but inaccurately. For this definition is too general, needing such additions as, "as we ought," "as we ought not," "when we ought," and all such other determinations as are logically possible. And we may therefore regard it as established that moral virtue is concerned in such a manner with pleasures and with pains as to produce from them the best possible results,—vice the worst. The following considerations will also serve to make the matter clear. There are three things that determine us for pursuit, and three (27.) for avoidance; the good, | the useful, and the pleasant, and their three contraries, the bad, the hurtful, and the painful. And with respect to all of these the judgment of the virtuous man is unerring, and that of the vicious man prone to error; but most of all is it so with respect to pleasure. For pleasure is a motive which man shares with the animals, and which is an element in all objects of choice; since even the good and the useful are both clearly pleasant. Moreover the love of pleasure has been nurtured within us from our cradle, and it is hard to bleach our lives of an emotion with which they have been thus ingrained. Moreover pleasure and pain are as a rule by which we measure our actions, some among us more exactly, some less. So that with them our treatise as a whole must perforce deal. For it makes no little difference to our actions whether we feel pleasure and pain as we ought, or whether we feel them as we ought not. Moreover it is harder to fight with pleasure than, as Heraclitus says, with anger. And it is always with that which is the more difficult that all art and all virtue are concerned; for in such a matter to do well is the more excellent. So that, for this reason again, both virtue, and with it the art political, the object of which is virtue, will be entirely concerned with our pleasures, and with our pains; which whoso uses well, the same will be good; whoso badly, bad.

Thus, then, have we shown that virtue is concerned with pleasures and with pains; and that, if the acts from which it has its birth continue to be done in like manner, it waxes; while, if they be done otherwise, it wanes; and, further, that the field wherein its acts lie is the same as that from which it had its birth.

4. But, again, a difficulty arises as to the exact meaning of our assertion that we must do just acts if we wish to become just, and temperate acts if we wish to become temperate. For, it may be said, if men do acts which are just and temperate, they cannot but be already just and temperate; exactly as, for a man to produce a grammatical or a musical result, he must already be a grammarian or a musician. But then is this quite true even of the arts? Is it not possible, for example, to spell a word correctly by chance, or from dictation? Whereas then, and then only, can a man be said to be a grammarian when he has produced a grammatical result, and produced it grammatically, that is to say in virtue of a know-
(28.) ledge of | grammar which he himself possesses. And, even were this not so, there is no analogy between the arts and the virtues. The excellence of art lies in its results, and it is therefore quite sufficient if these results be so produced as in themselves to fulfil certain required conditions. But moral acts are not said to be done virtuously, as justly, for example, or temperately, if in themselves they fulfil certain conditions, but only when certain conditions are fulfilled by him who does the act. In the first place, he must know what it is that he is doing. Secondly, he must

act with deliberate purpose, and must choose the act for its own sake. Thirdly, he must so act from a fixed and unalterable habit of mind. Now, as regards our artistic skill, none of these conditions need be taken into any account, except that we must know what it is that we are doing. But, where our virtue is concerned, such knowledge is of little or of no import, while the other conditions (which are to be acquired by repeated practice of just and of temperate acts) are so far from being of but little weight that they are the only things that are of any weight at all. Our actions, then, are said to be just and temperate when they are such as the just or temperate man would do. While the just or temperate man is not merely he who does such acts, but he who does them as do the just and temperate. So that it is with good reason that we assert that the just man becomes such by doing just acts, and the temperate man by doing temperate acts, while that, if he refrain from such acts, a man will never have even a prospect of becoming virtuous. But the many do not act upon this rule; they rather betake themselves to mere talk about what is right, deluding themselves into the belief that they are philosophers, and are consequently upon the high road to virtue; but, in reality, acting not unlike a sick man who listens attentively to his physicians, and then carries out none of their advice. And, as surely as such treatment will never give a healthy body, so such philosophy as this will never give a healthy soul.

5.   Let us, after this, inquire what is the genus of

virtue. Now, since there are but three possible kinds of mental states or conditions, to wit emotions, capabilities, and habits, one of these three classes must be the genus of virtue. As instances of emotions may be named lust, anger, fear, pride of strength, envy, (29.) delight, affection, | hatred, longing, emulation, pity, or in a word any immediate state of mind followed by a pleasure or by a pain; while a capability or faculty is that in virtue of which we are said to be capable of such or such an emotion, as of anger for instance, or of pain, or of pity; and a habit is that in virtue of which we stand in a certain relation towards our emotions for good or for bad: our relation to anger, for example, being bad, if we feel anger either too violently or over slightly, but good if we feel it in moderation. And so, too, is it with all the other emotions. Now neither the virtues nor the vices are emotions. For with reference to our emotions we are not called good or bad, as we are with reference to our virtues and our vices. And, again, with reference to our emotions no praise or blame is ever given to us. A man, for example, is never praised for being afraid, or for being angry; nor is a man blamed for simply feeling anger, but for the manner in which he feels it. But with reference to our virtues and our vices we are praised and blamed. Moreover, neither anger nor fear springs from purpose, whereas the virtues, if not to be absolutely identified with purpose, most certainly involve such purpose, and imply it. And, again, with reference to the emotions we say that a man is thus or thus affected, but with reference to the virtues and the vices we do not talk of his affection, but of his disposition. Hence, too, it follows that the virtues and the vices are not mere capabilities. For we are not said to be good or bad, nor are we praised or blamed, in that we are simply capable of feeling such or such an emotion. And, moreover, our capabilities are either innate or connate, which our virtues and our vices are not, as we have said before. So that, since the virtues are neither emotions, nor capabilities, it remains that they must be habits.

6. Thus, then, we have ascertained what is the genus of virtue. It remains to determine its differentia, and to say wherein it can be distinguished from other habits. We must premise that every excellence or virtue perfects that thing of which it is the virtue, and causes it to perform its function well. The excellence of the eye, for example, makes the eye good, and perfects its function; for it is only by the virtue of the eye that we can see well. So, too, the excellence of the horse makes it a good horse, swift, and strong to carry its rider, | and bold to face his enemies. And if this be true, as it is in all cases, it follows that the virtue of man will be such a habit as will make him a good man, and enable him to perform his function well. And how this is to be brought about we have already said; but we shall make the matter yet clearer if we consider wherein the nature of moral virtue consists. In everything that is continuous, and consequently capable of division, we can mark off an amount which will be either more than, or less than,

or equal to the remainder; and can do so either objectively, that is to say with reference to the matter in question, or subjectively, that is to say with reference to ourselves. Now that which is equal is a mean between excess and defect. And by the mean of the matter I understand that which, as is the point of bisection in a line, is equally distant from either extreme, and which is for all persons alike one and the same. But by the mean with reference to ourselves I understand that which is neither too much for us nor too little, and which consequently is not any one fixed point which for all alike remains the same. If, for example, ten pounds be too much and two pounds be too little, we take as the mean with reference to the matter six pounds, which exceed two pounds by as much as they are exceeded by ten. This is what is called a mean in arithmetical progression. But the mean with reference to ourselves must not be thus fixed. For it does not follow that, if ten pounds of meat be too much to eat, and two pounds be too little, our trainer will therefore order us six pounds. For this may be either too little for him who is to take it, or too much. For Milo, for example, it would be too little, while for one who is to begin training it would be too much. And in running, and in wrestling, the same rule holds good. And so, too, all skilled artists avoid the excess and the defect, while they seek and choose the mean, that is to say not the absolute but the relative mean. And since it is thus that all skilled knowledge perfects its results, by keeping the mean steadily in view, and by modelling its work upon it, whence it comes that we are wont to say, at the termination of any good work, that neither to it can anything be added, nor from it can anything be taken away; inasmuch as excess and defect destroy perfection, while moderation preserves it;—since, then, all good artists, as we have said, always work with the mean in view, and since virtue is, as also is nature, (11.) more exact | and higher than is any art, it follows that virtue also will aim at the mean. And when I say virtue I mean moral virtue, for moral virtue is concerned with our emotions, that is to say with our actions; and in these excess and defect are to be found, and also moderation. Fear, for example, and confidence, and desire, and anger, and pity, and, generally, any pleasure or pain, we can feel both more and less than we ought, and in either case we feel them not well. But to feel them when we ought, and at what we ought, and towards whom we ought, and for the right motive, and as we ought,—in all this lies the mean, and with the mean perfection; and these are the characteristics of virtue. And so, too, with reference to our actions, no less than our emotions, excess and defect are possible, and with them consequently moderation. Now virtue is concerned with our emotions and with our actions. It is in these that excess is an error, and that defect is blamed as a fault; while moderation meets with praise and with success, both of which things are marks of virtue. And hence it is that all virtue is a mean, in that it aims at that which is the mean. Moreover the forms of wrong are manifold (for evil is of the infinite, as said the allegory of the Pythagoreans, and good of the finite), while of right the form is but one. Hence the one is easy, the other hard; easy is it to miss, hard to hit our aim. And from this again it follows that to vice belong excess and defect, and to virtue belongs moderation.

> One path hath righteousness, but many sin.

Moral virtue, then, is a certain formed state, or habit of purpose, which conforms to the relative mean in action, and which is determined to that mean by reason, or as the prudent man would determine it. And it is the mean between two vices, one of which consists in excess, and the other in defect. So that the vices sometimes fall short of what is right in our emotions and in our actions, and sometimes exceed it, while virtue finds the mean and chooses it. So (32.) that in its essence, and by its real definition, | virtue is a mean; but as regards perfection and goodness it is an extreme. But it is not every action or every emotion that allows of moderation. There are some the very name of which is sufficient to class them with the vices; such as are, for instance, malice, shamelessness, envy, among our emotions; and, among our acts, adultery, theft, and homicide. For all these things, and all others such, are blamed in that they are absolutely bad, not in that the excess or the defect of them is bad. In such matters one can never act rightly, but is always wrong; nor can one talk upon such occasions of behaving ill, or of behaving well; as, for example, by committing adultery with

whom one ought, and when one ought, and as one
ought; for to do any one of these things is wrong,
whatever be the circumstances of the case. One
might as well insist upon a mean and an excess
and a defect of injustice, and of cowardice, and of
debauchery; so making a mean in an absolute excess
and in an absolute defect, and an excess in an absolute excess, and a defect in an absolute defect.
Whereas, just as there can be no excess or defect in
temperance, or in bravery,—such a mean being as it
were the indivisible point at the apex of a triangle,—
so, too, in the case of the vices above quoted, neither
a mean nor an excess nor a defect is possible; but
under whatever circumstances such acts are committed they are wrong. For, to sum up, the mean of
an excess or of a defect, no less than the excess or the
defect of a mean, is a self-contradictory conception.

7.   But we must not rest content with a statement
thus purely general; we must also confirm it by an
application to particulars. In all matters of human
action broad generalisations are apt to be void of
content, and consequently unsatisfactory, the truth
rather lying in particular propositions. For the field
of action lies in particulars, and with these particulars
our generalisations must concord. Our confirmatory
instances we will draw from the recognised catalogue
of the virtues. Now, with regard to the emotions of
fear and of pride of strength, bravery is the mean.
Of those who run into excess, he who shows excess of
fearlessness has no name (as, indeed, is the case with
many moral states), and he who runs into excess of

pride of strength is foolhardy; while the coward is he who is either over-fearful, or deficient in proper confidence. Temperance, again, is a mean, and debauchery (33.) is an excess, not with respect to all pains and pleasures, but only to some, and concerned with pleasures rather than with pains. That a man's sense of pleasure should be deficient is a case that rarely or never occurs, and hence such a character has as yet found no name. But, provisionally, such men may be called insensible or ascetic. With respect to the giving and the taking of money, the mean is liberality, the excess and the defect are prodigality and illiberality. These vices are contradictorily opposed to each other, each being an excess of that of which the other is a defect. For the prodigal runs into excess in the giving of money, but in taking his due into defect; while the illiberal man is over-greedy in the receipt of money, and in giving it falls short of the true mean. We are now giving a mere summary outline, such being for the present sufficient for our purpose. Hereinafter these various states shall be more minutely described. With regard to money there are also certain other moral states. Magnificence is a mean (the magnificent man differing from the liberal in that the latter is concerned with small matters, the former with great), while its excess is bad taste and vulgarity; and its defect is pettiness. These two vices differ from the excess and the defect of liberality; and wherein the difference consists we will hereafter show. And, again, with regard to honour and dishonour, the mean state is high-mindedness; its excess is what has been called "chirking vanity," and its defect is feebleness of spirit. And, in like manner as we said when we contrasted magnificence with liberality that liberality differed from it in that it was concerned with small sums, so, too, is there a virtue which stands in a similar relation to high-mindedness, dealing with small honour, while high-mindedness deals with great. For one can aim at honour both as one ought, and more than one ought, and less than one ought. He whose craving for honour is excessive is said to be ambitious, and he who is deficient in this respect unambitious; while he who observes the mean has no peculiar name. Indeed, all these states are really nameless, except that of the ambitious man, which is known as ambition. Hence it arises that those who have run into either extreme lay claim to the mean, as a kind of border march; and hence, too, we at times call him who is in the mean state ambitious, and at times again we call him unambitious.

(34.) And on some occasions we praise the ambitious man, and on others again the unambitious man. Our reasons for this shall be given hereafter; meantime let us complete our enumeration of the virtues, drawing our distinctions by the aid of the method which has guided us all along. Anger, again, admits of an excess, and of a defect, and of a mean. These states can hardly be said to have any names of their own; but, as we call him gentle who is in the mean state, we hence will call the mean state itself gentleness; while, of those who fall into the extremes, he who errs on the side of excess may be called hasty, and his vice is hastiness; he whose error is one of defect spiritless, and the defect in question want of proper spirit. And there are also three other mean states, which to some extent resemble one another, and are yet distinct. They resemble one another in that they are all concerned with the daily intercourse of men in their speech and in their actions, and they are distinct in that the one is concerned with what is truthful in such matters, and the other two with what is pleasant. And of these two latter, the field of the one is our recreations, that of the other all the circumstances of our daily life. We must then place these also in our list, so as to still further strengthen our conviction that in all cases the mean state is praiseworthy, the extremes neither right nor praiseworthy, but blameable. The majority of these states are nameless; but we must endeavour, as we have done with others, to coin a name for each of them, that we may thereby give precision to our treatise, and render its course intelligible. With regard to truth then he who is in the mean is the truthful man, and the mean state itself may be called truthfulness, while all pretence to more than our merits is braggartry, and he who advances such pretences is a braggart. And, on the other hand, all dissimulation of our own powers is irony, as it is to be seen in the ironical man. And, as regards the element of pleasure in our amusements, he who hits the mean is the witty man, and his moral state is wittiness, while the excess is gross buffoonery, and he who displays it is a buffoon; and, on the other hand, he who is deficient in wit is a boor, and his habit is boorishness. And, as regards the other aspect of pleasure in our life as a whole, he who is pleasant as he ought to be is friendly, and the mean state is friendliness, while he who runs into excess, if it be with no particular object in view, is over-polite, but, if it be to serve his own ends, is a sycophant; while he again who errs on the side of defect, and who never lays himself out to please others, is quarrelsome and peevish. There are more-(35.) over certain mean states in our | emotions, and in the circumstances with which our emotions are concerned. Shame, for instance, is not a virtue, and yet he who shows a proper shame is praised. For in these matters we say that such a man is in the mean, and that such another runs into excess, as does the over-bashful man who feels shame at all things, while he who is deficient in this respect, or he who never displays shame at all, is called shameless; and he again who hits the mean is said to show a proper sense of shame. Lastly, righteous indignation is a mean between envy and malignity. These are states concerned with the pleasures and the pains caused by the fortunes of our neighbours. For he who feels righteous indignation is grieved when he sees the ungodly in prosperity. The envious man, on the other hand, runs into excess, and is grieved at the prosperity of all alike; while the malignant man, so far from feeling pain at the prosperity of the ungodly, actually rejoices thereat. But concerning all these states we shall have fitting occasion to speak elsewhere; and so too concerning justice, which is a word unlike the analysis of a geometrical problem. Indeed, although all investigation is not deliberation, as we can see in the case of a mathematical investigation, yet all deliberation is a kind of investigation,* wherein the last term in our analysis of ends into their means forms the first term in the production of ends by their means. When, in deliberation, men come to a means which is out of their power, they abandon it to seek for another; as, for example, when, to gain a certain end, money is required, but money cannot possibly be procured. But, should the means be possible, they then endeavour to take them. By "possible" is to be understood that which our own agency can effect. Even that which is effected by our friends is, in a way, effected by ourselves: for such matters really begin with ourselves. At times our question is, what instrument is to be used, and, at times, again, which is the right method of its use. And so, too, in other cases, at times our enquiry is, by means of what is such or such an end to be attained; and, at times, again, in what manner, or by whose assistance. It would seem, then, as has been said, that man's actions originate in himself, that deliberation is concerned with those things alone that we ourselves can do, and that all our actions have an ulterior end in view; so that it is not the end which is the object of deliberation, but the means to that end. Nor do we ever deliberate when we have come to a particular question of fact. We do not, for example, deliberate

---

* Continue the parenthesis from ζητησις down to the end of the sentence in the next line, ending with γενεσις.

whether this be a loaf, or whether it has been properly baked. For upon such matters perception passes an immediate judgment. And, were everything alike to be matter of deliberation, the chain of analysis would be infinite. Thus, then, the object of deliberation and the object of purpose will be identical, save in so far as the latter is, *ipso facto*, distinguished from the former, in that we call that purposed which has, after due deliberation, been preferred to all other alternatives. In fine, a man ceases to deliberate as to how he is to act, when he has identified the efficient cause of the desired end with himself; that is to say, with that faculty in himself which takes the lead in action, or which purposes to take a certain set of means in preference to all others. Our meaning is clearly illustrated by the old constitutions described in the poems of Homer, and in which the Kings (46.) declared their purpose | to the Commons. Since, then, the object of purpose is a something in our power, upon which we have exercised deliberation, and the result of which is the gratification of a desire, it follows that purpose is a desire for a something in our own power, coupled with an investigation into its means. For, after an investigation into the means to the end which we desire, we choose some one particular set of means, and so make our desire for an end accord with our analysis of that end into its means.

Here, then, we will close our sketch of purpose, having stated what is its object-matter, namely, the means to such ends as we desire.

4. We have already said that the object of wish is the end of action. But, while some think that its object is that which is objectively and truly good, others think that it is only that which subjectively seems good to ourselves. Now those who assert that the object of wish is that which is objectively good, cannot avoid the conclusion that that cannot really be the object of wish for which he wishes whose choice is faulty. For, if it be the object of wish, it ought, on their showing, to be good; whereas it may, perhaps, in such or in such a case, be bad. And those again who assert that the object of wish is only that which subjectively seems good, must also admit that it is not the natural fitness of things, but rather each man's individual fancies, that determine the object of his wish. And, inasmuch as each man has his own point of view, it follows that of two contradictories each may equally be the object of wish. And, since neither of these conclusions commend themselves to us, is it not perhaps best to say that the abstract and true object of wish is that which is really good, while for the individual the object of his wish is that which he holds to be good? So that, while the good man wishes for what is really good, the bad man may wish for anything, whether good or bad: exactly as, when our bodies are sound, that diet is healthy for us which is really healthy, while, when they are diseased, sometimes one thing is healthy for us, sometimes another. And in like manner with things bitter, and things sweet, and things hot, and things heavy, and indeed with all such things as in any way affect us, the same

rule holds good. For it is the man whose condition, whether moral or bodily, is in each case perfect who in each case judges rightly, and at once perceives the truth. For, as our conditions vary, so do various things seem to us good or pleasant. And herein it is that the perfect man may be said to differ most widely from all others, in that in all such cases he at once perceives the truth, being, as it were, the rule and measure of its application. But the majority of mankind would seem to be beguiled into error by pleasure, which, not being really a good, yet seems to be so. So that they indiscriminately choose as good whatsoever gives them pleasure, while they avoid all pain alike as evil.

5. Inasmuch, then, as the end of action is the object of wish, while the means to that end are the object of deliberation and of purpose, the actions into which (47.) these means enter will be done | with purpose, and will consequently be voluntary. And it is with these means to such ends as we desire that all acts of virtue are concerned. And consequently virtue is in our own power, and, by parity of reasoning, so is vice. For, where it is in our power to do a thing, it is equally in our power to abstain from doing it; where refusal is in our power, assent is equally so. So that, if to do such or such a thing, which is noble, be in our power, to abstain from it, which is disgraceful, will be equally in our power; and, if to abstain from doing such or such a thing, which is noble, be in our power, then to do it, which is disgraceful, will be equally in our power. And if, in a word, it be in

our power to do what is noble and what is disgraceful, it is equally in our power not to do it. Or, in other words, it is in our power to be good men or bad. It rests, then, with ourselves whether we are to be virtuous or vicious. To say that

> No man of his own will bears evil plight,
> Or prosperous plight against his will enjoys,—

seems partly false and partly true. For against his own will no man can be happy; but all vice is voluntary. On any other assumption, we shall have to contradict all that we have been saying, and to assert that man is not the efficient cause of his own actions, and their sire, as he is of his offspring. But, if we are satisfied with our present conclusions, and can refer our actions to no causes beyond such as are in our own control, it follows that our actions, since their causes are in our own control, are themselves in our own control, and so voluntary. And to this witness would seem to be borne, no less by each man in his own life, than by legislators who make life their study. For they afflict with pains and penalties those who do what is wicked, save only where they have done it under compulsion, or from an ignorance for which they cannot be held responsible; while to those who do what is noble they hold out honour as a reward, with a view to encourage the latter, and to check the former. But, where a thing is not in our own power, and so not voluntary, no encouragement can make us do it; since it is but idle labour to endeavour to persuade a man not to feel heat, or pain, or hunger, or anything else of this sort. For, spite of all persuasion, we cannot but be thus affected. Nay, more, for our very ignorance they punish us, if that ignorance seem to be self-caused; double penalties, for example, being affixed to crimes done in drunkenness, inasmuch as they primarily originate in (48.) the volition of the agent. | For it was in his own power not to get thus drunk, and it was his drunkenness that was the cause of his ignorance. And, moreover, they punish those who act in ignorance of any particular enactment of the laws which ought to be known, and which it is not difficult to learn; and, indeed, in all cases of ignorance whatsoever, where the ignorance appears to be the result of negligence: since it was in the man's power to avoid such ignorance, in that he was perfectly able to give the matter all due attention. But, it may be urged, what if a man's character be such that he is incapable of this attention? To which it may be answered, that, for their becoming such, men are themselves responsible, in that they live dissolutely; in brief, that men bring upon themselves their own injustice or intemperance by wrong-doing, or by passing their time in drunkenness and other such follies. For, in brief, specific acts produce in their agent a correspondent character, as is clear from the case of those who are in training for a trial of strength, or for any other performance, and who continuously practise the particular act required. To be ignorant, then, that all habits are formed by the practice of particular acts, shows gross want of common sense. Indeed, it is absurd to

suppose that a man should persevere in unjust acts,
and yet not wish to be unjust, or in intemperate acts,
and yet not wish to be intemperate. But, if a man
persists in a course of conduct which cannot but
make him unjust, being at the same time well
aware that such will be its effect, he will become
unjust of his own free will. It does not, however,
follow that, should he so desire, he will cease to be
unjust, and will become just again, any more than
that a sick man can wish himself back into good
health. Let us, for example, suppose the case of a
man who has brought on a sickness of his own free
will, by incontinent living, and by contempt of his
physicians. It would once have been in his power
to have escaped this sickness, which it no longer is,
now that he has lost his self-control: exactly as,
when the stone has once left our hand, it is no longer
in our power to recall it; although it none the less
was once in our power either to pick* it up or not,
or to throw it or not, as we chose,—our own volition
being the efficient cause. And so, too, with the unjust
man, and with the intemperate,—originally it was in
their power not to become such, and consequently
they are such of their own free will. But, now that
they have become such, it is no longer possible for
them not to be such. And, indeed, not only are the
vices of our souls voluntary, but in some cases (those
that is to say where we award censure for them)
even the vices of our bodies. No one, for example,

---

* For ἀλλὰ read λαβεῖν with Argyropylus, Lambinus, Coraes, and others.

censures those who are mis-shapen by nature, but only those who have become so from want of proper exercise and care. And so, too, with all weakness and mutilation. No one, for example, would cast it in a man's teeth that he was blind by nature, or from (49.) sickness, or from | a blow, but would rather pity him; while all would censure him who had lost his sight from what is known as "drunkard's blindness," or from any other intemperate living. In a word, then, we are censured for such bodily-vices as it is in our power to avoid, and not for such as are out of our own power. And, if this be so, then, of all other vices whatsoever, it follows that those for which we are censured will be in our own power. But suppose it be urged that, although all men aim at what they conceive to be good, yet they are not masters of their own conceptions, but that, as is each man's character, such is his conception of the true end of action. To this it may be replied that, if a man be in any sense whatever responsible for his moral condition, in that same sense will he also be responsible for his conception of the true end; but that, if he be not so responsible, then no man can be held responsible for the evil which he does, but must be held thus to act through ignorance of the true end, and thinking by such means to attain the chief good: in other words, that it is not our own choice which determines the end at which we aim, but that a man must be born with what may be called a moral sight, by which he will judge rightly and will choose that which is truly good; and that he alone on whom nature has bestowed this gift in full, is of noble nature. For, where nature has given to a man in its full perfection and beauty the greatest and noblest of her gifts, which no man can either get or learn from another, but such as nature has given it him so only must have it, there surely we have perfect and true natural nobility. But, if all this be true, how can it be shown that virtue is any more voluntary than is vice? For, for both alike, for the good man no less than for the bad, their conception of the true end of life is given and determined either by nature or by some other agency, and they act, whether for evil or for good, in that they take certain means with reference to this end. Whether, then, each man's conception of the end, whatever that may be, be not determined for him by nature, but be a something dependent upon himself; or whether our conception of the end be determined for us by nature, while virtue is voluntary in that the good man voluntarily takes the means to this end; in either case vice cannot be shown to be less voluntary than is virtue. For the bad man no less than the good has free agency in his actions, even if not in his choice of the end. If then the virtues be voluntary, as we assert,—for we cannot but to some extent contribute to the formation of our habits, and, (50.) according as is our character, | such or such is the end which we propose to ourselves,—the vices also will be voluntary; for of both virtues and vices the same reasoning holds good.

Thus, then, as regards all the virtues alike, we have roughly described their genus, and asserted that they are mean states, and also more definitely that they are habits; and we have stated the acts by which they are produced, and have said that they of their own nature tend to make us repeat these same acts; and, further, that they depend upon ourselves, or are in a word voluntary, and that they are regulated as right reason orders. But our actions and our habits are not equally voluntary. For, provided we in each case know the details, we are masters of our actions from the beginning up to the very end. But, in the case of our habits, we are only masters of their commencement,—each particular little increase being as imperceptible as in the case of bodily infirmities. But yet our habits are voluntary, in that it was once in our power to adopt or not to adopt such or such a course of conduct.

We will resume, then, the detailed account of the individual virtues, saying what they are, and with what they are concerned, and how; and so will at the same time make it clear how many they are in number. And, first, let us treat of bravery. That it is a mean state, concerned with fear and confidence, has

6. already been said. What we fear is manifestly things terrible, or, to use a more general phrase, things evil; whence comes the definition of fear as the anticipation of evil. Now we fear evil of every kind; as, for instance, loss of reputation, poverty, disease, loss of friends, death. But with all these the brave man is not held to be concerned. For there are some things which a man ought to fear: to do so is noble, and not to do so is disgraceful. Loss of reputation is a fair instance. He who fears this is a good man, and shows

a proper shame, while he who fears it not is brazen-faced. But yet some people call even such a man as this brave, thus transferring the term because he has a certain resemblance to the brave man; for the brave man also is a fearless character. Poverty, perhaps, a man ought not to fear, or disease, or, indeed, anything that is not the result of vice, and for which he is not responsible. But yet he who is fearless of these things is not, on that account, a brave man, although we call him too brave, in virtue of his resemblance to the brave man. For some there are who, although cowards amid the dangers of war, are yet of liberal spirit, and throw away their money with a good
(51.) courage. Neither is a man a coward if he fears insult and injury for his children and his wife, or envy for himself, or anything of a similar sort; nor is he brave if he is of good courage when about to be flogged through the streets. With what kind, then, of terrible things is the brave man concerned? With the greatest, surely; for there is no one who will with equal fearlessness face what is dreadful. Now of all things death is the most terrible, for it is an absolute end, beyond which popular opinion assigns to the dead man neither good nor evil. But yet it is not with every form of death that the brave man would seem to be concerned, as with death at sea, for instance, or with death by disease. With what form of death, then, is he concerned? Surely with death under the noblest conditions. And such is death in war; for war involves the greatest and noblest of all risks. Testimony is borne to this by the rewards

which are given in free states and by absolute rulers. He then alone will strictly be called brave who is fearless of a noble death, and of all such chances as come upon us with sudden death in their train. And such especially are the chances of war. Not but that in sickness and at sea the brave will be fearless, although not in the same manner as are mariners. For the brave will have given up all hope of life, and will feel grief and indignation at such a death, while experience will make the mariners of good courage. And, moreover, we play the brave man where either our prowess can be shown, or our death will be noble; neither of which is the case in such a loss of life as are these.

7. Not only is that which is fearful not for all men the same, but we also recognize some things as being too fearful for any human strength. A danger of this kind will be fearful to anyone who is in his right mind, while things fearful in the ordinary course of human nature are some greater and some smaller, some more fearful and some less. And of things that inspire confidence the same rule holds good. Now the brave man, as judged by the ordinary standard, is never terrified out of his self-possession. He will consequently fear all things of this kind, but he will none the less face them as he ought, and as reason orders, having in view that which is beautifully good and noble, which is the end of all virtue. Now one may fear dangers of this kind more than one ought and less, and one may moreover fear that which is not fearful as if it were such. Our error sometimes

consists in fearing where no fear is, or sometimes in showing our fear as we ought not, or sometimes in showing fear at a moment when we ought not, or in something else of this kind. And similarly errors
(52.) arise with respect to those things | that inspire confidence. He then who with the right end in view faces what he ought, and fears it, and does so as he ought, and when he ought, and who in a similar manner faces with confidence that which ought to be so faced,—he is brave. For the brave man both suffers and acts as is right and as reason orders. Now the end in view in each particular act will be the end which is conformable to the habit of which that act is a manifestation. To the brave man his bravery is a noble thing. Such then will be the end which his bravery as a whole has in view; for in every case the attributes of a habit are determined by its end. And consequently it will be for the sake of that which is noble that the brave man faces danger, and achieves his acts of bravery. Of those who run into excess, he whose excess takes the shape of absolute fearlessness has no name (we have already said that there are many moral states with no name of their own), but he would be a simple madman, or insensible to all pain, were he to fear nothing, neither earthquakes nor breakers, as we are told of the Celts. On the other hand he who shows excessive confidence in matters really fearful is foolhardy. The foolhardy man would seem to be a braggart, and to lay claim to a courage which he has not. As then the brave man bears himself in what is fearful, so he wishes to seem to

bear himself, and therefore, where he can at all do so, he imitates the brave man. And hence the majority of such men are blusterers; for, although they are over confident where there is a semblance of danger, they cannot be brought to face what is really terrible. He, again, whose fear is excessive is a coward, and upon cowardice it is always consequent to fear what we ought not, and to fear it as we ought not, and to fall into all such other faults. The coward is deficient in confidence, but he is most easily detected by his excessive dislike of pain. He is moreover but of faint hope, for he fears all things alike. Quite other is the brave man: for confidence betokens good hopes. Thus, then, both the coward, and the foolhardy man, and the brave man, are concerned with the same matters, but stand to them in a different relation. For the coward and the foolhardy commit errors both of excess and of defect, while the brave man observes the mean, and acts as he ought. And the foolhardy are headlong and zealous before the danger, but in the midst of danger they hold aloof; while the brave are keen in action, but before the crisis are self-possessed.

(53.) As then has been said, bravery is a mean state concerned with things that inspire confidence and with things fearful, under the circumstances already described, and leading us to | choose danger and to face it, either because to do so is noble, or because not to do so is base. But to court death as an escape from poverty, or from love, or from some grievous pain, is no proof of bravery, but rather of cowardice.

For to fly from trouble is mere effeminacy, and such a man does not face death because it is noble to do so, but merely that he may escape from present evil.

8. True bravery, then, is such as has been described. But there are also five other forms of bravery generally recognized. First among these we will describe what has been called political bravery, for it is the most like to the true. It is so called because citizens would seem to face danger under influence of the penalties and disgraces which the laws inflict, and of the honours which they hold out. And hence it is that they would seem to be bravest among whom cowards are infamous, and the brave are held in honour. Homer has told us in his poems of men who were brave after this wise, as Diomed for instance, and Hector,—

> Polydamus will of all men be first
> To heap reproach upon me;

and Diomed, too, says—

> Hector will boast among the Trojan lords,—
> "Tydides by my hand——."

This kind of courage is most like that described above, in that it has its origin in virtue; for it arises from a proper shame and from a desire to win what is noble, to wit | honour, and to avoid stigma, which is disgraceful. Along with bravery of this kind may be classed the courage of those who are forced by their officers into battle, but which is however inferior to it in that they act thus not from a proper sense of shame but rather from fear, and that what they desire to avoid is not so much disgrace as pain. For they who are set over them drive them into action, as did Hector,—

> Whom so aloof from fight I cowering find,
> Him hounds shall surely rend.

And they who post cowards among the ranks of the veterans, and then have them beaten if they give ground, act in a similar way; as also do they who place their lines immediately in front of a trench, or in some similar position. For they all force their troops into action; whereas our bravery ought not to be forced, but to be a free act prompted by desire of what is noble. Secondly, experience of certain particular details would seem to be a species of bravery. And hence it was that Socrates thought that all bravery was knowledge. This kind of experience will, according to the circumstances of the case, be possessed by various people, and in war by professed soldiers. For war would seem to have many empty terrors, which they, most of all men, have learned to understand; and hence they appear by comparison brave, in that their fellows do not know how slight the danger is. And, moreover, their experience enables them better than others to inflict wounds and themselves to remain unwounded; for they are skilled in the use of arms, and have moreover such as are best adapted to wound the foe and to protect the wearer. Such men, then, when they fight, are like armed troops contending with unarmed, or professional wrestlers with amateurs. For in contests of this kind it is not the bravest who make the best fight, but those who are strongest, and in

best condition. Nay, more, professional soldiers will
sometimes even play the coward, when the danger is
too great for them, and when they are short in num-
bers and deficiently equipped; for then they are the
first to take to flight; while the volunteer contingent
dies at its post, as happened in the battle near the
temple of Hermes. For, for the latter, flight is disgraceful, and death is preferable to safety gained at
such a price; while the former originally faced the
the risk trusting to their superior strength, and when
they learn their weakness take to flight, fearing
death rather than disgrace. Far other is the brave
man. Anger, too, has sometimes been ascribed to
bravery. For, because the brave are also highspirited,
it has been held that they too are brave who in a fit
of anger rush like wild beasts against those who have
wounded them. Anger is indeed the keenest of all
spurs to risk. Whence says Homer,

    Strength to his wrath she gave;

and again,

    His might and wrath she roused;

and again,

    Up through his nostrils surged the bitter wrath;

and again,

    His blood boiled over;

for all such phrases as these would seem to indicate
the uprising and onset of anger. Now the truly
(55.) brave | act as they do for the sake of what is noble,
and in their actions anger has its proper share,
whereas beasts act from fear of pain. It is because
they have been wounded, or because they are afraid;

for, if they are safe in a wood, or in a swamp, they
never commence the attack. The fact that they are
driven by pain or by passion to rush against danger,
foreseeing none of its terrible results, does not make
them brave. From such a point of view even asses
would be brave when they are hungry, for however
much they are beaten they will not leave their pas-
turage. And adulterers, too, are led by their lust to
do many deeds of daring. Beasts, then, are not to be
accounted brave when they are driven by pain or
anger to encounter danger. This quasi-courage of
anger is of all kinds of courage the most physical; but,
if there be added to it a proper purpose, that is to say
a good motive, it becomes identical with true bravery.
When men are provoked to anger they feel pain, and
when they revenge themselves they feel pleasure.
But those who engage in battle with these motives
show pugnacity rather than bravery, for they do not
act with that which is noble in view, nor as reason
orders, but are led by passion. They, therefore, to
a certain extent only, resemble the truly brave.
Neither ought those who are over-sanguine to be
called brave, for their only confidence in danger is
that they have conquered many enemies, and often.
They resemble the brave, however, in that, like them,
they are full of confidence. But the brave are confident from the reasons we have given above; the sanguine because they think that they are the stronger,
and that they will meet with no return of injury.
(Drunken men act in much the same way, for they
too become full of confidence.) But, when the result

proves other than they had hoped, then they take
refuge in flight; whereas the brave man ought rather
to face that which, as judged by a human standard,
is fearful, and which seems such; because to do so is
noble, and not to do so is disgraceful. And so, too,
it shows more bravery to be fearless and untroubled
in sudden terror, than in foreseen; for to act thus is
more the result of a settled habit, or in other words
is less the result of previous preparation. For, where
a man can anticipate danger, he might perhaps choose
it after some reflection and reasoning; but towards
sudden danger the bravery which we exhibit is the
immediate result of our character. They, too, appear
to be brave who are ignorant of the presence of danger.
Their bravery is but little removed from that of the
sanguine, but yet inferior to it, inasmuch as, unlike
(56.) it, it involves no self-confidence. And hence the
sanguine will stand their ground for awhile; whereas
they who have been deceived as to the extent of the
danger, as soon as they learn that it is greater than
they had suspected, take to flight; as did the Argives
when they encountered the Spartans whom they had
taken to be Sicyonians. Thus, then, we have said
what kind of men are the brave, and also what kind
of men are they who are wrongly reputed to be such.

9. Now, although bravery is concerned both with confidence and with fear, it is not equally concerned with
each, but has rather to do with things fearful. For he
who is untroubled amidst these, and who bears himself as he ought concerning them,—he is to be called
brave, rather than is he who bears himself as he ought

in circumstances that inspire confidence. Men are indeed called brave, as we have already said, for withstanding what is painful. And hence bravery involves pain as its consequent, and is with justice praised; for it is more difficult to withstand what is painful than to abstain from what is pleasant. Not but that the end of bravery would seem to have a pleasure of its own, although obscured by the circle of its environments, as is the case also in gymnastic contests. For, for the boxers, the end, having which in view they contend, to wit the crown and the honour, has a pleasure of its own. But the blows which they receive, and the toils which they undergo, must needs be grievous and painful to them, since, after all, they are but flesh and blood. And, since they have many troubles of this kind to undergo, the true end for which they labour, being in itself but a small thing, seems at first sight to have no pleasure of its own. Since, then, with regard to courage the same rule holds good, it will follow that death and wounds will be grievous to the brave man, and be sorely against his will; but that he will none the less face them, because to do so is noble, and not to do so is disgraceful. And the more that he possess every virtue, and the happier that he be, the more grievous will death be to him. For to such a man life is of the highest value, and yet he consciously deprives himself of the very greatest goods: and to act thus is a grievous task. He is, however, none the less to be held brave on this account, but perhaps even more so, in that he chooses war's noblest prize in place of all other worldly goods. All virtuous acts, indeed, are not as a rule pleasant, save only in so far as their true end is attained. Nor does it perhaps of necessity follow that it is men such as we have described who make the best soldiers, and not rather men with (57.) less bravery, and with naught else about them good. For such men are ready to face all kinds of danger, and for a little lucre will barter their lives.

About bravery, then, thus much suffices, for, from what we have said, it is not difficult to shape an out-
10. line of its nature.

After bravery we will consider temperance, for these two would seem to be the virtues of the irrational portions of our soul. Now that temperance is a mean state concerned with pleasures we have already said; for with pains it is less concerned, or at least not equally; its field being, in fact, identical with that in which intemperance manifests itself. It remains, then, to determine with what kind of pleasure it is concerned. And, first, there is a clear distinction between the pleasures of the body on the one hand, and those on the other of the soul, such as are the love of honour and the love of learning. For, while the ambitious man and the student each takes pleasure in their special object of pursuit, it is yet not their body that is in any way thereby affected, but rather their understanding. And those who are concerned with pleasures of this kind we neither call temperate, nor yet intemperate. And the same holds true of all pleasures that are not distinctly bodily. For those who are fond of listening to long stories, and who love the

sound of their own voice, and who waste their days
upon trifles, we call idlers, indeed, but yet not intemperate; neither do we call those intemperate who
are grieved at the loss of money, or of friends.
Temperance, then, is concerned with the bodily
pleasures; but yet not with all of even these. For
those who take pleasure in the presentations of sight,
as in colours, and in outlines, and in paintings, are
neither called temperate, nor yet intemperate, although it would none the less seem to be possible
to take pleasure in such things as one ought, and
more than one ought, and less than one ought. And
of the presentations of the hearing the same rule
holds good. For no one calls intemperate those who
take an excessive pleasure in music, or in acting, nor
calls those again temperate who take in such things
the pleasure which they ought. Nor do we call
those intemperate to whom the sense of smell gives
pleasure, unless it be indirectly. For we do not call
those intemperate who take pleasure in the smell of
fruit, or of roses, or of incense, but rather those who
(5B.) take pleasure in the smell of unguents and of made
dishes; for in the smell of these it is that the intemperate rejoice, because they are by it reminded
of the objects of their desire. One may indeed
observe that all men as a rule, when hungry, take
pleasure in the smell of food. But to consistently
take pleasure in such things is a mark of intemperance, for it is only to the intemperate man that
these things are objects of desire. Nor do even
animals derive any pleasure from these senses, except

indirectly. For it is not in the scent of the hare that the hounds rejoice, but in the eating of it,—it being the scent by which they perceived its presence. Nor does the lion rejoice in the lowing of the ox, but rather in the devouring of it,—it being the lowing by which he perceived that the ox was near, and in which he consequently seems to rejoice. Nor, in like manner, does he rejoice because he sees a deer or a wild goat, or because he comes upon its traces, but because he knows that he will have food to eat. Temperance, then, and intemperance are concerned with pleasures of that kind in which even the animals share, and which consequently appear slavish and brutal; and these are the pleasures of touch and of taste. But of taste the intemperate seem to make but little or no use. For to the taste properly belongs the distinction of flavours, which is the task of those who taste wines and who season made dishes. But in flavours, as such, the intemperate take but little pleasure, or rather none at all, their pleasure being rather in that enjoyment which is to be derived from eating, and drinking, and venery, and which is entirely a matter of touch. And hence it was that a certain man who was a glutton prayed for a gullet longer than that of a crane, since it was the actual touch of the food from which he derived his pleasure. The pleasure, then, with which intemperance is concerned is that of the most widely spread among our senses, and would seem with justice to be held in censure, since it belongs to us in that we are animals, not in that we are men. And to rejoice in pleasures of this

kind, and to love them better than all others, is brutal. For the most liberal of all the pleasures of touch must be excluded, such as the pleasures which in the gymnasium are given by the friction, and by the warmth. For the peculiar sense of touch from which the intemperate man derives his pleasure is not spread (59.) over his entire body, but is restricted to [certain
11. portions of it. Among our desires, again, some would seem to be common to all men, and others to be peculiar and acquired. The desire for food, for instance, is natural to man; for every one who is in want either of meat or of drink feels a desire for it; and sometimes a man feels a desire for both at once; and he who is young, and in the prime of his strength, feels, says Homer, the desires of sex. But it is not all men alike, nor is it even always the same men, who desire this or that particular kind of meat or drink, or who are enamoured of this or of that particular style of beauty. And hence, to this extent at least, our desires are clearly our own, and peculiar to ourselves. Not but that, however, such particular modifications of desire have in them a something natural. For different men take pleasure in different things, and there are some things in which all men alike take more pleasure than in aught else. Now in the matter of their natural desires but few men fall into error, and that error always takes the one shape of excess. For to eat or to drink what is put before us until we are filled to repletion is to exceed what is natural in the matter of amount, inasmuch as our natural desires extend only to the satisfaction of our actual wants.

And hence men who act thus are called "cormorants" (which word etymologically signifies "belly-mad"), inasmuch as they fill themselves beyond all bounds. And such do they become who are of a disposition excessively slavish. But in the matter of their own peculiar desires many men fall into error, and in many ways. For a man may have given to him the phrase "over-fond of" such or such a thing either because he takes pleasure in what he ought not, or because he takes more pleasure in his particular object than he ought, or because he takes pleasure in it as do the uneducated many, or because he takes pleasure in it in a way in which he ought not; and in each and all of these points the intemperate run into excess. For they take pleasure in some things in which they ought not to take pleasure, inasmuch as they are absolutely hateful; and, if there be any among the objects of their desire in which it is right to take pleasure, then they take in it a pleasure which is greater than they ought, and such as is felt by the uneducated many. It is self-evident, then, that excess in the matter of pleasures constitutes intemperance, and calls for blame. But with regard to pains a man is not herein, as in the case of bravery, called temperate because he faces pain, and intemperate because he does not; but the intemperate man is so called in that he is more pained than he ought to be if he does not obtain what gives him pleasure (and so it is his very pleasure that gives him pain); whereas the temperate man is so called in that he is not pained by the deprivation of what gives him pleasure, and in that he can abstain from it.

The intemperate man, then, desires things pleasant as a whole, or desires the most pleasant among them, and his desire leads him to choose these things in place of all else. And consequently he feels pain (60.) when he fails to attain these things | and yet continues to desire them, for an element of pain enters into all desire. And yet it seems a strange thing that our very pleasures should give us pain. Men whose sense of pleasure is deficient, and who feel pleasure less than they ought, are not really to be met with; for insensibility of this kind is not human. Even animals can distinguish between different flavours, and take pleasure in some, and do not take pleasure in others. And were nothing to yield a man pleasure, and were all objects indifferent to him, his nature would be far from being human. And it is only because such a character is never really to be met with that it has no name by which it is designated. But the temperate man bears himself in these matters moderately; for neither does he take pleasure in those things in which the intemperate man especially delights, but rather looks upon them with indignation; nor, in a word, does he delight in what he ought not, nor does he take excessive pleasure in any such thing, nor does it give him pain to be deprived of it, nor does he ever long for such things, except moderately, nor does he long for them either more than he ought, or when he ought not, nor in a word does he ever fall into any error of this kind. But his appetites are set moderately, and as is right, upon all such things as are at once pleasant and good for health, or for bodily condition, and upon all such other pleasures as do not thwart these by leading to any violation of noble conduct, or to any expense not justified by his means. For for a man thus to go astray is a proof that he estimates such pleasures above their worth; and this the temperate man would never do, for he judges all pleasures by the standard of right reason.

12. Intemperance would seem to be more voluntary than is cowardice. For intemperance arises in the love of pleasure, cowardice in the fear of pain—and we naturally choose pleasure and avoid pain. And pain upsets and altogether destroys our natural balance, while pleasure does nothing of this kind, but is rather voluntary; and so to give way to it is more disgraceful. Besides, it is more easy to accustom ourselves to its influence, for there are many occasions in life upon which this can be done, and the process of habituation is unattended by any risk. But of things terrible exactly the reverse holds good. And, again, the habit of cowardice as a whole would seem to be more voluntary than are particular acts of cowardice. For in cowardice as a whole no pain is involved; but in particular acts of cowardice men are so upset by pain that they throw away their arms, and do many other unseemly acts; and hence particular acts of cowardice have even been held to be compulsory. But in the case of the intemperate man, on the other hand, his particular acts of intemperance are voluntary, for they proceed from his own desires and appetites. But his intemperance as a whole is not so voluntary, for no man really desires to be intemperate.

The term intemperance, or wantonness, is also applied to the faults of children, which to some extent resemble the faults of the intemperate. It matters not for our purpose which of these two uses of the term is derived from the other; but it is clear that the most appropriate application was also the earliest, and gave rise to the other. Nor was the transference inapt. For that which yearns for what is disgraceful, and which waxes apace, ought to be tempered and chastened. And desire is very much of this kind, as also is a child. For children lead a life of desire, and in them especially the appetite for pleasure shows itself. Unless, then, this desire be made obedient and subject to authority, it will go to great lengths. For in the fool the desire for pleasure is insatiable, and he seeks it from every source. And, moreover, our desires wax and grow with each act of their gratification; and, when they have come to be great and violent, trample out even reason itself. And so our desires ought to be moderate and few, and in no respect to run counter to our reason. And, where they are such, we say that they are obedient, and tempered, or chastened. For, as a boy ought to live by his tutor's rule, so desire ought to act by the rule of reason. And, consequently, the desires of the temperate man ought to move in harmony with his reason. For the mark at which each alike aims is that which is noble; and the temperate man desires what he ought, and desires it as he ought, and when he ought. And so, too, does reason order him. Of temperance, therefore, the foregoing may be accepted as our account.

IV.

1. NEXT in order we will treat of liberality, the popular conception of which is that it is that mean state which is concerned with property. For it is not with regard to his conduct in war that praise is given to the liberal man, nor with regard to those matters (62.) with which the temperate man is concerned, nor | with regard to his justice in legal matters, but with regard solely to the giving of property and the taking of it, and most especially with regard to giving. By property we must be understood to mean everything the worth of which can be expressed in money. Prodigality, moreover, and illiberality are manifestations of excess and defect with regard to property. Illiberality we never attach except to those who busy themselves about property more than they ought; but prodigality is a term which we sometimes apply to denote a combination of vices. For those who are incontinent, and who spend money upon their intemperance, we call prodigals; and such men are held to be most depraved, for they have many vices at once. But still, even to such, the term is not applied appropriately; for by the prodigal ought to be understood he who has but one vice, namely, that he wastes his substance. For the word "prodigal" etymologically signifies one who is brought to

destruction by himself; and to waste one's substance
would seem to be a kind of self-destruction, since
life necessarily involves such means and supports.
It is in this strict sense, then, that we shall understand the term "prodigality." Such things as have
a use can be used for good or for evil. Wealth is a
utility. He in each case puts a thing to the best use
who has the virtue which is concerned with it. He,
consequently, will put wealth to the best use who
has the virtue which is concerned with property;
and he it is whom we mean by the liberal man.
Now the true use of money would seem to consist
in the spending of it, and the giving of it; for the
taking of it, and the careful keeping of it, would
rather seem to be forms or modes of its acquisition.
And, consequently, the liberal man shows himself to
be such by giving to those to whom he ought, rather
than by taking whence he ought and not taking
whence he ought not. For virtue rather shows itself
in treating others as we ought, than in being treated
as we ought; and in doing noble acts, rather than in
abstaining from disgraceful acts. And it is clear that
in the act of giving is involved the benefiting our
neighbour, and the doing what is noble; while the
act of taking involves the being benefited by our
neighbour, and, at the most, the abstaining from what
is disgraceful. And it is to the giver that gratitude
is due, rather than to him who abstains from taking;
and the same is true of praise. And, moreover, it is
far easier to abstain from taking than it is to give.
For men as a rule are far more disposed to abstain from

taking that which is another's than to give up that which is their own. And, moreover, those who give (63.) are called liberal, while | those who abstain from taking are not praised for their liberality, but rather for their justice; whereas those who make a practice of taking meet with no praise at all. Of all the virtuous it is the liberal who, perhaps, would seem to be loved the most; for they are useful to others, utility being involved in the act of gift. All virtuous acts are noble, and are done for the sake of that which is noble. And so the liberal man will in the distribution of his gifts have that which is noble in view, and he will award them rightly. For he will give to whom he ought, and as much as he ought, and will give it when he ought; and his gift will, in a word, have all the determinations that a right gift implies. And all this he will do with pleasure, or, at any rate, without pain; for virtuous action, if not always pleasant, is at least devoid of pain, and never positively painful. And hence he who gives to whom he ought not, or without having that which is noble in view, but influenced by some other motive, must not be spoken of as liberal, but must be called by some other name; as also must he who is pained at making a gift, for such a one would rather choose money than a noble action, and to act thus is not the mark of the liberal man. Moreover, the liberal man will avoid taking from improper sources, for such a receipt is not the mark of one who does not hold property in great esteem. Nor will he be prone to cry "Give, give!" For he who loves to benefit others will not over-lightly receive good offices. But from right and proper sources the liberal man will take,—as, for instance, from his private estate,—not on the ground that it is noble to do so, but rather on the ground that it is necessary in order that he may have wherewithal to make gifts to others. Neither will he neglect his private fortune, since there are others whom by means of it he wishes to assist. He will also avoid making his gifts without distinction of persons, that thus he may be enabled to give to whom he ought, and when he ought, and where it is noble so to give. But of all the marks of the liberal man, the most pre-eminently distinctive is that he makes the measure of his gift so great as to leave for himself the smaller share; for it is a mark of the liberal man to disregard himself. But yet a man's liberality must always be considered with reference to his means; for true liberality is not to be measured by the magnitude of the gift, but rather by the disposition of the giver, which must be such that his gifts are proportioned to his means. And thus it is perfectly possible that he may be the more liberal who makes the smaller gift, provided that he make it from a scantier income. And hence they would seem to be the more liberal who have not made their own fortune, but have inherited it; for they have never had experience of want; and, besides, what (64.) men most love is what they have made for themselves, as we can see in the case of parents and of poets. For a liberal man to be rich is no easy task, since he neither cares to take money from others, nor to keep it for himself, but is open-handed, and values wealth not for its own sake, but rather as a means wherewith to make gifts. And hence Fortune is held to blame because those who deserve the greatest wealth often have the least. But yet this is only as might well be expected; for it is with money as with all things else—he cannot have it who labours not to acquire it. On the other hand, the liberal man will not give to those to whom he ought not to give, nor when he ought not to give, nor will he fall into any other such error; for he would not then be acting liberally, and, having thus exhausted his property, would no longer be able to spend it upon worthy objects. For, as has been said before, the liberal man is he who spends his money as suits his means, and upon worthy objects; and the prodigal is he who transgresses either of these two rules. And so a tyrant cannot properly be called prodigal, for the multitude of his possessions is such that excessive making of gifts or excessive expenditure is for him a thing almost impossible. Now, since liberality is a mean state with respect to the giving of money and the taking of it, it follows that the liberal man will give and will spend his money to a proper amount, and upon proper purposes, and that he will do so in little matters no less than in great, and that he will take pleasure in doing so; and further that his receipts will only be from proper sources, and of a proper amount. For, since the virtue of liberality is a mean state with respect both to giving and to taking, it follows that the liberal man will both give and take as he ought. Good gifts, indeed, involve and imply good and proper receipts, any other kind of receipts being incompatible with them; and gifts and receipts that are compatible with one another can form a part of the life of the same man; which cannot possibly be the case with gifts and receipts that are absolutely incompatible. Moreover, should the liberal man happen to have fallen into an expense neither proper nor noble, he will be grieved at it, it is true, but his grief will be moderate and proper. For virtue always shows itself in that a man feels pleasure and pain at right objects, and feels them as he ought. And, in all transactions where money is involved, the liberal man is easily to be dealt with; for it is easy to overreach him, inasmuch as he holds money in no esteem. And he is more grieved if he has not spent money where he ought, than pained if he has spent money where he ought not; and so thinks (65.) but poorly of the wisdom of Simonides. | But the prodigal man errs in all these matters; for neither does he take pleasure at what he ought, nor as he ought; nor pain; and this we shall see more clearly as we proceed. We have already said that prodigality and illiberality are the excesses and the defects with which we are at present concerned; and that they manifest themselves in two matters, in giving, that is to say, and in taking, —expenditure being classed along with giving. Prodigality, then, is an excess in the matter of giving and of not taking, for in the matter of taking it is a defect; while illiberality, on the other hand, is a defect in the matter of giving, while in the matter of taking it is an excess,—provided that such receipts must always be small. And hence the two chief elements of prodigality seldom coexist in their full entirety; for it is not easy to take from no one, and to give to every one. Where private persons make a practice of bestowing gifts their property quickly fails them; and it is persons of this kind who are generally held to be prodigals. But, were the combination practically possible, such a prodigal would be many degrees better than the illiberal man. His faults are such as increasing years or straitened means easily remedy, and it so becomes in his power to hit the proper mean. He already, indeed, possesses the two chief characteristics of the liberal man, for he gives to others, and abstains from taking: only he does neither of these rightly and properly. So that, if by a course of habituation, or by any other means, he were to modify his conduct, he would become a liberal man; for he would then give to fitting persons, and would not receive from unfit sources. And so it would seem that he must not be accounted a really bad man; for to make over-large and over-frequent gifts, and to altogether abstain from taking, does not so much argue vice and ill-breeding, as folly. And a prodigal of this stamp is far better than an illiberal man, not only from the reasons already given, but also because he actually benefits many others; whereas the illiberal man benefits no one—no, not even himself. But the majority of prodigals, as has already been said, have the additional fault of taking from improper sources, and so are in this respect illiberal. They become thus over-anxious to take, because they desire to run into expense, and cannot do so as easily as they would wish; for their resources soon fail them, and so they are compelled to seek for supplies elsewhere. And because, moreover, they have no regard for what is really noble in conduct, they become heedless, and will take from any source whatever; for their sole desire is to make presents to others, but how these presents ought to be made, or whence they ought to be procured, matters to them nothing. And so their gifts cannot even be termed liberal; for they are not noble, nor do they aim at what is noble, nor are they made as is right. For the prodigal will at times enrich those who only deserve to be poor; and to men of fair character, and who avoid all extremes, they will give nothing, but upon flatterers, or upon those who furnish them with any pleasure, they will bestow large sums. And hence the majority of them are also intemperate; for they spend their money recklessly, and waste large sums upon their vices: and, because their life is not regulated by the standard of what is noble, pleasure tempts them astray. Thus then the prodigal, if due care be not taken of him, falls into these yet further vices; but, if he meet with careful supervision, will ultimately arrive at the right and proper mean. But illiberality is incurable; for men would seem to be made illiberal by old age, and by all such other hopeless infirmities. It is, moreover, more akin to human nature than is prodigality, the majority of men being far more fond of accumulating wealth than of making presents. It is a vice of wide range, and appears in many shapes,—the recog-

(66.)

nised forms of illiberality being manifold. For, although it involves two principal characteristics, the giving, that is to say, of too few presents, and the taking of too many and of too large sums, yet it does not in all cases manifest itself in its entirety, its two members having sometimes a distinct existence; so that while such or such a man, for instance, is over-greedy to take, such or such another is too sparing of his gifts. Those, for instance, who are called by such names as "thrifty," "tight-fingered," "mean," are all too spare of gifts, but yet neither covet the property of others, nor desire to take gifts from them; and such conduct is, in some cases, the result of a certain amount of real good feeling and desire to avoid discredit. For their tight watch upon their own property would seem to arise (so at least they assert) from the fear of being ever compelled to do anything discreditable. Of this kind is the "skinflint," and all such other characters, who are so named because they can under no circumstances whatever be induced to make a present. Then there are others again who are afraid to touch their neighbour's property, on the ground that it is not easy to take presents from others, unless you also make them gifts; their rule, therefore, is "to have no giving and taking." On the other hand, there are others who are over-greedy for receipts, taking from any quarter whatever, and whatever they can get. Such are all they who ply illiberal trades, as those, for instance, who keep houses of ill-fame, and all persons of that class, and usurers who lend out small sums at exorbitant rates; for all of these take from improper sources, and take more than they ought. The element common to them all is clearly that of making disgraceful gains. For they all submit to public infamy for the sake of gain, and that gain, moreover, a small one. For those who acquire great wealth to which they have no right, and from wrong sources, as, for instance, tyrants who sack cities and pillage temples, we do not call illiberal but, rather, wicked; that is to say, sacrilegious and unjust. But among the illiberal are classed sharpers, such as are dicers, and thieves, such as are stealers of clothes, and footpads; for both sharpers and thieves practise their craft, and submit to the infamy which it involves, for the sake of small gains; and thieves in pursuit of their booty will run the greatest risks, while sharpers make a profit out of their friends, upon whom one ought rather to bestow gifts. And so they both desire to make a profit from an improper source, and are hence rightly held to be traffickers in disgraceful gains,—all such receipts whatever being illiberal. And it is with good reason that by the term "illiberality" is implied the contradictory of liberality; for illiberality is in itself a greater evil than is prodigality, and it leads men into errors both more numerous and more great.

Such, then, is our account of liberality, and of the vices which are opposed to it.

2.   Next in order, magnificence must be adequately discussed, for it, too, is a virtue which has property for its object. But its range does not, like that of liberality, extend to all transactions into which pro-

perty enters, but is strictly confined to such as are expensive; and in these it exceeds liberality in magnitude; for, as its name points out, it is an expense in the magnitude of which consists its beauty. Magni-
(68.) tude, of course, involves | some standard of reference; for it does not become the captain of a privateer to go to the same expense as does the leader of a sacred embassy. In estimating what expense becomes a man, we must take into account, first, who the man is; secondly, the object upon which he spends his money; and, thirdly, the amount which he spends.* He who puts himself to a fitting expense in small or in ordinary matters, as, for instance,

Oft to a vagrant have I given alms,

is not called magnificent,—but only he who acts thus in great matters; for, although every magnificent man is also liberal, it does not follow that every liberal man is magnificent. Magnificence, then, being such as we have said, its defect is called pettiness, while its excess is known as vulgarity, or as want of taste, or by some other such name, and does not consist in too great an expenditure on proper objects, but in over-ostentation manifested upon improper occasions, and in a wrong manner; and about this we shall speak hereafter. To be magnificent would seem to involve some special kind of knowledge, for a magnificent man knows exactly what becomes the occasion, and can spend great sums with good taste. The determinants of each moral state are, as we have

---

* For περὶ ἃ read ἃ, with the New College Manuscript as Michelet advises.

already said, the acts by which it manifests itself, and the objects with which it is concerned. Now the expenses to which the magnificent man puts himself are great and becoming; and, therefore, the results of his expenditure must be also such; for so only can the expense be properly called a great expense, and one that becomes its object. The object, in a word, must be one worthy of the expense, and the expense must be one worthy of the object, or even more than worthy of it. Expenses of this kind the magnificent man will incur that he may thereby make his conduct noble as a whole; for the Beautifully-good and Noble is the one common end of all the virtues; and he will, moreover, take pleasure in such expenses, and will spend his money with an open hand; for to economise in details is narrow-minded. And his first question will be, how he can produce the most noble and becoming result; not what will be the expense, and how can it be brought to a minimum. And, consequently, the magnificent man must of necessity be liberal, for the liberal man will always, where he can, expend a fitting sum in a proper manner. But, in all such expenses, although liberality and magnificence are concerned with the same objects, the characteristic of the magnificent man is magnitude of scale, as, for example, the spending his money upon an object of bulk actually great; and, with an expense no greater than that incurred by another man, he will produce a more magnificent result. Nor must it be forgotten that the glory of the possession which a man acquires is one, and that the glory of the result which he produces is another. For the glory of the possession is measured by its worth, as is the glory of gold, but the glory of the result by its bulk and beauty. For such a result is (69.) wondrous to behold, and | all that is magnificent ought to be wonderful. Thus, in a word, the glory of a result is magnificence, manifesting itself in greatness of bulk.

Now there are certain expenses which are recognised as ennobling him who incurs them, such as are offerings made to the Gods, or a new temple, or a public sacrifice, or indeed any other religious service whatsoever; and, with these, all those public expenses in which the citizens vie with one another; as when, for instance, it is desired to put a play upon the stage in brilliant style, or to equip a privateer, or to give a banquet to our fellow-citizens. And on all such occasions, as has already been said, the standards by which we measure the result produced are the position of the donor and his circumstances. For the expense to which he puts himself must be such as suits his rank and his fortune, and must become, not only the occasion, but also him who occupies it. And, consequently, a poor man can never display magnificence, his income not being sufficient to warrant a large and becoming expense; and to attempt such a display is in him only a mark of folly, violating that rightness and propriety which all virtue involves. Such an attempt becomes those alone who have a large estate, either acquired by themselves, or inherited from their forefathers, or relations, and who are also of noble birth, and of high public position, and so forth; for in all these requisites is involved that magnitude and dignity which the position of the magnificent man ought to imply. Such then ought the position of the magnificent man distinctly to be; and such, as we have already said, are the expenses upon which magnificence ought to be manifested; for such expenses are the greatest, and are held in the highest honour. And to these may be added all those private occasions of expense that occur but once in a lifetime; as, for instance, a marriage, or any other occasion of equal importance; and any other private expense in which interest is taken by the city as a whole, or by the leading citizens: to which also may be added public entertainments given to great men from other countries upon their arrival and upon their departure, and the making of gifts to distinguished foreigners, or the sending of gifts to them in return. For the expenses of the magnificent man ought to be made in the public interest, and not in his own; and in this point a gift has a certain resemblance to an offering to the Gods. The magnificent man will, moreover, equip his house as becomes his wealth, for he thereby adds a certain lustre to his position; and he will prefer such expenses as lead to the most durable and permanent results, for such are the most noble. Above all he will always consider what most becomes the particular occasion. For the fitting expense with which to honour the Gods is one, and that with which to honour men is another; and the fitting cost for a temple is one, and that for a tomb is (70.) another. | Each expense, in a word, is great according to its kind; and the most magnificent expense is a great expense upon a great object, and among such expenses again it is their greatness which is the measure of their magnificence. But, still, greatness as a matter of result must be carefully distinguished from greatness as a matter of expense. For a ball or a flask, if it be the most beautiful of its kind which can be procured, is a magnificent present to give a child, although its actual value is so small that to consider it would be illiberal. And hence we can see that, whatever the magnificent man undertakes, he will carry it out with a magnificence that suits its kind; for so he will produce a result not easily to be surpassed, and worthy of the expense incurred in its production. Such then is the character of the magnificent man. But he who runs into the excess of vulgarity errs, as we have already said, in transgressing the proper measure of expense.

Such a man will upon small occasions spend large sums, and affect an ill-timed and inharmonious splendour. When, for instance, his turn comes to entertain his breakfast club, he will give them a wedding collation; and, when he has to equip the comic chorus, he will dress them in purple for their opening song, as do the Megarians. And he does things of this kind, not from love of what is really noble, but merely from a desire to parade his wealth, and with hope of being thereby wondered at. And, in a word, where he ought to spend much, he spends little; and, where he ought to spend little, he spends much. The petty-minded man, on the other hand, does everything upon a deficient scale; and, even where he has put himself to what is for him the greatest expense, will ruin the

effect for some trifle; and he delays over everything
that he undertakes, that he may consider how to
spend a minimum upon it; and even that minimum
he regrets, and always believes that he is doing more
than is required of him. Vulgarity, then, and with
it pettiness must be ranked as vices; although no
great opprobrium attaches to them, because neither
do they injure a man's neighbours, nor do they to
any great extent violate decency.

3. High-mindedness, as its very name would seem to
show, is concerned with high and great matters; and
what these are, we must first determine. It is indifferent for our purpose whether we consider the
habit or the man in whom it is manifested. We shall
find that the high-minded man is he who, being really
worthy of great things, holds himself worthy of them;
for he who holds himself thus worthy beyond his real
deserts is a fool, and no man possessed of any virtue
whatsoever can ever be a fool or show want of under-
(71.) standing. Such then is | the high-minded man; he
who, being worthy of but small things, holds himself
worthy of them, being properly-minded indeed, but
still not high-minded. For high-mindedness involves
greatness of scale, just as true beauty requires a great
body—little men being neat and symmetrical, indeed,
but still not beautiful. He who thinks himself worthy
of great things, being in reality unworthy of them,
shows what is commonly called "chirking vanity," or
conceit,—although to overestimate one's own merits
need not of necessity imply conceit,—and he, on the
other hand, who holds himself worthy of less than his

merits is little-minded, no matter whether the merits which he thus underrates be great, or moderate, or small. And he is most little-minded if his merits be really great. For, if they had not been such, what would his estimate of himself have been? The merits, then, of the high-minded man are extreme, but in his conduct he observes the proper mean. For he holds himself worthy of his exact deserts, while others either overestimate, or else underestimate their own merits. And, since he is not only worthy of great things, but also holds himself worthy of them, or rather indeed of the very greatest things, it follows that there is some one object which ought most especially to occupy him. Now, when we speak of what a man is worth, or of what he is worthy, it is always with reference to external goods. We hold, moreover, that to be the greatest of all things which we give to the Gods as their just due, and which is the chief aim of all great men, and the recognised reward for the noblest exploits. And to this definition honour answers, for it is the very greatest of all external goods. And it is honour, consequently, and with it by implication dishonour that are the objects with which the virtue of the high-minded man is concerned. It is indeed too self-evident to need any proof that it is honour with which the high-minded occupy themselves; for it is to honour, most of all things, that men of high position lay claim, inasmuch as they rightly estimate their own worth. The little-minded man, on the other hand, forms an estimate of himself which falls short of his own merits, and *à fortiori* of those of the high-minded man; whereas the conceited man has an estimate of himself which exceeds his own merits, although it does not exceed those of the high-minded man. Now the high-minded man, since his deserts are the highest possible, must be among the best of men; for the better a man is, the higher will be his deserts, and the best man will have the highest deserts. True high-mindedness, therefore, cannot but imply virtue; or, rather, the criterion of high-mindedness is the conjoint perfection of all the individual virtues. And so the high-minded man will never under any (7ª.) circumstances | take to a coward's flight, legs and arms at once, nor will he ever commit a fraud. For what adequate object can he who holds nothing in great esteem possibly have for a disgraceful act? In short, whatever we suppose to be the circumstances, the more we consider the character of the high-minded man, the more will the notion of any demerit in him appear ridiculous. And indeed any such demerit would deprive him of his claim to honour; for honour is the prize of virtue, and it is only given to the good. High-mindedness, then, would seem to be the crown, as it were, of all the virtues; for it not only involves their existence, but it also intensifies their lustre. And, consequently, there is nothing so difficult as to be truly high-minded, for it is impossible to be such without perfect nobility of character. It is with honour, then, and with dishonour that the high-minded man is most especially concerned. And, where he meets with great honour, and that from upright men, he will take pleasure in it; although his pleasure will not be excessive, inasmuch as he has obtained at the outside only what he merits, if not perhaps less—for for perfect virtue adequate honour cannot be found. He will, however, none the less receive such honour from upright men, inasmuch as they have no greater reward to offer him. But honour given by the common herd, and upon unimportant occasions, he will hold in utter contempt, for it will be no measure of his deserts. And dishonour of all kinds he will equally disregard, since it cannot justly concern him. It is with honour, then, as has already been said, that the high-minded man is most especially concerned; not but that with regard to wealth also, and hereditary family power, and indeed all great good fortune and bad, whatsoever may take place, he will bear himself with such due moderation that neither will good fortune exceedingly elate, nor bad fortune exceedingly depress him. For he does not even bear himself towards honour as if it were the very greatest of all goods. And yet family rank and wealth are only to be desired for the honour which they bring. Those, at all events, who possess them seek to acquire honour by their means. Now he who makes but little of honour must needs make but little of all things else, and hence it is that the high-minded are held to be arrogant. But yet good fortune would seem to some extent to contribute to high-mindedness; for those who are nobly born claim honour as their due, as also do those who have high family rank or great possessions; for all such have a something wherein they exceed other men; and the greater the

excess of good the greater always is the consequent
honour. And hence it is that all good fortune of this
kind makes men more high-minded than they would
(73.) otherwise have been, for there are | certain quarters
in which it brings them honour. Really and truly
it is the good man alone who ought to be held in
honour; but whoso has both virtue and great prosperity will lay claim to the more honour on that
account. But those who have such good fortune
without virtue cannot justly advance any great claims,
nor can they properly be called high-minded: for
to make such claims, and to be so called, involves
and implies perfect virtue. Those, then,* who have
good fortune such as this, and nothing more, end by
becoming arrogant and insolent. For without virtue
it is difficult to bear gracefully the honours of fortune; and, since men cannot so bear them, and believe
themselves superior to their fellows, they look down
upon others, and to their own conduct pay not the
least regard. And so they imitate the high-minded
man, although not really like him,—that is to say, they
do so where they can. And hence they combine
contempt for their neighbours with entire absence on
their own part of really noble conduct. Now the
high-minded man justly despises his neighbours, for
his estimate is always right; but the majority of men
despise their fellows upon insufficient grounds. The
high-minded man is not fond of slight danger; nor
does he court danger as a whole, since there are but
few things which he holds in esteem; but a great

* Omit καὶ before οἱ τὰ τοιαῦτα ἔχοντες, as Michelet suggests.

danger he will encounter, and upon such an occasion is unsparing of his life, since he holds even life upon certain terms to be dishonour. He also loves to confer a favour, but feels shame at receiving one; for the former argues superiority, the latter inferiority. And he always repays a favour with a greater; for so he who first commenced the exchange of kindly offices ends by being laid under an obligation for the kindnesses which he has received. The high-minded would, moreover, seem to bear those in mind to whom they have done kindnesses, but not those from whom they have received them. For he who has received a kindness stands in a position inferior to that of him who has conferred it, whereas the high-minded man desires a position of superiority. And so he hears with pleasure of the favours he has conferred, but of those which he has received with dislike. And hence it is that we are told that Thetis did not remind Zeus of her good offices; as neither did the Lacedæmonians the Athenians, but only spoke of the benefits which they had received. It would seem, too, that the high-minded man asks favours of no one, or, at any rate, asks them with the greatest reluctance, but that he is always eager to do good offices to others; and that towards those in high position and prosperity he bears himself with pride, but towards ordinary men with moderation; for in the former case it is difficult to show superiority, and to do so is a lordly matter; whereas in the latter case it is easy. And to be haughty among the great is no proof of bad breeding, but haughtiness among

(74) the lowly is as base-born a thing | as it is to make trial of great strength upon the weak. Neither will the high-minded man seek ordinary opportunities of honour, or occasions where others than himself hold the first place. He will rather be given to inactivity and to delay, unless great honour or some other great result is at stake. And hence his achievements will be but few, but those great in themselves and of great repute. Moreover, he cannot but be open in his enmities and open in his love; for to conceal either hatred or affection argues fear. And he regards truth rather than report, and in both speech and action he is frank and open; for he speaks boldly from contempt of others. And hence, too, he will be truthful, except where he speaks ironically; but to the many his bearing will be ironical. Neither will he submit to mould his life for any other than for his friend; for to do so is the part of a slave—all flatterers being of slavish spirit, and all weak-souled men flatterers. Neither is he given to wonder, inasmuch as there is nothing which he holds great. Nor does he bear malice; for high-mindedness does not show itself by long memory of past events, especially of past injuries, but rather by entire neglect of such things. Neither is he a babbler: for he neither talks about himself, nor about other men, since he cares not either to hear himself praised, or to hear others blamed; while, on the other hand, he is also sparing of his praise. And so, too, he speaks evil of no man; no, not even of his enemies, unless it be in the pride of strength. And about the necessi-

ties of life, or about trifles of any sort, he is the last of all men to make complaints or requests; for to do so argues over-zeal about such matters. And he will prefer possessions that are noble, and that bear no profit, to such as are of profit and utility, for he thus more thoroughly shows his independence. The high-minded man, moreover, ought to move slowly, and his voice ought to be deep and his utterance deliberate; for he who busies himself about but few things will not be given to haste, nor will he who thinks nothing great be of shrill quick speech; for a high-pitched voice and a hasty step come from these reasons. Such, then, is the high-minded man; while the deficiency of high-mindedness is little-mindedness, and its excess is vanity. But yet little-mindedness and vanity are not to be counted as vices; for, though they argue error, they do not result in any actual harm to others. For the little-minded man has merits that deserve a certain reward, and yet he deprives (75.) himself of his | just deserts. And so he would seem to some extent to be in fault, in that he does not duly estimate his own merits, and so shows ignorance of his true character. Otherwise he would certainly have striven to gain the true reward of his deserts, inasmuch as that reward is good. But yet such men must not be held to be foolish, but, rather, diffident. And the opinion which they have of themselves tends to exaggerate their weakness. For, while all other men aim at what they conceive to be their true deserts, these men stand aloof from noble actions and noble pursuits, believing that they are not worthy of them; and in the same way, too, do they hold themselves aloof from all external goods. But the conceited are fools; and, moreover, full of self-ignorance, and that, too, manifestly. For they attempt occasions of honour, as if they were worthy thereof, and are then detected therein. And by their dress, and gesture, and such other means, they endeavour to produce a great effect; and they further desire that their prosperity may be seen of men, and their talk is about themselves, (that by all these means they may be held in honour. But yet it is little-mindedness rather than conceit which contrasts itself with high-mindedness, for it is a more frequent fault, and involves a greater error.

4. High-mindedness is then, as we have said, concerned with great honour. But there would also seem, as indeed was said before, to be another virtue, which also is concerned with honour, and which stands in the same relation to high-mindedness as does liberality to magnificence; for both it and liberality make us stand aloof from things great, and bear ourselves properly in matters moderate and small. Exactly, then, as in the taking and in the giving of money there is a mean, and an excess, and a defect; so, too, a man can aim at honour more than he ought, and less than he ought, and can also seek it from proper sources, and as he ought. For we blame the ambitious man as being one who craves for honour more than he ought, and who seeks it from improper sources; and we also blame the unambitious man as one who will not receive honour, even as the price of a noble achievement.

(76.) And at times, again, we, as | has been said before, praise the ambitious man as being a true man, and a lover of fair fame; and at times we praise the unambitious man, as one who shuns excess, and who is sober-minded. And it is clear that, inasmuch as the phrase "lover of" such or such a thing admits of a variety of shades of meaning, we do not always use the phrase "lover of honour," or "ambitious," in the same signification; but, when its connotation is one of praise, it denotes a man who desires honour more than do the many; while, when its connotation is one of blame, it denotes a man who desires honour more than is right. Since the mean state herein has no name of its own, it becomes a sort of waste land to which its border marches, the extremes, lay claim; for, where excess and defect exist, there also exists the mean. Now men do, as a matter of fact, aim at honour more than they ought, and less than they ought, and sometimes also as they ought: it is at least clear that there does exist such a habit as we have described, that it is praiseworthy, that it is a mean state with regard to honour, and that it has no name of its own. As compared with ambition, it would seem to be a want of ambition; and, as compared with the want of ambition, it would seem to be ambition; and, as compared with both, it would seem, to a certain extent, to be both at once: and this is a rule that would seem to equally hold good of the other virtues. The reason why those who run into the extremes herein seem to be opposed to one another is because he who observes the mean has no name of his own.

5. Gentleness is properly a mean state with regard to anger; but, inasmuch as he who observes the mean with regard to anger has no recognised name, as indeed hardly have those who fall into either extreme, we apply the term "gentleness" to him who observes the mean, implying thereby a tendency in him towards the defect—which defect has no name of its own. The excess is not inaptly called wrathfulness; for the emotion underlying it is wrath, or anger, of which the exciting causes are many and diverse. He, then, who becomes angry at what he ought, and with whom he ought, and further as he ought, and when he ought, and for as long as he ought,—he is praised: and he it is who ought to be called gentle, since it is gentleness alone that is to be praised. For the gentle man ought to be of unruffled temper, and not to be led away by passion, but, exactly as reason orders, so only, and upon such occasions alone, and for so long only, to bear bitterness. But, if anything, he would seem to err on the side of defect, for he loves pardon rather than revenge. The absolute defect, whether it is to be called "want of anger," or whatever other name is to be given to it, is to be blamed. For those who do not feel anger at what they ought are held to be weak and foolish; as also are those who do not feel anger as they ought, or who do not feel it when they ought, or with whom they ought. For such a man seems to have no feeling and no sense of pain, and the absence of all anger argues the absence in him of proper resentment. For to submit to insult, or to overlook an insult offered to our friends, shows a

slavish spirit. The excess, on the other hand, can take almost every shape. For we can be angry with those with whom we ought not to be angry, and at things at which we ought not to be angry, and we can be more angry than we ought, and we can become angry more quickly than we ought, and remain angry for a longer time than we ought. But still the same man does not fall into all of these faults. This he could not possibly do. For anger is an evil that destroys itself, and if it come in its fullest intensity is no longer to be borne. And so, first of all, we find the irritable, as those are called who become angry quickly, and with those with whom they ought not to be angry, and for matters which ought not to make them angry, and who are more angry than they ought to be, but whose anger is quickly over. And this last is the best point in their character. And the reason of it is that they do not brood over their wrath; but their quick temper betrays them into open and immediate reprisal, and then their anger ceases. The excess of irritability is found in the passionate, who are keen to take offence, and who become angry at everything, and upon every occasion; and hence it is that they have their name. Then, in the second place, there are the sulky, with whom it is hard to be reconciled, and who remain angry for a long time; for they brood over their wrath. When such a man has made reprisals, then his anger ceases; for revenge substitutes a pleasure for the previous pain, and so makes his anger cease. But, if they cannot do this, they continue their grievance; for, since it does not openly manifest itself, there is no one who can reason with them, and to digest one's spleen within one's self needs time. Such persons cause infinite trouble, both to themselves and to their dearest friends. Lastly, we call those "nasty-tempered" who become angry at things at which they ought not to be angry, and who are more angry than they ought to be, and for a longer time, and who will not be reconciled without they have revenged themselves or punished their enemies. It is the excess rather than the defect that we ordinarily oppose to gentleness. In the first place it is more frequently met with than is the defect, for love of revenge is more natural to man than is apathy; and, in the second place, it is worse to have to pass one's life with those who are nasty-tempered than with those who are apathetic. The present is, moreover, a good instance by which to illustrate what has been elsewhere stated. For it is no easy matter to exactly determine how, and with whom, and for what, and for how long, a man ought to be angry; and up to what point a man acts rightly herein, and at what point he begins to err. For he who steps but little wide of the good is (78.) not | blamed, whether he incline towards excess or towards defect; for at times we praise those who manifest anger too little, and call them meek, and at times again we call those who manifest wrath manly, and say that they are fit to govern their fellows. And yet it is no easy matter to determine by precise rule up to what point, and how far, such transgression of the mean can take place without blame; for all such questions as this are in their very nature particular matters of fact, which must be decided by immediate perception, and not by argument. But still thus much at least is clear, that that which is praiseworthy is the mean state, in virtue of which we are angry with whom we ought, and at what we ought, and as we ought, and so forth: while the excess and the defect, in whatever shapes they occur, are blameable, being but slightly blameable if they go to but a slight extent, more blameable if they proceed further, while, if they go to great lengths, they are absolutely to be condemned. And so it is clear that we must do our

6. best to hold fast to the mean state. Here closes our account of those states of mind which have anger for their object matter. In society, on the other hand, that is to say in spending our life in the company of others, and in the commerce both of words and of deeds which we have with them, there are some men who are held to be obsequious, who lavish praise upon everything that they may please their listeners, who never contest any point whatever, and whose idea of duty is that it consists in giving no offence to those with whom we come into contact. And there are others who do the exact opposite to all this, who contest every point, and who never consider for a moment whether they annoy their neighbours; and these are called surly and contentious. It is, of course, easily to be seen that the habits which we have just described call for blame; and that that which is praiseworthy is the mean state, in virtue of which a man tolerates what he ought, and tolerates it as he ought, and regulates his resentment by similar rules. This state of

mind has had no name given to it, but it very closely resembles friendship: for he in whom this mean state is manifested is, with the one addition of affection, exactly the person whom we should describe as a good friend. But still this habit differs from friendship because it involves no element of emotion or of affection for those with whom we associate. Such a man does not receive the conduct of others rightly because he, as the case may be, either likes or dislikes them, but rather because it is his character so to receive it. For, whether he be associating with those of whom he is ignorant, or with those whom he knows, or with those with whom he is acquainted, or with those with whom he is absolutely unacquainted, his conduct will be guided by exactly the same rules, except that he will in each case act as suits the particular occasion; for it is not right to pay equal regard to the feelings of friends and of perfect strangers, nor on the other hand to be equally regardless of the pain which one may give them. Upon the whole, then, such a man will, as we have (79.) said, bear himself in society | as he ought; but still he will always be guided by the standard of what is noble and of what is expedient, and his aim will be to contribute to a mutual pleasure where he possibly can, or at any rate to avoid the giving of pain. He would indeed seem to be concerned with those pleasures and pains which originate in society; and, with regard to these, wheresoever it is not noble for him to contribute to a mutual pleasure, or where it is really detrimental to do so, there he will scout the notion of giving such a pleasure, and will rather prefer to inflict pain. And should, moreover, the act be one such as to bring disgrace, and that, too, no small disgrace, upon the doer of it, or, it may be, material injury, while the refusal on the other hand gives but little pain, he will not tolerate such an act, but will give an unmistakeable refusal. He will moreover bear himself differently according as he has to associate with men of great position or with men of none, and according as his company is well known to him or not; and in all other cases where a similar distinction can be made he will follow the same rule, treating each person as he ought to be treated, and, as an abstract rule, preferring to contribute to a mutual pleasure and taking all care to avoid giving pain, but still being guided by results, accordingly as they may preponderate, or, in other words, keeping what is noble and what is expedient steadily in view. And hence it is that for the sake of a great pleasure in the future he will sometimes inflict a slight pain at the present. Such then is the man who observes the mean in his social conduct. To him no name has as yet been given; but, of those whose aim is to impart a mutual pleasure, he whose sole object is to appear agreeable, and who has no ulterior end in view, is called obsequious; while he who acts thus that he may receive therefrom some pecuniary or material benefit is a flatterer. He, on the other hand, who treats everybody roughly is, as we have already said, called surly and contentious. And the two extremes would seem to be opposed to one another because the mean has no name of its own.

K

7. What is called "the mean state with respect to boastfulness" is concerned with almost the same object-matter as the virtue just discussed; and, like it, has no name of its own. But yet it is best that all such moral states should be adequately discussed; for, for a full knowledge of human character, a detailed discussion of particular moral phenomena is essential; and the best way in which to strengthen our conviction that the virtues are mean states is to ascertain that the rule holds good in each particular case. We have already spoken of those whose intercourse with us in daily life is so directed as to yield us either pleasure or pain: and we will now treat of those whose conduct is either truthful or untruthful, whether it be in speech, or in action, or in the pretensions which they advance. The braggart would seem to be he who lays claim to qualities usually held in esteem, and which he does not really possess, or who lays (80.) claim to them in a greater degree | than is justified by facts; while the ironical man, on the other hand, either denies the merits which he actually possesses, or else depreciates them; and, lastly, he who observes the mean herein is a kind of "plain blunt man," truthful both in life and in speech, who acknowledges his own merits, and who neither exaggerates nor depreciates them. Each of these three types of character may be assumed to serve some particular end, or may be assumed with no such ulterior object. And, indeed, as is each man's character, so he speaks, and so he acts, and so he lives, unless he have some special motive to the contrary. Moreover, falsehood

of any kind, considered entirely by itself, and without
reference to circumstances, is disgraceful and blameable, while the truth is noble and praiseworthy. And
so the truthful man, who observes the mean in these
matters, ought to be praised; while those who practise
deceit are each of them to be blamed, but the braggart
most of the two. We will proceed to describe each
of these two types of character; and also the truthful
type, with which we will commence. We are not
herein concerned with him who is truthful in his
agreements and bargains, or in those matters which
come under the scope of injustice and of justice (for
with these matters it is altogether another virtue that is
concerned), but rather with him who, where no such
question is at issue, is truthful in his speech and in
his life, because it is his character to be such; and a
man of this character cannot but be esteemed as good.
For he who loves the truth, and who is truthful in
unimportant matters, will be all the more truthful in
matters that are important. For, since it was his
custom to avoid a falsehood in itself and independently
of all circumstances, he will surely all the more avoid
it when it involves disgrace: and such a man as this
deserves praise. If anything, however, his statements will fall a little short of the truth; for a slight
depreciation of this kind would seem to be in better
taste, inasmuch as exaggeration in any form is
odious. He, on the other hand, who lays claim to
more than his merits, and who does so with no particular object in view, to a certain extent resembles a
bad man, for otherwise he would not take pleasure

in falsehood; but he clearly is not so much to be held a wicked man, as a fool who talks at random. He who exaggerates his merits with an ulterior object, if that object be reputation or honour, as in the case of the braggart, is not so much to be blamed; but his conduct becomes more disgraceful when his object is money, or any form of material advantage. It is not then the mere power of exaggeration that constitutes the braggart, but rather the end to which that power is intentionally put. A man is a braggart as a matter of habit, and because it is his character to be such; much as there is one type of liar who loves a lie for its own sake, and another who lies to win reputation (81.) or to make | money. Those then who play the braggart for the sake of reputation, lay claim to those qualities for which men gain repute, or for the possession of which they are accounted happy; while those whose object is gain, make a pretence of qualifications which are of use to their neighbours, and the absence of which can be successfully concealed, as, for instance, skill in soothsaying, or in medicine. And hence it is that the majority of men advance claims of this description, and play the braggart about them; inasmuch as all such claims have the advantages which we have mentioned. The ironical, on the other hand, whose conversation tends to depreciate themselves, are of a more pleasing type of character; for it would seem that they do not so much mould their conversation with a view to profit, as from the wish to avoid pomposity. And so what they most especially disclaim is any quality held in high estimation; as used to be the habit of Socrates. But those who disclaim unimportant merits which they evidently possess, are known as "mock-modest," and are simply despicable. Such mock-modesty is at times a mere form of braggartry, as is the over-simple dress of the Spartans; for over-modesty can be as braggart a thing as over-boastfulness. Those however who avoid all excess in their irony, restricting it to matters that are not too commonplace and obvious, manifest their good taste. And it is the braggart whom we contrast with the truthful man, inasmuch as the extreme into which he runs is the worst of the two.

8. Since the business of life calls for rest, and rest involves recreation and amusement, it follows that upon such occasions it is possible to adopt a bearing which is in good taste, or, in other words, to say what one ought, and to say it as one ought, and to observe a similar rule as to what it is to which one listens. And it also, of course, will matter much whether we are speaking ourselves among men of such or such a kind, or whether we are listening to them. It is clear, then, that in such matters one can both exceed the mean, and fall short of it. Those who push the ridiculous to excess are called buffoons, and are rightly held to be of vulgar mind; for their desire for merriment is reckless, and their object is rather to raise a laugh by any means whatever, than to say what is seemly, and to avoid paining those at whom they mock. Those, on the other hand, who would on no account indulge in a joke themselves, and who take offence at all who do so, are held to be savage and austere. Those however whose

jokes are in good taste are called witty or quick-witted, as if their wits moved quickly; for it would (82.) seem that | the character, no less than the body, is capable of such movements; and, exactly as the body is judged by its movements, so too should be the character. And, since the ridiculous has a wide range, and since most men take more pleasure than they ought in fun and ridicule, even buffoons are often called witty, on the ground that they are agreeable. But that there is a difference, and that no small one, between buffoonery and wit, is clear from what has been said. The peculiarity of the mean state is the tact which it involves. For a man of tact will make and listen to such jokes only as become a good and liberally-minded man. There are, indeed, certain jokes which it is not unbecoming for such a man either to hear or to make by way of amusement; and there is a great difference between the amusement of the liberally-minded and that of the slavish, and between that of the educated and that of the un-educated. This can be distinctly seen from a comparison of the Old comedies with the New; for the wit of the Old comedies consisted in their grossness, while that of the New lies rather in innuendo; and, from the point of view of good taste, there is no little difference between these two. What then is to be the definition of decorous ridicule? Is it that we are to say nothing that does not become a liberally-minded man;—or that we are on no account to pain our hearer;—or that we are absolutely to gratify him? Or is it not rather true that about such matters no exact rules can be laid down, inasmuch as the likes and dislikes of no two men whatever are identical? In any case the jokes to which the witty man will listen will be regulated by similar rules; for the jokes which a witty man makes will be such only as he will submit to hear. And consequently the witty man will not indulge in every kind of ridicule. For all ridicule is a species of abuse, and legislators, inasmuch as they forbid certain forms of abuse, ought perhaps also to have forbidden certain forms of ridicule. And the man of culture, who is liberally-minded, will bear himself according to these rules, being, as it were, the law for his own actions. Such then is the man who observes the correct mean,—whether it is tact which we are to say that he has, or wit: whereas the buffoon can never resist the ridiculous, and, provided only that he can raise a laugh, will spare neither himself nor anyone else, and will say things which no gentleman would ever say, and sometimes even things to which no gentleman would submit to listen. The savage man, on the other hand, is absolutely useless in any society which has amusement for its object; for he contributes nothing to the general amusement, and takes offence at anyone who endeavours to do so;—and it ought perhaps to be observed that recreation and amusement are necessary (83.) for active life. | Such then are the three mean states which are possible in the conduct of life, and which are all concerned with our intercourse in speech and in action, but which differ from one another, in that the object of the one is truthfulness, and that of the other two pleasure. And of these last two the one is concerned with pleasure as it enters into our amusements, the other with pleasure as it enters into all the other forms of daily intercourse to which life gives rise.

9. To speak of shame as a virtue would seem incorrect, for it rather resembles an emotion than a formed state of character. Indeed, its very definition is "the fear of evil repute," and in its results it very closely resembles the fear of danger. For those who are ashamed blush, while those who are in fear of death turn pale. And both these affections are clearly physical. And physical affection is more characteristic of an emotion than of a habit. Moreover, shame does not become all ages alike, being only appropriate to youth. For we hold that the young ought to have a proper sense of shame, inasmuch as, their life being governed by the passion of the moment, they would fall into many errors, were they not restrained by shame. And so we praise those among the young who show a proper shame. But no one would praise an old man for being thus sensitive, inasmuch as we hold that no man of such an age ought to do anything of which he need be ashamed. For even shame itself, if it be felt for disgraceful acts, is no mark of a good character; inasmuch as we ought not to do such acts. And to urge that some acts are really disgraceful, while others only offend against convention, is no answer. For we ought not to commit either, and then we should have no occasion for shame. It is, of course, only a bad man who is dis-

posed to do disgraceful acts. And, consequently, to
be so disposed as to feel shame were one to commit
such an act, and to lay claim to any merit on that
account, is absurd. For shame need only be felt for
such acts as are voluntary; and a good man will never
voluntarily do what is disgraceful. And, consequently,
shame is only good upon a certain assumption, namely,
that a man would feel shame if he were to do such or
such an act. And of none of the virtues does this
rule hold good. For, even although barefacedness
and utter absence of all shame at a disgraceful act be
had, it does not, on that account, follow that to feel
(84.) due shame at a disgraceful act is good. Neither is |
self-restraint a virtue, unless it be of a mixed kind;
its nature shall be pointed out hereafter. And now
we will proceed to the consideration of justice.

V.

1. NEXT follows the consideration of Justice and of Injustice,—with what actions it is that they are concerned, and in what sense it is that justice is a mean, and what are the extremes between which that which is just constitutes the mean. The method of our investigation will be inductive, as it was in the case of the virtues previously discussed. Now it is clear that all men understand by justice, a habit such that those who possess it are disposed to do just acts, and act justly, and desire that which is just; and so too with injustice, which makes men act unjustly, and desire that which is unjust. These statements, then, in this general form, we may assume as granted. Now, habits differ from faculties, and from the various sciences. For one and the same science, and one and the same faculty, can be concerned with contradictory objects, while with a habit this is never the case. The habit of health, for instance, produces healthy results alone, but never unhealthy results. And hence we say of a man that he walks healthily, when he walks as he walks who has the habit of health. And so sometimes a habit is known when we know the contradictory habit, and sometimes when we know its manifestations. If, for instance, we are clear as to what is a healthy habit of body, then we are, *ipso*

facto, clear as to what is an unhealthy habit; while, again, knowledge of the symptoms of a healthy habit involves knowledge of the habit, and knowledge of the habit involves knowledge of the symptoms. If, for example, firmness of the tissues be a symptom of health, then flabbiness of the tissues will be a symptom of disease, while that which produces firmness of the tissues will be productive of health. And, again, it is (85.) generally the case that the | various significations of a pair of contrary terms will correspond to one another. If, for example, "just" have a variety of acceptations, then will "unjust" have a corresponding variety. Now justice and injustice would seem to have a variety of acceptations; but, because the shades of meaning vary so slightly, the ambiguity escapes us, as it would not if the difference were wider. Physical shape, for instance, is a clear difference, removing all ambiguity between "key," with which to lock a door, and "key," the clavicle of men or animals. Let us then enumerate the various meanings of the word "unjust." He who violates the law is held to be unjust, as also is he who grasps at more than his share, and he who aims at inequality. And hence it is clear that he will be just who observes the law, and who aims at equality. Hence, too, that will be just which is in accordance with the law, and which is equal; and that will be unjust which transgresses the law, and which is unequal. And since, moreover, the unjust man grasps at more than his share, he will be concerned with such things as are good,—but yet not with all even of these, but with such alone as admit of good fortune or of bad, and which are always in the abstract good, but yet not good in certain particular cases. These are the class of goods that is the object of human prayer and effort; whereas men ought rather to pray that such things as are in the abstract good may be good also for themselves, and to pursue such things only as are in the concrete good for themselves. But yet the unjust man does not always strive for more than his share; for he will sometimes, in the case of things absolutely bad, strive for what is less. It is because the lesser evil is held in a sense to be a good, and because the object of all overreaching is the good, that the unjust man seems to grasp at more than his share. But at inequality he always aims,—this being the generic and common attribute of all injustice. Again, since we said that the transgressor of the law was unjust, and that he was just who observed the law, it is clear that all that the law commands is in a sense just. Now the commands of law are co-extensive with the axioms of the science of legislation, and we hold that each and every one of these commands is just. Law, moreover, is universal in its range; its object being either that which is for the interest of all, or that which is for the interest of the best and noblest, or that which is for the interest of the powerful few; while it adopts for its standard either virtue, or some other similar criterion. And hence, in one acceptation of the term "just," we apply it to all such acts as tend to produce or to preserve for the body politic either happiness as a whole, or any of its constituents. And hence the law orders us to act as does the brave man—as, for instance, neither to break the ranks, nor to fly from the fight, nor to throw away our arms; and to act as does the temperate man—as, for instance, neither to insult our neighbour, nor to lie with our neighbour's wife; and to act as does the evenly-tempered man—as, for instance, to abstain from blows, and from evil-speaking; and so forth, as regards all other virtues and vices, the law lays down parallel commands and prohibitions, the merits of which will vary accordingly as it has been sagely ruled, or made at hap-hazard. Thus, then, this kind of justice may be regarded as perfect virtue,—virtue, that is to say, not viewed abstractedly, or as regards the individual alone, but as regards the individual considered in his relation to his fellow-man. And hence it comes that justice is oft-times held to be noblest among the virtues,—

> Nor even-star, nor morning star so fair.

And, again, as the proverb says,

> In justice lies the whole of virtue's sum.

And herein especially is it counted as perfect virtue, in that it consists in the practice of perfect virtue,—perfect, in that the just man can make use of it for the good of his fellow-man, and not for his own good alone. For many there be who can make good use of their virtue in their own matters, but not towards their fellow-man. And, hence, Bias would seem to have said well, saying that,

> It is authority that shows the man.

For whosoever is in authority stands *ipso facto* in relation to his fellow-man, in that he is a fellow-member of the body politic. And for this same reason it is that justice alone among the virtues is held to be "another's good," in that it alone among the virtues involves a relation to our fellow-man. For he who is just does that which is to the interest of another, whether that other be a ruler set over him, or a fellow-member of the body politic. Worst of men is he whose wickedness affects not himself alone but his fellow with him; best of men is he whose virtue affects not himself alone but his fellow with him; for such an one has in all sooth a hard task. Justice, then, after this kind, is not any portion of virtue, but rather virtue as a whole, whilst the injustice that is opposed to it is no portion of vice, but rather vice as a whole. And, moreover, it will be clear from what we have already
(87.) said wherein justice after this kind is distinct from virtue. It is generically the same, but specifically distinct; for, in so far as it involves any relation to our fellow-man, it is justice, but, in so far as it involves such or such an abstract type of character, it is identical with virtue in the abstract.

2. But there is also, as we assert, a justice and a corresponding injustice, which form a portion only of virtue and of vice as a whole; and it is of these that we are now in search. In confirmation of this assertion we may observe that, in the case of all the other vices, he who does the bad deed acts unjustly, it is true, but still gains nothing over and above his share; as, for instance, when he throws away his shield from

cowardice, or speaks evil of his neighbour from churlishness, or refuses to give pecuniary assistance from niggardliness. But, when by the act in question he gains more than his share, his conduct is often not referred to any one among these above-named vices, nor yet to all of them collectively, but yet to a definite vice, inasmuch as we blame his conduct,—that is to say, to injustice particular. And so there is another kind of injustice, which is a part of injustice as a whole, and a corresponding unjust, which is a part of that unjust as a whole of which the essence is transgression of the law. Moreover, if a man lie with his neighbour's wife for the sake of gain, and make a profit thereby, while another man act thus from desire, spending his substance thereon, and incurring a loss, the latter would be held to be incontinent rather than overreaching, while the former would be held to be unjust, but not incontinent; the difference plainly consisting in his wrongful gain. Moreover, in the case of all unjust acts that involve no gain, we always make reference to some definite vice, as to incontinence if a man has committed adultery, to cowardice if he has deserted his coverer, to hastiness if he has committed an assault; but, if he has made a gain, we refer his act to no one of these vices, but to injustice alone. And hence it is clear that there is another kind of injustice, particular, and distinct from injustice as a whole, but yet called by the same name, since its definition involves the same generic quality. For both the particular and the universal injustice involve a relation to our fellow-man; but the former is concerned with honour, or with property, or with personal security, or with that, whatever it be, the common name of which embraces all these, and has primarily to do with the pleasure of gain; while the latter is concerned with all such actions as distinguish the good man.

(88.) | Thus then it is clear that there are more kinds of justice than one,—that there is, in short, a justice particular, distinct from virtue as a whole. It remains to determine its genus and its differentia. That which was unjust we divided into that which transgressed the law, and that which violated equality; and that which was just we divided into that which observed the law, and that which aimed at equality. And the injustice of which we have already treated is co-extensive with transgression of the law. Now, exactly as we saw that to aim at inequality and to grasp at more than one's share were not always identical, but were related as are whole and part (for when we grasp at more than our share we always aim at inequality, but when we aim at inequality we do not always grasp at more than our share), so in like manner we can see that the unjust and the injustice co-extensive with inequality are not identical with but distinct from the unjust and the injustice co-extensive with illegality, the latter being the whole of which the former is a part. For this the particular injustice is a part of injustice as a whole, and similarly this the particular justice is a part of justice as a whole. It remains then to treat definitely of particular justice, and along with it of particular injustice, and of that which is specially just, and along with it in like manner of that which is specially unjust. Here, then, we dismiss further consideration of the justice co-extensive with virtue as a whole, and of the injustice parallel with it, the one of which consists in the practice of virtue as a whole to the benefit of our neighbour, the other in the practice of vice as a whole to his detriment. Nor is there any doubt as to the determination of that which is just and of that which is unjust with reference to this kind of justice and of injustice. For, as a rule, the enactments of legislation are co-extensive with the acts that characterise virtue as a whole. The law, indeed, orders us so to rule our life that we may practise each virtue, and avoid each vice. And, moreover, those practices that tend to the formation of virtue as a whole are comprised in the enactments whereby public education is regulated. With regard, however, to that especial education which each one of us requires for his ultimate perfection, we must hereafter determine whether or not it falls within the province of the science of politics, inasmuch as the perfection of the man is not perhaps in all cases identical with the perfection of the citizen. Of particular justice, and of the just that is co-extensive with it, one kind is concerned with the distribution of honour, or of money, or of all such other things as are shared in common by the members of the body politic (for in all these matters one man can in relation to another have what is an equal or what is an unequal share), and another kind, the corrective, is concerned with transactions or contracts. And this latter is again divided into two (89.) kinds; |—transactions being either voluntary or invo-

luntary. Voluntary transactions, or contracts, are such
as are purchase, sale, loan, sceurity, hire, deposit, letting,
and are called voluntary because they originate in an
act of free-will. Involuntary transactions are either
fraudulent, such as are theft, adultery, administration
of noxious drugs, procuring for defilement, kidnapping,
assassination, perjury, or else are forcible, such as are
assault and battery, violent detention, murder, rape, assault with intent to do grievous bodily harm, abuse,
3. insult. Now the unjust man being he who aims at inequality, and the unjust being that which is unequal,
it will be clear that the unequal will imply a mean, and
that that mean will be the equal. For, in any action
whatsoever in which a man can take either more than
another man's share, or less, he can also take an amount
exactly equal to it. Since then the unjust is unequal,
the just will be equal. This is too commonly recognised to need proof. And since, moreover, that which
is equal is a mean, that which is just will also, in a
certain sense, be a mean. Moreover, equality involves
at least two terms. And thus it follows that that
which is just will be both a mean and also equal, and
that it will involve reference to a standard, and will
concern certain persons, and that in that it is a mean
it will involve two other terms (the greater, that is
to say, and the less), and that in that it is equal it
will again involve at least two terms, and that in that
it is just it will have reference to at least two persons.
And, therefore, that which is just will of necessity involve at least four terms; for there will be two persons
at least whose rights will be involved in that which is

just, and two shares at least into which the matter of the action will be divided. And justice will involve an equality between the persons concerned therein similar to the equality between the things; for, as is the ratio of the things to one another, so too must be the ratio of the persons. If the persons be in a ratio of inequality, then their shares must be in the same ratio. Indeed, contention and dispute always originate in the fact that those who stand in an equal ratio to one another have acquired unequal shares, or that those who stand in an unequal ratio to one another have acquired equal shares, either by appropriation or by distribution. Indeed, this is clear from the very phrase "by such or such a standard." For all men are agreed that a just distribution must involve reference to some standard, although they are not agreed as to what that standard ought to be; democrats asserting that the standard ought to be individual freedom, while oligarchs propose wealth, others noble birth, and true aristocrats personal merit. And hence, again, that which is just involves a proportion, or similarity of ratios. For proportion can obtain not only in abstract number, but in all things that are capable of a numerical expression. Proportion is an equality of ratios, and involves four terms at least. Discrete proportion obviously involves four terms; and so too does continuous proportion, which by repeating one term makes it do duty for two, as

(90.)

$$A : B :: B : C$$

the term B herein being repeated, and such repetition producing in reality four proportionate terms. Justice, then, involves four terms at least, between the first and the second of which there will be a ratio similar to the ratio between the third and the fourth, inasmuch as the things in question will have been divided in a ratio similar to that in which the persons stand to one another. As then A (Achilles) is to B (Ajax), so must C (the meed of Achilles) be to D (the meed of Ajax). Then, *alternando*, as is A to C, so must B be to D. Then lastly, *componendo*, as is A to B, so must A *plus* C, be to B *plus* D; thus,

if A : B :: C : D
then, *alternando*, A : C :: B : D
and then, *componendo*, A : B :: A + C : B + D.

This is the connection which the distribution effects, and which it will effect justly if it effect it in accordance with this proportion. Thus, then, it is just in a distribution to connect A with C and B with D; and thus it is that that which is just is a mean between the two possible violations of proportion—that which is proportional being a mean, and that which is just being proportional. It is this kind of proportion that mathematicians call geometrical. For it is in geometrical proportion that the terms stand to one another in a similar ratio, whether they be taken severally or jointly. Moreover, this proportion which we have given above is not continuous, inasmuch as one and the same term cannot represent both a person and a thing. Thus then this species of justice consists in proportion, and the corresponding injustice in the violation of proportion. Proportion may be violated either by excess or by defect. And this is what actually takes place; for, as a matter of fact, he who commits the wrong act gains more good than he ought, while he who is wronged obtains less. While with that which is evil the contrary takes place, the lesser evil as compared with the greater being reckoned as a good. For the lesser evil is always more choiceworthy than is the greater; and, since that which is choiceworthy is *ipso facto* good, it follows that that which is the more choiceworthy will be the greater good. The above described is then one kind of particular justice. There remains yet one other kind, the corrective, which has its place in transactions or contracts whether voluntary or involuntary. This kind of justice differs specifically from the former.

4.

(91.) For distributive | justice is always concerned with those goods to which all the citizens have some claim, and with reference to these goods it employs the proportion which we have described. Suppose, for instance, that a public dividend be announced, the payments made will be proportionate to the values of the original deposits. And the injustice which is the contradictory of this kind of justice consists in a violation of this same proportion. But that which is just in the case of transactions or of contracts implies equality, and that which is unjust implies inequality, not in geometric, however, but in arithmetic proportion. For it does not matter whether a good man has cheated a bad, or a bad man a good, or whether a good man has debauched the wife of a bad, or a bad man the wife of a good. If A. has committed and B. has suffered a wrong, or if A. has injured and B. has been injured, the law only looks to the actual nett result of the injury, and draws no distinction between the parties. So that this kind of injustice is one which involves an inequality, which inequality the juror endeavours to equalise. For, if A. has struck a blow and B. has been struck, or if A. has committed murder and B. has been murdered, the amount of injury involved in the action has been divided into two unequal shares; and these shares the juror endeavours to equalise by the infliction of a penalty, so taking something away from the gain of the injurer. For in such cases, even although the term may not always be appropriate, we, using wide and general terms, speak of "gain," as of "the gain" of him who has struck the blow, and of "loss," as of "the loss" of him who has been so struck. But it is only after that the amount of the damage has been assessed that the terms "gain" and "loss" can be correctly applied. Now that which is equal is a mean between that which is too much and that which is too little; and gain and loss are respectively too much and too little in two distinct ways,—gain implying too much good and too little evil, while loss implies the exact contrary. The mean between the two is that which is equal, or, as we call it, just. Hence, that which is correctively just will aim at the mean between loss and gain. And so, after a dispute, men betake themselves to a justice; and, to betake one's self to a justice is to betake one's self to that which is just,—a justice being abstract justice embodied in a concrete person. And thus they seek for a justice as an impersonification of the mean (justices, indeed, are called by some, "arbitrators," a word which etymologically signifies "middle-men"), on the assumption that, if they obtain that which is in the mean, they will then obtain that which is just. And so, since the justice is the impersonification of (92.) the mean, that which is just will be | in the mean. And so, too, a justice produces equality in the same way as if, a line having been divided into two unequal segments, one were to take the excess of the greater segment over and above the exact half of the line so divided, and were to cut it off from the greater segment, and to add it to the less. For, when the whole has been divided into two parts, and the parties have each received an equal share, then men say that they have that which is their own. That, then, which is equal after this wise, is the arithmetical mean between that which is too much and that which is too little. And hence the word "just" is used, because it etymologically signifies "that which is bisected"; while a "juror," or "justice," signifies "one who bisects," For, if from the one of two given equal straight lines a given segment be cut off, and be added to the other, then shall this other exceed the remainder by twice this given segment. Whereas, if the given segment be cut off from the one line, but be not added to the other line, then shall this other line exceed the remainder by one such segment. The other line shall, then, when increased by the given segment, exceed the original line (which is the mean) by one such segment; and the mean, again, shall exceed the re-

mainder by one such segment. And by the use of
this theorem we shall discover what to take away from
him who has more than his neighbour, and what to
add to him who has less. For one must add to him
who has less as much as is that by which the exact
mean exceeds his present share; and one must take
from the greater share that by which the mean falls
short of that share.

```
A               D          A
B                          B
C               F    C          E
```

Let the lines AA, BB, CC, be all equal to one another.
From AA cut off a given segment AD, and then add
that segment to CC, so that CC is produced to E.
Then shall the entire line CE be greater than AD by
FE, and greater than BB by CE. And this same
theorem holds good of interchange in the arts, which
depend for their very existence upon the fact that
production and consumption are equal to one another
both in quantity and in quality. In fact, the very
terms "gain" and "loss" are borrowed from the
phraseology of voluntary barter, wherein "to gain"
means to conclude barter in possession of more than
one had at first, and "to lose" means to conclude
in possession of less; as is the case, for instance, in
buying, and in selling, and in all those other contracts to which the law, by its recognition, guarantees
security. But when, by buying and selling,[*] men
have got neither more nor less than they had at first,

---

[*] The reading ὠνῇ δὲ πράσει and the rendering given above are both
due to Mr. Chandler, of Pembroke College, Oxford.

but exactly the same, then they say that they "have their own," and have neither lost nor gained. And (93.) hence corrective justice | is a mean between the gain and the loss which are involved in involuntary transactions, and is such that each party has the same both before the transaction and after it.

5. Now some have held that the one form of all justice is simply retaliation. This was the opinion of the Pythagoreans, who defined justice simply as "exact retaliation." But the conception of retaliation will not suit either distributive or corrective justice. And yet they would have it that it is this that is meant by "Rhadamanthine justice":—

> When a man suffers that which he has done,
> Then upright Justice shows herself.

But there is a wide difference between the two on many points. If, for instance, an officer has struck a private, he ought not to be struck in return; whereas, if a private has struck an officer, he ought not only to be struck in return, but also to be in addition punished. Moreover, a great distinction must be made between voluntary and involuntary wrongs. But, in all contracts of sale and of barter, the bond of union between the parties is a justice of this kind, consisting however in a retaliation made not according to numerical equality, but according to proportionate value. Indeed, retaliation or reciprocity of proportionate values is the bond of union of the body politic. For either a man desires to requite evil with like evil, which not to be allowed to do is held to be sheer slavery; or else he desires to repay good with like good, which when men cannot do then no mutual interchange can take place; and by mutual interchange it is that citizens are held together. And hence men make to themselves a Temple of the Graces in the public streets, that they may remember to return good for good. For gratitude is the especial gift of the Graces. And a man ought in his turn to minister again to one who has done him an act of grace, and then himself to make a new commencement with such another act again on his own part. The proportion in which all return ought to be made is given us by the conjunction of the diameter with the two sides.

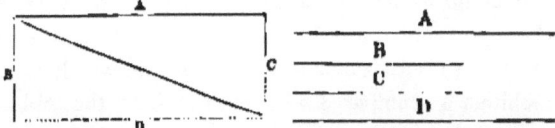

Let the line A represent an architect, and the line B a cobbler, then shall C represent a house, and D a pair of shoes. Now the architect has to receive from the cobbler a portion of his produce, and to give him in return a portion of his own produce. If, then, proportionate equality of value be first secured, and then exact retaliation take place, the justice of which we have spoken will be the result. But, otherwise, there will be no real equality, and consequently no permanent bond of union. For there is | no reason why the produce of the one man should not be more valuable than is that of the other, and so the two kinds of produce must first be equalised.* For con-

* Omit the words ἐστὶ ἐὶ τοῦτο—τοσοῦτον καὶ τοσοῦτον, as does Andronicus.

tracts of exchange are not entered into between physician and physician, but between physician and husbandman, or, in a word, between people who differ from one another, and who are not of the same class, but whom the bargain ought to place upon equal terms. And hence it is a necessity to have some kind of common measure for all such things as are exchanged for one another. And to meet this want was the origin of a currency, which serves, as it were, for a mean between things that differ in value; for it is the one common measure of all commodities, so that it can measure their relative excess or deficiency in value, and so determine how many pairs of shoes are the equivalent in value of a house, or of a given amount of provisions. As then is the worth of the architect as compared with the worth of the cobbler, so must be the number of pairs of shoes as compared with the house, or with, it may be, the given amount of provisions; or otherwise all barter and all contract will be an impossibility. And this cannot be the case unless the two kinds of produce be in some way equalised. And thus it comes about that we must, as we have said before, have some one common measure by which to measure all commodities. And this common measure is in reality demand, which is the one bond of union in all contracts. For if men stood in no need each of the produce of another, or if their mutual needs were not in that relation of equality in which as a matter of fact they now are, then there would either be no exchange at all, or at any rate there would be a different kind of exchange from that which there now is. Now a currency is a kind of conventional representative of demand, and the term "currency" signifies that its value is not intrinsic but conventional, and that it is consequently in our power to adopt a new representative of value, and so to make the old useless. Exact retaliation then must not take place until after such an equalisation has been effected that the husbandman is to the cobbler as is the produce of the cobbler to the produce of the husbandman. After, however, that the exchange has once taken place the parties must not be represented as being still in a relation of mutual superiority and inferiority, or otherwise the one of the terms will be having an allowance made for its superiority twice over, and in two distinct ways. When the result of the contract has been such that each party has got that which is fairly his, then they are equalised, and fairly represented in the contract, in that there can result between them the following relation of equality,

$$A : B :: D : C$$
$$\text{or } A \times D = B \times C$$

in which, A being the husbandman, C so much provision, and B the cobbler, D represents an amount of the produce of the cobbler equal in value to C. And, unless reciprocation were to take place after this wise, there would be no transactions between man and man. And that it is mutual need that binds together diverse wills into the accidental unity of contract, is clear from the fact, that, when men stand in (95.) no need of one another, | or even when the one of two men is in no need of his fellow, then no exchange takes place between the two; as it does when one man happens to want that which another has, as, for instance, wine, and gives for it a portion of an export of corn, which portion will first have to be equalised in value to the amount of wine which he receives. Money, moreover, acts as a security to us for the possibility of exchange hereafter, should a want arise which we do not perhaps at present feel; for money ought to serve as a legal tender for any required commodity. It also obeys the same law as do all other commodities, for its value is not always identical. But yet its value has, of all values, the greatest tendency to be permanent. And hence all things ought to have assigned to them a definite money value; for so barter will become possible, and, along with barter, intercourse between man and man. A currency, then, serves as a kind of common measure, by means of which one commodity can have its value expressed in terms of another, and so be equalised with it. Unless barter existed there could be no intercourse between man and man; unless different commodities could be equalised there could be no barter; and different commodities could never be equalised unless there were some common standard of value. Of course, things so widely different cannot really be referred to any common standard; but still, for all practical purposes, we can make such a reference with sufficient accuracy. There must, therefore, be some one common representative of value, which, as the name "currency" indicates, will depend upon convention for its use. And, since money is the one common measure of all values, the use of money enables us to express the value of any one commodity in terms of another.

$$A = \frac{B}{2} = 5 C \begin{cases} A = \text{a house} = 5 \text{ minæ.} \\ B = 10 \text{ minæ.} \\ C = \text{a bed} = 1 \text{ mina.} \end{cases}$$

Let A, for instance, be a house, B be ten minæ, and C be a bed. Then, if a house be worth five minæ, that is to say, be equivalent to them in value, A will be equal to the one-half of B. Further, let C, a bed, be equal to the one-tenth part of B. It thus becomes clear how many beds are equal in value to a house—namely, five. It is, moreover, clear that, before the invention of a currency, barter took place in this fashion; for it matters nothing whether one give five beds for a house, or whether one give the value in money of five beds.

Thus then we have described both that which is unjust, and that which is just. And from our description it will follow clearly that just treatment will be a mean between doing wrong and suffering wrong. For to do wrong is to take more than one's share, and to suffer wrong is to get less than one's share. And justice is a mean state, not in the same way as are the virtues which we have before described, but in that it aims at producing that which is in the mean; whereas injustice aims at producing one or the other of two extremes. Moreover, justice is a habit in virtue of which the just man is said to be disposed to do deliberately and of free purpose that which is just, and to make a distribution, whether between himself and another, or between two others, not such that he (96.) himself secures the | larger share of advantage and his neighbour the less, and of disadvantage the exactly contrary; but rather such that he only secures for himself that which is his equal share according to a fair proportion, and observes a similar rule in his decision as arbiter between two claimants. Injustice, on the other hand, aims at producing that which is unjust, and which consists in such an excess or defect, as the case may be, either of the advantageous or of the disadvantageous, as to violate the rules of proportion. And hence injustice is both an excess and a defect, in that it aims at producing both an excess and a defect,—in one's own case, that is to say, an excess of that which is in the abstract advantageous and a deficiency of that which is disadvantageous; while, when the unjust man acts as arbiter between two claimants, the character of his act as a whole obeys the same rule, but the particular violation of proportion that takes place may be to the interest of either of the two parties to the suit. In fine, in an unjust act, to get less than one's share is to be wronged, and to get more than one's share is to commit a wrong.

6. Concerning particular justice, then, and with it particular injustice, and concerning the nature of each respectively, the foregoing may be taken as our account; as also of that which is just and of that which is unjust universally. But, inasmuch as a man need not *ipso facto* be unjust in that he does an unjust act, shall we inquire what are the several kinds of unjust acts,—

such, for example, as theft, or adultery, or highway robbery,—the commission of which in each case *ipso facto* stamps a man as unjust? Surely this is not the distinction which we require. A man might, for example, lie with his neighbour's wife, and do so knowingly, yet not deliberately at all, but in a fit of uncontrollable passion. Such a man would commit an unjust act indeed, but yet would not on that account be unjust; much as a man need not be a thief, but yet may have committed a theft, or need not be an adulterer, but yet may have committed adultery; and in other instances the same rule will hold good. Now we have already stated how retaliation and justice are connected, and we must further remember that that of which we are in search is justice in its simplest acceptation,—justice, that is to say, such as it exists between fellow-members of the body politic, who lead life in common, with a view to the perfect satisfaction of all their wants, and who are further free, and also equal,—if not equal man to man, yet at least proportionately equal, when their several and respective claims have been referred to one common standard. Where men do not stand in this relation to one another, then there is for such no justice political in their mutual dealings, but only a certain spurious justice, falsely so called, in so far as it may resemble the true justice. Justice cannot exist unless there be a law between man and man; and the very existence of law implies the possibility of wrong, inasmuch as an adjudication is nothing more than a distinction between that which is right and that which is wrong.

Now, where wrong is possible, there one can always (97.) commit a wrong; | but to simply commit a wrong does not in all cases prove the presence of wrong;— to commit a wrong being to allot to oneself the larger share of what is abstractedly good, and the smaller share of what is abstractedly evil. From these considerations it is that we do not allow an individual man to rule, but only a general principle, lest the individual should rule for his own good alone, and so prove himself a despot. Indeed the sole duty of a ruler is to keep watch over that which is just, and so by implication over that which is equal. Now, if he be a just man, he will by thus ruling gain nothing for himself. He will not allot to himself a larger share of what is abstractedly good, unless his merits deserve such a proportion. He acts, that is to say, in the interest of others; whence comes the common definition of justice, which we have given before, as another man's good. He must then have allotted to him a reward of some kind. This reward will take the shape of honour and dignity. And whoso are not content with these, they make themselves despots. But justice between master and slave, or between father and son, is not the same as is justice political, but only like unto it. One cannot wrong that which is absolutely one's own. Now one's property, and equally with it one's son (as long as he is only of a certain age, and so has not yet separated himself from his parents), is, as it were, an integral portion of one's self. And, since no man can deliberately purpose to do him-

M

self an injury, it follows that for a man to commit a wrong against himself is an impossibility. Justice and injustice political have consequently no place in the relations of a man either to his children or to his slaves. For justice political is dependent upon law, and so can, as we have already said, exist amongst those alone whose mutual relations are naturally regulated by law, that is to say amongst those who can both hold rule and submit to rule upon equal terms. Hence justice has much more place between a man and his wife, than between a man and his children, or his property. This kind is the justice economic —a kind which, like the justice between father and son, is not to be confounded with justice political.

7. Justice political may be subdivided into two kinds, the natural and the conventional. The natural kind is that which is in all places equally valid, and which, whether it be accepted or whether it be rejected of men, will equally be just; while the conventional kind is that which might originally have been determined either way with equal justice, but which, when once it has been determined, is then no longer indifferent; as, for example, that the ransom for a prisoner of war should be one mina, and that sacrifice should be made with a she-goat, and not with two sheep; and, in addition, all bills passed to meet special and particular occasions, as that sacrifice should be made to Brasidas, and all resolutions of the general assembly. Some, indeed, there are who hold that all justice whatsoever is of this kind, inasmuch as that which exists by nature is— say they—unalterable, and everywhere alike holds equally good; as, for instance, is

the case with fire, which burns here exactly as it burns among the | Persians; while that which is just experience shows to vary. Now the matter is not exactly as they state it, although to a certain extent it is. Amongst the Gods, perhaps, that which is just may be absolutely immutable. Amongst men there is a kind of natural justice, although all human justice is conceivably liable to change. But still the distinction between that which is natural and that which is not natural none the less holds good. And it is self-evident what kind of things contingent exist by nature, and what kind by positive law and by convention,— although both alike are conceivably variable. The distinction is one which can be drawn in all other similar cases. The right hand, for instance, is by nature stronger than the left; and yet it is none the less possible for men to be ambidextrous. That justice which depends wholly upon convention and expediency may be compared to a standard of measure. For moist and dry measures are not of equal capacity in all places alike, but are larger among buyers and smaller among sellers. And so, in like manner, is it with that justice which is not by nature, but of men; for it is not in all places alike, as neither are forms of government,— albeit that there is by nature but one form of government, which is in all places alike the best. Moreover, each rule of justice and of law is as a universal which contains under itself many particulars. For the actions of men are many, while each rule is but one, for it is a universal. Moreover, we must distin-

(98.)

guish between that which is wrong in fact, and that which is wrong in principle; and between that which is right in fact, and that which is right in principle. That which in principle is wrong, is so either by nature or by convention. And this same, when put into actual practice, is then a wrong in fact; but, before it has been put into practice, is not such, but is only a wrong in principle. And of acts of right, also, the same rule holds equally good. The phrase "act of righteousness" is, however, the more general; the term "act of right" being usually restricted to the righting of an actual wrong. And, as regards particular acts of righteousness and of wrong, what kinds of them there are, and how many, and with what things they are concerned, we must consider hereafter. That which is just, and that which is unjust, is, then, such as we have said; and to act justly or unjustly consists in the doing of such acts voluntarily. For, when a man does such acts involuntarily, he neither acts justly nor yet unjustly, save only incidentally,—the act itself, in such cases, being just or unjust only incidentally. Indeed, the justice or injustice of an act is determined by the question whether it be voluntary or not. | When it is voluntary, then only do we attach blame to it, and then only is it properly an unjust act. And so an act may answer to the abstract definition of injustice, and yet not be, *ipso facto*, an unjust act, unless it be also voluntary. A voluntary act we define, as before, as one which is at the discretion of the agent, and which he, the agent, does with full knowledge of the person thereby affected, and of the means employed, and of the result (as, for instance, when a man knows whom he strikes, and with what he strikes him, and what will be the effect of the blow), and which in each several case has been done neither incidentally, nor under compulsion. If, for instance, A. seizes the hand of B., and with it strikes C., then B. acts under compulsion, and not voluntarily, inasmuch as the act was not done at his own discretion. Or if, again, the man whom you have struck should happen to have been your father, and you were to have been aware that he was a man, or that he was one of the bystanders, but were to have been ignorant that he was your father, you would then have done wrong only incidentally. And, with regard to the result of the act, or, indeed, to the act itself as a whole, the same distinctions may be drawn. Wherever, in a word, we are ignorant of what we do, or wherever we are not ignorant, but yet the act itself is not at our own discretion, but is compulsory, what is done is involuntary. We are, for example, conscious of many purely physical acts and feelings, which are neither voluntary, nor yet strictly involuntary,—as of growing old, for instance, or of the act of death. That, then, which is unjust can, equally with that which is just, be done incidentally as well as directly. For, if a trustee restore a deposit under compulsion and from fear, he cannot be said to do that which is just, or, in other words, to act justly, directly, but only incidentally. And, in like manner also, he who, under compulsion, and against his will, refuses to restore a deposit, can only incidentally be said to act unjustly, and to do that which is unjust. Of our voluntary acts, again, some we do deliberately, and others not. We do deliberately all such acts as we have planned beforehand; acts not previously planned not being deliberate. In the intercourse of man with man three kinds of wrong can occur. A simple tort is a wrong done in ignorance; as, for example, when the act has affected some other person than the agent expected, or when the act itself has proved to be other than he expected, or when its instrument or its result has proved to be such,—as, for instance, when A. had not intended to strike B., or did not think that he had used such or such a weapon, or did not think that B. was such or such a person, or did not think that the result of the blow would be such as it was—the result proving to be other than he had expected,—as if, for instance, he had not intended to wound his man, but only to touch him; or had not intended to wound this man, but another; or had not intended to wound him | in so deadly a manner. When, then, the injury which has been inflicted is contrary to all rational expectation, it is an accident. But, when it might have fairly been expected, but yet has involved no evil purpose, it is a simple tort:—the distinction between tort and accident being that, in the former, the efficient cause of the injury is the agent, who is, consequently, responsible; while, in accident, the efficient cause is extraneous. But, when a man acts knowingly, indeed, but still not from premeditation, then his act is a wrong. Such are all those acts into which men are betrayed through anger, and through other unavoidable and purely physical emotions. In such cases a man injures his fellow, it is true, and so commits a tort, or, more properly, does a wrong; and the act so done is a wrong. But the doer of such an act need not be, on that account, unjust and criminal. The wrong done did not originate in the criminality of the agent. It is only when the wrong is done deliberately that the doer of it is unjust and criminal. And hence it is that assaults committed in anger are rightly decided not to proceed from malice prepense, for such acts do not originate in the volition of the man who has been angered, but rather in that of the man who so angered him. Moreover, the question at issue is not one of the facts of the case, but of the rights of it,—for anger is provoked by what one conceives to have been a previous wrong to one's self. We are not here, as in civil contracts, concerned with a question of fact. In such cases one of the two parties must be a rogue, unless the dispute originate in forgetfulness. But here the fact of the injury done is admitted, the question raised being as to the rights of the case. Now, when a man has deliberately committed a breach of the peace, he cannot have so acted unconsciously. And hence it is that, in cases such as those of which we are speaking, he who has been assaulted holds that he has been wronged; while he who under provocation so assaulted him, holds that he has been rightly served. Of course, in all those cases in which a man has deliberately injured another, he has committed a wrong. And it is for the commission of wrongs of this latter kind alone, wherein fair proportion or equality has been deliberately set at nought, that men are held to be unjust. And so, too, in like manner, that man alone is held to be just who deliberately pursues just dealing. And he alone properly pursues just dealing who thus acts of his own free will. Of involuntary wrongs, on the other hand, some are excusable, and some are not. For, when men commit a tort, not only in ignorance, but actually from ignorance, their offence is excusable. But, where the wrong done does not actually originate in the ignorance of the agent, but is only done in ignorance,—which ignorance has been brought on by some passion neither natural nor human,—then it is inexcusable.

9. A further doubt arises, whether our determinations in respect of doing wrong and of suffering wrong are sufficient. And, first of all, is the statement of Euripides, inconceivable as it appears, yet conceivable?

(101.)
  I slew* my | mother,—I,—the tale is brief;
  I with my will, she here,—else here, not mine.

Can we, that is to say, really suffer wrong with our own will, or can we not; and is not rather all suffering of wrong involuntary, exactly as all wrong doing must be voluntary? And is this rule to be made absolute? Must, that is to say, all suffering of wrong whatsoever be involuntary, in the same way as all wrong doing is voluntary; or may some suffering of wrong be voluntary, and some not? And with regard to right treatment also a like doubt arises; for all just

  * Read *aorizras* with Corael.

action must be voluntary. And hence, in so far as the voluntariness or the non-voluntariness of the act is concerned, justice and injustice, both in agent and in patient, ought to be symmetrically opposed. But yet it seems inconceivable that all those who submit to just treatment should do so voluntarily; for some men certainly submit to just treatment against their will. And a further doubt is possible,—namely, whether every one who has a wrong done to him is really thereby wronged, or whether the suffering of wrong may not have its voluntariness decided by the analogy of that of the doing of wrong. For, in the case of just dealing, both agent and patient may be concerned with what is just only incidentally. And the same rule clearly holds good of what is unjust. For he who does that which answers to the abstract definition of the unjust does not in all such cases commit a wrong, nor does he who suffers that which answers to the abstract definition of the unjust always suffer a wrong. And the same rule holds good of just treatment both in agent and in patient. No one, that is to say, can suffer a wrong, unless another has intentionally done him a wrong; or experience just treatment, unless another intentionally treat him justly. And, again, since wrong doing simply consists in voluntarily doing an injury to another,—" voluntarily" meaning, knowing to whom the wrong was done, and by what means, and in what manner,—and since the incontinent man voluntarily injures himself;—it follows that he is voluntarily injured, and hence that it is possible for a man to wrong himself. And, indeed, the question, whether it is possible for a man to wrong himself, is one of the points that remain to be raised. Moreover, a man might through his own incontinence be injured by another person, who might also be acting voluntarily. And thus it would be possible to be wronged with one's own will. The answer is that our definition of wrong doing is not yet perfect, but that to the words "knowing to whom the wrong was done, and by what means, and in what manner," we must further add the words "and that it was against the patient's will." For, although a man may indeed be injured voluntarily, and so may suffer treatment which answers to the abstract definition of wrong, yet no man can be actually wronged with his own consent. For no man ever wishes to be wronged,—no, not even the incontinent man: for he in reality acts against his own (102.) will. No man, indeed, can really wish for that which he does not think to be good; and even the incontinent man does not act as he knows he ought to act. Even he who makes a losing gift, such as that which Homer tells us that Glaucus made to Diomed,—

<blockquote>Golden for brass,—a hundred beeves for nine,—</blockquote>

even he is not wronged. It depends upon himself, it is true, whether he shall make the gift or whether he shall not, but it does not depend upon himself alone whether or not he shall be wronged; for, for him to be wronged, there must first be some one else to wrong him.

Thus, then, as regards the being wronged, it is clear

that it can never be voluntary. There remain, however, yet two more of the questions which we proposed; namely, whether it is he who makes an unfair award, or he who receives it, who commits the wrong; and also whether it is possible for a man to wrong himself. For if, in the case of the first question, the former of the two assumptions be true, and it is he who makes the unfair award who really does the wrong, and not he who receives it, then it will follow that, if a man knowingly and willingly award to another a larger share than to himself, he will thereby do himself a wrong. And this it is that the modestly-minded are held to do; indeed, the equitable man may be said to seek that which is less than his fair share. But then, is this an adequate account? May not such a man obtain, perhaps, a larger share of another kind of good, as of reputation, for instance, or of that which is good in the highest sense of the word? Moreover, the very definition of wrong doing resolves our difficulty. For no man can suffer a wrong against his own will. And so, in the case in question, he does not suffer a wrong, but only a loss. Moreover, it is clear that it is he who makes the unjust award, and not he who, in the given case, receives it, who does the wrong. For it is not he to whom that attaches which answers to the abstract definition of injustice, but only he who voluntarily commits an act of such a kind, who can be properly said to commit a wrong. Now an act is done voluntarily by him in whom it actually originates. And, in the case in question, the wrong originates in the volition of him

who makes the award, and not in that of him who
receives it. And, again, inasmuch as there are many
senses in which we may be said to do a thing,—a lifeless instrument, for instance, may be said to kill a
man, or another man's hand, or a slave acting under
orders to assassinate,—so he who receives the unjust
award does not indeed commit a wrong, but yet none
the less does that which answers to the abstract definition of wrong. And, again, if the award was made
in ignorance, the judge has not done that which is
wrong in the eye of the law, nor is his decision in this
sense unjust. But yet unjust, in a certain sense, it
is; for legal justice is one thing, and natural justice is
another. But, if the unjust award was made know-
(10J.) ingly, then the judge must himself have made an
unfair gain, in the shape either of a gratuity from
him whom the verdict favoured, or of vengeance
wreaked upon the other party to the suit. Exactly
as is the case when one receives a share in the profits
of a wrong, so here he who gives an unjust verdict,
whether from cupidity or from revenge, may be said
to make an unjust gain. In the case, for instance, of
receiving a share in the profits of a wrong, he who
unjustly awarded the field which was in dispute, may
have received, not a portion of the field itself, but the
equivalent in money of such a portion. Now men
hold that it is in their power to commit or not to
commit a wrong, and that so it is an easy matter to
be just. But this is not really the case. For, albeit
that to lie with one's neighbour's wife, and to smite
one's neighbour, and to actually deliver a bribe, are

easy matters, and to do them or not to do them rests with a man's self; yet, to do these acts, and to be at the same time in a certain definite state of mind with reference to them, is no easy matter, and does not rest with a man's self. For the same reason it is that men hold that it requires no great wisdom to know what is just and what is unjust, because it is no difficult matter to understand what the laws order. But that which is ordered by the laws is not, as such, just; it is only just incidentally; it does not, indeed, become distinctly just, until the act has been done, or the award has been made, in a certain definite spirit. And for a man to act in this spirit is a more difficult matter than it is for him to acquire a knowledge of what is good for health. In the case of medicine, for instance, it is easy to know what is honey, and what is wine, and what is hellebore, and what is cautery, and what is excision. But to know how all these ought to be applied with a view to health, and to whom, and when, amounts, in fact, to being a physician. And hence, too, it is that men are led to suppose that the just man is capable of unjust equally with just acts, in that the just man is able to do each and all of these acts, not only no less, but, perhaps, even more than is the unjust man. For the just man can lie with his neighbour's wife, and can smite his neighbour, much as the brave man can also fling away his shield and take to flight in any direction that comes first. But, to play the coward, or to commit a wrong, does not consist in merely doing these particular acts (except in so far as it incidentally involves the doing of them), but in doing them with a certain definite frame of mind,—exactly as to make sound and to be sound does not consist in the mere use of the knife or of drugs, or in the mere abstinence from their use; but rather in such use, or in such abstinence, under certain definite conditions. In fine, just acts can have place among those alone who partake of things that are in the abstract good, and who can have of such things either more or less than their fair share. For some beings, as, perhaps, the Gods, cannot have more than their share of good; while others, again,— the incurably depraved,—find no share of good things a blessing; but to them all good things whatsoever are a curse. Others, again, there are for whom a certain amount of good things is to be desired. And thus we can see that justice is a human matter.

10. Next in order we must treat of equity, and of that which is equitable, and of the relations between equity and justice, and between that which is equitable and that which is just. Upon consideration, we shall see clearly that, while, upon the one hand, justice and equity are not absolutely identical, yet, on the other hand, they are not specifically distinct. At times, for instance, we praise that which is equitable, and with it the equitable man; and so transfer the name, together with the praise which it implies, to other objects which we had usually called good; proving thereby that we hold that the more equitable is an act the better it becomes. And yet, at times, it would seem, upon reflection, inconceivable that the equitable, although it has been contradistinguished from the

just, should yet call for praise. For if, on the one
hand, the just be distinct from the equitable,* then it
must follow that either justice is not good, or else
equity is not good. While, if, on the other hand,
both justice and equity be good, then they must be
identical. Such, or nearly such, then, are the grounds
of this difficulty concerning equity. And yet all the
premisses in question are, to a certain extent, true,
and in no way self-contradictory. For the real truth
is that the equitable is superior to the just, as being
an intensified form of the just, and not as being distinct from the just in kind. The just and the equitable are thus identical,—each being good, but the
equitable the best. The real source of the difficulty
is that the equitable is just, not in that it agrees with
positive law, but in that it is a rectification of it.
And this is possible, because all positive law is ex-
pressed in general propositions, whereas cases can
occur to which general propositions are inapplicable.
Wherever, then, on the one hand, an abstract and
general rule is a political necessity; and, on the other
hand, such a rule is too abstract to be practically
true; there the law is content if its applications be
upon an average correct, although aware that, within
certain limits, an error has been made. Nor must
the law herein be accounted wrong, inasmuch as the
error originates neither in the law nor in those who
framed it, but rather in the nature of the cases to meet
which it was framed. For all matter of action is in
its very nature such that abstract rules when applied

* Read ἢ τὸ ἐπιεικὲς οὔ, ἢ καιτοι τὸ αὐτό, with Michelet.

to it are only true upon an average. Whensoever, then, the terms of the law are abstract and universal, and the particular case cannot in consequence be brought under them, then it is but right, where the framer of the law falls short from over abstractness, (105.) to correct this error, and to supply that decision which the legislator would have given, had he been present at the case in question, and which he would have comprised in his law, had he foreseen the case. And so, consequently, that which is equitable is also just, and is superior to certain forms of the just,— not, that is to say, to that which is absolutely just, but to that which, because just in the abstract, errs in the particular. The essence, in a word, of equity is that it should correct positive law wheresoever such positive law fails from its over abstractness. And hence, too, it is that all matters indiscriminately do not come within the range of positive law, because there are certain cases for which it is impossible to lay down a positive law in general terms, and for which we consequently require a special and particular enactment. For that which is in itself irregular requires an irregular rule, exactly as the Lesbian walls of uneven masonry require a leaden rule by which to measure their actual length. For, much as such a rule is not inflexible, but adapts itself to the configuration of the stones, so does the special enactment adapt itself to each particular case. Thus, then, it is clear what the equitable is, and that it is also just, and moreover that it is superior to certain forms of the just. And from the nature of the equitable the nature of the equitable man is also clear. For whosoever fixes his purpose upon such acts as we have described, and does them, and does not wrest the letter of the law to his neighbour's wrong, but rather aims at less than his legal right, although he has the law at his back,—such a man as this is equitable, and his habit of mind is equity; which equity is a species of justice, and not a habit of mind specifically distinct from justice.

11. As regards the question whether a man can wrong himself or not, the answer to it is clear from what we have already said. For, in the first place, one class of just acts consists of those actions which are enjoined by the law as being co-extensive with virtue as a whole. The law, for instance, nowhere bids a man kill himself; and that which the law does not bid, it by implication forbids. And when, too, a man in violation of the law injures another, and that not by way of just retaliation, and does so willingly (knowing, that is to say, whom he injures, and with what instrument, and how), that man commits a wrong. He, then, who from rage kills himself, does so willingly, and in violation of right reason, and, further, does that which the law does not allow, and so commits a wrong. But whom does he wrong? Surely it is the State which he wrongs, and not himself. For he suffers the injury in question willingly; whereas no man can be wronged with his own will. And hence it is that it is the State which punishes him, and that civil infamy attaches to him who kills himself, on the ground that he thereby wrongs the State.

And, in the second place, it is impossible for a man to wrong himself in the sense in which he is a wrongdoer who commits acts of particular injustice, and who yet is not entirely and absolutely bad. These two kinds (106.) of injustice are | distinct from one another. For he who is unjust in this, the particular sense, is a bad man, much as the coward is a bad man,—bad, that is to say, not absolutely and entirely, but only in a particular and limited sense. But yet, even in this sense, he does not wrong himself. Were this so, then the same person could have the same thing both taken from him and given to him; and this is impossible,—justice and injustice always involving more persons than one. Moreover, a wrong must be voluntary, and deliberate, and aggressive,—by which latter qualification we understand that he who, because he has suffered an injury, inflicts a similar injury upon his aggressor, is not held to commit a wrong. Now here, in the case in question, a man inflicts an injury upon himself. He therefore both suffers and inflicts the same wrong. And, again, could a man wrong himself, then would it be possible to be wronged with one's own will. In addition, it may be argued that no man can commit specific wrong without doing some specifically wrong act, and that no man can, for instance, commit an adultery with his own wife, or a burglary upon his own premises, or a larceny of his own goods. But, after all, the most comprehensive answer to the question is to be found in the definition of justice and of injustice, by which it is settled that to suffer wrong cannot be voluntary.

It is, moreover, clear that to suffer wrong and to do wrong are both bad; for the one is to obtain less, and the other is to obtain more than that which is the fair mean; and herein we may compare the analogies of health in medicine, and of condition in training. But, still, to do wrong is morally the worst. For to do wrong involves conscious vice, and so is blameable. And the vice which it involves will be either complete and absolute, or approximately such; for all voluntary injuries do not imply conscious wrong-doing. While, on the other hand, to suffer wrong involves no such consciousness of vice and of injustice. In itself then, and apart from its consequences, to suffer wrong is less bad than to do wrong. But the suffering of wrong may none the less incidentally lead to results far worse than follow from the doing of wrong. All, however, that is incidental strict science must ignore. Medicine, for instance, asserts that a pleurisy is a greater danger to health than is a stumble; and yet a stumble may none the less incidentally lead to greater damage than does a pleurisy, as when, for instance, a man stumbles, and then, as the indirect result of the fall, is captured by the enemy, and put to death. Lastly, by a metaphorical or analogical use of language, we may be allowed to speak of justice as subsisting, not between a man and himself, but between the man as a whole and certain parts of his nature. But yet it will not be every kind of justice that can thus subsist, but only that justice which can subsist between master and slave, or between a father and his family; for a relation of

this kind it is that exists between the rational and the irrational parts of the soul. And from a considera-
(107.) tion of this fact it has been held that a man can | wrong himself, inasmuch as the possession of these distinct parts involves the capability of a treatment that runs counter to one's own desires. And hence it has been said that justice can subsist in a certain relation between these two parts of the soul, analogous to that between ruler and ruled.

Concerning justice, then, and with it the other moral virtues, such are the determinations which we have to advance.

VI.

1. Now, since we have already said that a man ought to choose the mean, and not the excess or the defect, and that the mean is as right reason orders, it remains to determine what this right reason is. In all the moral habits of which we have spoken (as indeed in all others), there is a definite mark at which he who acts with reason aims, exactly as one aims and shoots at the centre of the target; there is a definite limit to the mean, which mean lies, as we have said, between excess and defect, and is determined by right reason. But this account, although true, is yet not sufficiently definite. For, although, in all practical applications of any scientific rule, it is true to say that we must neither be over accurate, nor yet careless, but must aim at that mean which right reason prescribes, yet the mere knowledge of this rule leads to nothing further. What, for instance, would a man know about the treatment of the body, if merely told to apply all that medicine orders, and to apply it as the physician prescribes? And, consequently, in describing the mental states we must not rest content with such a mere abstract truth, but must further seek a definite statement as to what this right reason is, and what are the limits which it prescribes.

In our division of the virtues, we said that some of

them were moral, and others intellectual. Having fully treated of the moral virtues, we will now proceed to discuss the others; and our discussion must be prefaced by certain statements concerning the soul.
(108.) We have already | said that the soul may be divided into two parts—the rational, and the irrational; and we will now make a similar division of the rational part. We will, that is to say, assume that the rational soul may be divided into two parts—the one that deals with such truths as are universal and necessary, the other that deals with such as are contingent. For, to correspond with object-matters that are specifically distinct, nature must have framed parts of the soul that are specifically distinct: since their knowledge of their respective object-matter cannot but depend upon a certain similarity to, and affinity with it. These two parts we will, respectively, call the speculative, and the deliberative. For deliberation means nothing more than an analysis of an end into its means; and no one attempts such an analysis in matter which is universal and necessary. Thus, then, to one of the two parts of the rational soul we apply the term "deliberative." It remains to determine what is the best formed state of which these two parts are respectively capable; for this it is that will be the highest specific excellence, or virtue, of each. Moreover, the excellence of each thing cannot be considered except as in relation to that special work
2. which it has to do. Now, of all the five parts of the soul, there are but three which are in any way concerned with either moral action or with truth,—to

wit, the sensitive, the rational, and the appetitive. But in the sensitive part alone moral action never originates; as is shown by the fact, that beasts, although they possess sensation, yet have no share in moral action. Now, assertion and negation in reason correspond to pursuit and avoidance in impulse; and, consequently, inasmuch as moral virtue is a formed-state of purpose, and purpose is impulse followed by deliberation, it results that, if our purpose is to be good, not only must our analysis of the end into its means be correct, but also our impulse towards the end must be right,—and, moreover, that the deliberation must give its assent to that at which the impulse aims. Such, then, is the reasoning, and such is the truth involved in moral action. For the speculative reason, on the other hand, which does not enter into our analysis, either in action or in production, it is abstract truth and abstract untruth which form the standard of good and of bad. So that, while truth as a whole is the object of the entire rational part of our soul, the especial object of that part which deals with reason as involved in action, is true analysis into means correspondent with good impulse towards an end. Thus, then, all action originates in purpose,—that is to say, in the choice of means to a given end, not in the mere conception of, or impulse towards that end,—purpose consisting in impulse towards an end, followed by an analysis of that end into its means. And purpose,

(109.) consequently, involves reason, that is to say | a process of reasoning, no less than it involves a determinate moral character, to which the impulse will

correspond. Free action, whether for good or for
bad, is inconceivable, without, on the one hand,
reason, and, on the other, a certain definite bent of
character. And, in like manner, action never originates in mere analysis, but only in that analysis of a
desired end into its means which all action involves.
Hence comes our determination to act, even in the
analytic processes of art. For every artist has, in the
execution of his work, an ulterior end in view; so that
the work itself is not an absolute end, but is subordinate to and dependent upon a something beyond
itself. But moral action is, in itself, an absolute end,
—the end of the action being nothing more than that
it should be done well, and the impulse having no
further aim than this. Hence it follows, that purpose
may be defined, either as reasoning resultant upon
impulse, or as impulse coupled with reasoning. And
in this sense and thus it is, that man's acts originate
in himself. Hence, moreover, purpose has nothing to
do with the past: no one, for example, purposes to
have sacked Ilium. For an analysis into means is not
applicable to that which is past, but only to that
which is in the future, and, consequently, in our
power. What is past cannot possibly be other than
it is, as Agathon has well said, saying—

> One thing alone not even God can do,
> To make undone whatever hath been done.

Thus, then, each of the rational parts of our soul has,
for its especial province, a specific kind of truth.
And, consequently, the highest excellence of each

part will be that particular formed state, or habit, by which each, respectively, will best arrive at truth.

3. Here, then, we will resume, and commence an account of the intellectual habits. Now, the soul arrives at truth, whether affirmative or negative, by the aid of five instruments,—by the aid of art, of deductive science, of prudence, of philosophy, and of induction. Supposition and opinion are omitted from the list, for they can lead to error no less than to truth. What is to be understood by demonstrative science will be at once clear, if we are to use our words in their strictest sense, and to avoid being misled by any transferred application of terms. We all hold that the object-matter of science is necessary; for, of matter which is not necessary, we can predicate nothing with certainty beyond the actual limits of our experience. The object-matter of science will, consequently, be necessary, and its truths will be immutable. For truths necessary in themselves, not necessary *ex hypothesi*, are always immutable; and the (110) objects of immutable truth | are unaffected by the phenomenal changes of becoming or of ceasing to be. Moreover, science is, in all cases, inferential: its truths can be taught and learnt. Now all inference involves some previous knowledge, as has been pointed out in the Analytics, and will, in its form, be either inductive or deductive. Universal propositions presuppose a previous induction; deduction proceeds from these universal propositions. Deduction, therefore, will ultimately presuppose, as its premisses, truths which cannot be arrived at by deduction itself; and which

must, consequently, be the result of induction. Science, in fine, is a habit of deductive demonstration; and, to complete its definition, all those determinations must be added that are given in the Analytics. A man, strictly speaking, has scientific knowledge, only when he has a certain specific kind of belief, —a belief, that is to say, in conclusions deduced from premisses of which he is assured. If he be not better assured of his premisses than he is of his conclusion, then his knowledge is scientific at best but incidentally: it has the deductive form without the deductive certainty. Let this, then, be accepted as our definition of science.

4. Matter that is contingent may be divided into the object-matter of art or of production, and the object-matter of action. Even popular language bears sufficiently valid testimony to the distinction between morality and art. And from this it follows, that the habit of free rational action must not be confounded with the habit of conscious rational production. Neither of the two contains the other under it. No moral action is ever a case of art, nor is a process of art ever a case of moral action. Now architecture is an instance of an art, for it comes under the class of habits of methodical production. And, since there is no art which is not a habit of methodical production, nor any habit of methodical production which is not an art, it follows that the definition of art is "a habit of production in conscious accordance with a correct method." Art, moreover, is always occupied with production. The artist has to plan and to consider

how to produce a something which it is possible either to bring about or to leave undone,—a something, that is to say, the efficient cause of which is the producer, not the product itself. Hence all necessary matter, whether immutable, or variable in accordance with fixed law, is beyond the sphere of art: as likewise are all natural phenomena; for these latter are their own efficient causes. Since, moreover, moral action and production are distinct, it follows that it is production, and not action, which is the province of art.

(111.) | And, to a certain extent, the object-matter of art will also be the object-matter of chance, as Agathon has said, saying—

<blockquote>Art loveth chance, chance art, with sister's love.</blockquote>

Art then, is, as we have said, a habit of production in conscious accordance with a correct method—if the method be faulty, it is not art that we have, but bungling—and is concerned with matter which is contingent, and so alterable by human agency.

5.   Prudence will be best defined by an examination of the grounds upon which we apply the term "prudent." The popular conception of the prudent man is that he is able to take the right means to those ends that are good and expedient for himself; and that not in any limited or special matter, as, for example, the means to health, or the means to strength, but, more generally, the means to a good and happy life. In confirmation of this, it may be observed that the term "prudent" is applied to those who have any special knowledge, only when they occupy themselves with the best means to some good end beyond the

province of their own special art. Thus then, speaking generally, the prudent man is he who can analyse ends into their means. As no one ever applies such an analysis to necessary matter, nor, indeed, to any matter not in his own power, it follows that prudence and science will be distinct: for, on the one hand, the method of science is deductive, and deduction is impossible except from premisses necessarily true, as otherwise our conclusions will have but a contingent certainty;* and, on the other hand, an analysis of ends into means is useless in necessary matter. And prudence must also be distinguished from art. It is distinct from science in that the matter of action is contingent, and from art because moral action and production are specifically distinct. Necessary matter and production being thus excluded, it remains that prudence is a conscious habit of correct reasoning on matters of action, and concerned with what is good or bad for man. And it will thus be distinct from art: for, in a process of production, the end proposed is distinct from the process itself; which is not the case in moral action, where the end proposed is nothing more than that the action should be done well. Hence it is that Pericles and men like Pericles are held to be prudent, because they can see what is good, not only for themselves, but also for mankind in general; and hence, too, we hold those to be prudent who are good managers of a household, or good statesmen. | It is for this reason, moreover, that the word "temperance" etymologically signifies "that

* Terminate the parenthesis at ἄλλως ἔχειν.

which preserves prudence"; for temperance does, as a matter of fact, preserve in us a right conception as to that which conduces to our real good. Inordinate pleasure and pain do not destroy or pervert all our conceptions—as, for example, our conception of a triangle, as having, or not having, its inner angles equal to two right angles—but only those conceptions that are concerned with matters of moral action. The ultimate principles of moral action state the ultimate motive of our acts. But, when a man has been corrupted by pleasure or by pain, then, of course, such principles are to him no longer self-evident truths; and he no longer believes that he ought to regulate his every purpose, that is to say, his every action, by reference to such or to such an end; for the practice of vice has a tendency to destroy our appreciation of moral principles. And thus we find ourselves again obliged to define prudence as "a conscious habit of correct reasoning on matters of action, concerned with that which is good for man." Art, again, admits of degrees of excellence, while prudence does not; and in art a voluntary error is not so blameable as an involuntary, while in prudence, as in every other virtue, the reverse of this holds good. Hence it follows that prudence is itself a definite virtue, and consequently must not be confounded with art. And, as the rational soul has two parts, prudence will be the virtue, or highest excellence, of that part whose province is opinion,—the object-matter of opinion, and consequently of prudence, being matter which is contingent, and so alterable by human agency. And yet prudence is something more than a mere habit of conscious reasoning, such as art or science; a proof of which is, that such a habit can, in course of time, be forgotten, whereas to forget prudence is impossible.

6. Again, since science involves a conception of certain universals, the matter of which will be necessary, and since all deduction, and consequently all science (the method of science being deductive), must have certain premisses from which to proceed, it follows that it cannot be science itself that supplies those premisses which scientific knowledge involves. Neither can it be art or prudence that will give us these premisses; for scientific knowledge is gained by deduction, and its matter is consequently necessary, while art and prudence have to do with matter which is contingent. Neither will these premisses be given us by philosophy, inasmuch as there are certain subjects which even the philosopher treats deductively, and for which he will consequently stand in need of premisses. Since, then, the faculties which, without possibility of error, always lead us to truth, whether in necessary or in contingent matter, are science, prudence, philosophy, and induction,—and since we see that three of these, that is to say, prudence, science, and philosophy, | cannot possibly supply our universal premisses,—it therefore remains that induction is the one faculty left, to which the discovery of these premisses must be ascribed.

7. "Wisdom" we, in the case of the arts, ascribe to those whose knowledge of their specific art is most absolutely exact; as, for example, when we call

Phidias a "wise" sculptor, and Polyclitus a "wise" statuary, meaning by this use of the word "wisdom" nothing more than the highest perfection of which art is capable: while in some cases again we say that a man is "wise" in a general sense, and without reference to any such specific knowledge as is implied in the phrase "wise in naught else," used by Homer in the Margites—

> Him neither ditcher made the gods nor ploughman,
> Nor wise in aught besides.

And hence it is clear that "wisdom," used as the equivalent of philosophy, will signify the most absolutely exact scientific knowledge: so that the philosopher must not only be assured of the truth of his conclusions, as deducible from such or such principles, but must further be assured that his principles are absolutely true. Thus, then, philosophy will be the combination of inductive with deductive knowledge, —knowledge, so to say, at once deductive and inductive, of the noblest and highest objects,—

> Fair body, and with fairest head complete.

It is indeed inconceivable to hold that statesmanship, or that prudence, is the highest knowledge, unless we also hold that man is the noblest object in the universe. And since, moreover, that which is healthy and that which is good will be one thing for men and another for fishes, while that which is white and that which is straight will under all circumstances whatever be identical, and since all men would admit that philosophy is concerned with the immutable, prudence

with the variable—for that being, whether man or animal, which can in each particular case well discern its own interests, men would assert to be prudent, and to it, consequently, would entrust the charge of these interests; so that we call in some cases even beasts prudent, when they display a power of forethought for their material welfare—from all this it will clearly follow that philosophy is distinct from statesmanship, and from all other kinds or forms of prudence. And suppose it be urged that philosophy merely means knowledge of what is for one's own good, then, it may be answered, there will be many philosophies: for there cannot be but one, having for its object what is good for all animals alike, but each animal must have a philosophy of its own: otherwise there will have to be but one science of medicine for all living things. And suppose it be further urged that man is the noblest of all living things, and that it is with his good that philosophy is concerned; yet even this in no way helps the argument, since there are things of a na-
(114.) ture | far more divine than is the human, such as are, to take a most obvious example, those heavenly bodies, of whose harmony the universe is composed. Thus, then, we have said enough to show that philosophy is the union of deductive with inductive knowledge of objects in their own nature the most noble. And hence we say of Anaxagoras, and Thales, and thinkers such as these, not that they are prudent, but that they are philosophers; inasmuch as we see them entirely ignorant of their own interests: and we say of their speculations that they are strange, and won-

derful, and arduous, and divine, but also that they
are useless, in that the question of what is good for
man is not the object of their investigation. Prudence, on the other hand, is concerned with human
affairs, and with such objects only as admit of deliberation. We indeed assign to the prudent man,
as his special province, good deliberation, deliberation
being never concerned with necessary matter, nor,
indeed, with any matter that does not subserve to
some end, and that end a good attainable by human
agency. And in the most general sense he shows
good deliberation who, by the use of his reason, hits
upon that which is for man the best attainable result.
Now prudence does not consist in knowledge of the
universal alone, but, in addition to this, a knowledge
of singulars is necessary; for prudence ought to
determine our action, and singulars constitute the
field of action. Indeed, men who have no knowledge
of the universal are often more successful in action
than are those who have such knowledge; and most
especially so are those who have an empiric knowledge of particulars. Suppose a man to have a
scientific knowledge of the law that all light meat
is easy of digestion, and consequently good for health,
but not to know what particular meats are light—such
a man will not be able to make us healthy. He rather
will make us healthy who knows, as a particular matter of fact, that the flesh of birds is good for health.*
Now, inasmuch as prudence is useless unless it influence our action, it follows that it is best to know

---

* I have ventured to omit the words τοὖ̣ρα καὶ before ὀρνιθ.

8. both the universal and the singular; failing this, to know the particular alone; although, of course, this latter kind of knowledge is subordinate, and the former supreme. Again, statesmanship and prudence are generically the same, although specifically distinct. Statesmanship, as a whole, has a supreme branch, concerned with universals, and known as the theory of legislation; while that branch which deals with particulars engrosses the generic name, and is called "statesmanship" *par excellence*. This latter kind of statesmanship is practical: it analyses ends into their means. A bill is a practical measure, and forms the last step in the analysis of ends into their means; and hence we confine the term "statesmen" to actual politicians, to whom, as to handicraftsmen, actual

(115.) practice is confined. Prudence, again, is held | most especially to consist in foresight for one's own individual self. This it is that engrosses the generic name of prudence, and is so distinguished from the good management of a household, from the theory of legislation, and from statesmanship and its two branches, the deliberative and the judicial. Knowledge of what is good for one's own individual self is, of course, only a branch of the knowledge of what is good for man: but still it is far the most distinctive branch. And hence it is that he who knows what is good for himself, and who busies himself herein, is held to be prudent; statesmen being troubled with much serving, as says Euripides—

> How call me prudent?—in whose power it was,
> Numbered among the many of the host,
> No busy body, to enjoy at ease
> An equal share of fortune with the wise.

> High-blown is human pride. For, whosoe'er
> Is over-skilled, and meddles over-much,
> We honour, as a hero in the state.*

The prudent are indeed chiefly held to be such, in that they confine their attention to what is good for themselves, and hold that herein their duty mainly lies; although perhaps even one's own good requires for its perfect realisation true conceptions as to the management of the family and of the state, and is moreover an uncertain matter, calling for much consideration. A further confirmation of the distinction we have drawn between philosophy and prudence may be found in a consideration of the fact that a boy can become a geometrician, or arithmetician, and can grasp these subjects philosophically, but yet cannot become really prudent. The reason of this is that prudence consists in rightly dealing with singulars, and that for a full knowledge of singulars experience is required. Such experience, for the acquisition of which a considerable time is necessary, is out of the reach of a boy. Suppose, however, the objection be raised, why can a boy acquire a philosophic grasp of mathematics, and not of metaphysics, or of physics?—to this the answer can be given that mathematics deal with pure abstractions, while the universals of physics and of metaphysics are gained by generalisation from experience; so that of these latter the young can have no genuine conviction, but must repeat them without understanding; whereas the first principles of mathematics are self-evident. Again,

---

* The verses are given in full, as they stand, conjecturally restored, in the small Leipsic edition of the Fragments.

prudence may be thus distinguished from philosophy. In an analysis of ends into their means an error of fact is quite as possible as an error of principle. We may, for instance, be ignorant, either that all heavy water is bad for health, or else that this particular water is heavy. And, again, prudence is clearly dis-
(116.) tinct from | deductive science of any kind. For, as we have said, it is entirely concerned with particular matters of fact,—all matters of action being such. Lastly, prudence, in its aspect as moral perception or practical reason, is the logically opposite pole to that analytic reason of which induction is the function. This latter mediately gives us those first principles that transcend all proof; while the practical reason gives us the ultimate singular, which is below the limits of science, and is immediately apprehended by the moral perception—a perception distinct from that of the localised bodily senses, and rather analogous to that by which we perceive that such or such a particular figure is three-sided, which is an ultimate fact, and beyond all demonstration. But yet this mathematical perception is more definitely a sense than prudence is, and differs from the moral perception in kind.

9. Between investigation and deliberation a distinction must be drawn, deliberation being a species of investigation. And we have now to determine wherein consists good deliberation. Is it a peculiar kind of scientific knowledge, or of unscientific opinion? Or does it consist in happiness of conjecture, or in any similar intellectual power? From science it is clearly

distinct: for men never investigate that about which they already have scientific knowledge; whereas good deliberation involves reflection,—he who deliberates going through a process of investigation or calculation. Neither is it happiness of conjecture, which is a something quick in its nature, as involving no process of reasoning; whereas men deliberate for some time, and we are told that we ought to act with decision upon our deliberation, but to deliberate slowly and deliberately. Moreover, good deliberation is entirely distinct from quick perception of causes, or sagacity, which is but a species of happiness in conjecture. Neither does good deliberation consist in any special kind of unscientific opinion. But, since he who deliberates ill errs, while he who deliberates well is said to deliberate rightly, it is clear that good deliberation is a rightness of some kind; but yet not a rightness of science, nor of unscientific opinion. For in the case of science rightness is no more possible than is error; while the rightness of unscientific opinion is that it should be true: and, moreover, that, whatsoever it be, of which we have an opinion is *ipso facto* determined, and no longer matter for deliberation. But yet good deliberation involves a reasoning process of some kind. It follows, therefore, that it can only be rightness in the process of analysis of an end into its means; for such an analysis is a purely investigatory process, committing us to no definite statement; whereas, while, on the one hand, opinion is not a mere process of investigation, but in its very nature a definite assertion, on the other hand he who deliberates (whether he deliberate well, or whether ill) goes through a process of investigation and of calculation. It is settled then that good deliberation consists in rightness of consideration, so that we must first inquire what consideration is, and with what objects it deals. Now since there are many kinds of rightness, it is clear that it is not every kind that constitutes good deliberation. For the incontinent (117.) man | and the bad man will obtain from their deliberation the results which they desire, and will, so far, have deliberated rightly, but will none the less have brought upon themselves a great evil; whereas, to have deliberated well would seem to be a good thing; for good deliberation is a rightness of reflection such that by it we arrive at a good result. But yet, again, a good result may be arrived at by false reasoning; so that a man may obtain the end which he ought, but not in the way which he conceived, his rationale of the process being altogether untrue. Good deliberation, then, cannot but be a something more than an analysis of this sort, in result of which we do indeed attain the right end, but not by use of the right means. And, again, a man may attain the right end after a long deliberation, or after a short. In the former case he will still have fallen short of good deliberation, which requires correctness of judgment upon our interests, directed towards the right end, attaining it by the appropriate means, and completed in a reasonable time. Moreover, of good deliberation there are two kinds—the general, and the specific: the former that which correctly aims at the true end of life as a whole, the latter that which aims at some specific end. In fine, since to deliberate well is a characteristic of prudent men, it follows that good deliberation is a correct conception of that which conduces towards a certain end, of which end the true conception is given by prudence.

10. Again, appreciation, or want of appreciation (in respect of which we say of men that they show or do not show appreciation), is not generically the same as is science, or as is unscientific opinion—in which case all men would possess it—nor is it identical with any specific science, as with medicine for example, which treats of things good for health, or with geometry, which treats of dimensions. For appreciation is not concerned with matter eternal and immutable, nor with every kind of contingent matter, but only with such contingent matter as admits of practical doubt, and of deliberation concerning means. In a word, it deals with precisely the same matters as prudence, with which however it is not on this account identical. For prudence speaks in the imperative. Its end is what we ought to do, and by implication what we ought not; while appreciation is purely critical. Moreover, appreciation must be understood to mean good appreciation, and those to show appreciation whose appreciation is good. Now appreciation does not merely consist in the possession of prudence, nor in the acquisition of prudence, but, exactly as when (118.) a man | uses critically scientific knowledge which he already possesses we call the process of inference through which he then goes "appreciation,"

so we apply the term "appreciation" when a man uses his knowledge of contingent matter to form a proper critical judgment on a something which lies within the province of prudence, and of which he has been told by others—a proper judgment being a good one. Hence it is that appreciation, in virtue of which men are said to show good or proper appreciation, derives its name,—from the above-mentioned use of the term in cases of scientific inference critically exercised; of which, if correctly performed, we often say that it exhibits appreciation.

11. What is called "consideration," in respect of which we say that men are considerate, and show consideration, consists in the correct judgment of the equitable man critically exercised. This is shown by the fact that we say of the equitable man that he is disposed to show forbearance, and that it is only equitable in certain cases to show such forbearance. And forbearance, which is etymologically connected with consideration, is merely the consideration of the equitable man correctly exercised in judgment upon the actions of others,—such correctness being an intellectual rather than a moral matter.

Now all these habits of mind above described, tend, as might be expected, in the same direction. We speak of consideration, and appreciation, and prudence, and of a practical reason, or moral perception, and say of the same individual that he has consideration, and with it, of course, a right moral perception, and that he is prudent, and shows appreciation. For all these faculties have for their object-matter ultimate moral facts. It is in that a man can form a good critical judgment upon those matters with which prudence is concerned that he is said to show appreciation, and consideration, or forbearance. For to act equitably in all their mutual relations is the common characteristic of all good men. Now all matters of action are in their very nature ultimate and particular facts. These facts the prudent man must be able to recognise in their true aspect. And, again, appreciation and consideration are concerned with these same ultimate facts that constitute the matter of action. Moreover it is reason that gives us the moral first principles of each kind; for it is reason, and not deductive inference, which not only finds for us the highest moral universal, but also apprehends the ultimate moral fact; the one kind of reason, that which deduction presupposes, furnishing us with our immutable and absolute universals, the other, the province of which is those propositions that relate to particular matters of action, apprehending for us the ultimate and contingent fact, which forms the minor premiss of the moral syllogism. From reflection upon such facts it is that we arrive at our conception of the ultimate end of life, gaining the universal by induction from particulars. For the immediate apprehension, then, of these facts an appropriate perception is required: and this perception is what is called the practical reason, or moral perception. Hence too it is that these faculties are supposed to, as it were, grow up in us. No man, it is said, finds philosophy grow up in him in the same way as does considera-

(119.) tion, and appreciation, | and a right moral perception. And this is illustrated by the fact that we hold these faculties to be consequent upon a certain length of life, and say that at such or such an age comes a right moral perception, and power of consideration, since they will by this time have grown up in us. Lastly it is reason that begins and reason that completes the scale of moral truths. From universals given by inductive reasoning moral demonstration proceeds; with particulars apprehended by the practical reason it is concerned. And hence it follows that where men have experience, and age, or in a word are prudent, we must pay no less regard to their unproved assertions and opinions than we should to a moral demonstration. For experience has trained their eye to correct vision.

12. Thus then we have defined both prudence and philosophy, have assigned to each a determinate object-matter, and have shown that each is the virtue, or highest specific excellence, of one of the two parts of the rational soul. It is however a question in what respect either of them is of any actual use. Philosophy in no way considers the means by which happiness is to be acquired, production of any kind being beyond its sphere. And, although prudence does do this, yet it is hard to see wherein we stand in need of it: for prudence consists in the knowledge of what is just, and noble, and good for man, that is to say in knowledge of what the good man will do. But such knowledge does not in any way lead us to act thereupon, since the moral virtues consist, not in know-

ledge merely, but in a formed state of the character; exactly as no result necessarily follows from knowledge of good health, or of good condition (knowledge, that is to say, not of the efficient causes of these states, but of their essential manifestations). For the mere knowledge of medicine or of gymnastic produces no result upon our action. And, if we are to assume that the object of prudence is not mere knowledge such as this, but the actual acquisition and possession of virtue, it follows that prudence will be useless both to those who are already good, and to those who are not so. For in the latter case it will be immaterial whether they have prudence of their own or whether they follow the advice of others who are prudent; the latter course—as in the case of health—being all that is really necessary. For, although we desire to have good health, we do not on that account study medicine. Lastly, it seems inconceivable that prudence should be inferior to philosophy, and yet her mistress, as indeed she is. For in every case all authority and all practical rules for each thing originate with the faculty concerned with its production. Having then thus raised these difficulties, it remains that we should discuss them. And in the first place it must be
(120.) observed | that, even although prudence and philosophy give no practical rules for the acquisition of happiness, they yet cannot but be choice-worthy in and for themselves, being each the highest excellence of one of the parts of the soul. And, secondly, philosophy (and with it prudence) does produce happiness, not in the same way as medicine produces a healthy

state of body, but rather as health itself may be held to do so. For, being an element in human excellence as a whole, it makes a man happy in that he not only possesses it, but also manifests it in action. And, again, the function of man as man requires for its perfect manifestation, prudence on the one hand, and moral virtue on the other; the latter to make the end of action right, the former to point out the best means thereto. The fourth part of the soul, the nutritive, has no such virtue; it is neither in its power to act, nor to refrain from action. So that, with regard to the difficulty that prudence, which consists in knowledge of what is noble and just, does not any the more dispose us to such acts, we must carry our analysis a little deeper, and therefrom commence our demonstration. Exactly as we do not say that men are just merely because they do just acts—as for example is the case with those who do what the laws order, either under compulsion, or through ignorance, or with some ulterior end in view beyond the just act itself—although such men do indeed do everything which is right, and which the good man ought to do—so too it would seem that, for the performance of the various virtuous acts to imply the possession of the various virtues, certain conditions must be fulfilled in their performance. Or, in other words, they must be done from deliberate purpose, and for their own sakes. Now it is virtue that gives our purpose a morally right end; but the correct means thereunto are given, not by virtue, but by another faculty, to which we must now direct our attention, and give of it a clear account. There is, then, a certain faculty which is called "cleverness," and which is such that the clever man can take, that is to say can hit upon, those means that tend to the end proposed. If this end be good, then cleverness is praiseworthy; if bad, it becomes identical with cunning; so that we sometimes call even the prudent clever, and so by dislogistic imputation cunning. Now prudence is not convertible with mere cleverness, although it presupposes such cleverness. This cleverness is, as it were, an eye of our soul, which cannot acquire a habit of right vision without moral virtue. We have made this statement (121.) before, and it is, indeed, self-evident. All moral action involves a syllogism, having for its major premiss " such or such a thing "—what, is unimportant: for, for the sake of argument, it may be what we choose—" is the end of all action, that is to say, the chief good." But, unless a man be virtuous, he does not perceive the truth of this principle: for vice perverts the soul, and leads it to false conclusions upon moral principles. And thus it is plain that a man cannot possibly be prudent, unless he be also virtuous.

13. It remains, therefore, again to discuss virtue. Exactly as prudence is related to cleverness, which it resembles, but with which it is not on that account identical, so is true virtue related to our natural virtuous instincts. There is a certain sense in which all the moral virtues may be said to be innate. From our youth upwards we are to a certain extent just, and temperate, and brave, and so forth; but the real object of education is true virtue, or the possession of these natural instincts after they have undergone

certain definite modifications. Even children and beasts possess these virtuous instincts; which, however, until formed and modified by reason, as often result in evil as in good. Nay, more, experience shows that, exactly as great physical strength devoid of sight, because so devoid, cannot but result in a grievous fall, so too is it with our instinctive moral impulses; but that, if in addition a man acquire reason by which to guide them, his actions become distinctively virtuous, and his new habit of mind, which will resemble the old, will be true virtue as opposed to instinctive. Thus then, exactly as that part of the intellectual soul, the province of which is the contingent matter of action, has two habits or conditions, cleverness and prudence; so too there are two conditions of the moral soul, instinctive virtue and true virtue, for the existence of the latter of which prudence is necessary. And hence some people are misled to suppose that the various moral virtues are only so many forms of prudence. Socrates was partly right herein, and partly wrong; wrong in asserting that the virtues were merely so many forms of prudence, right in asserting that they necessarily involved prudence. Our meaning may be thus illustrated. The usual definition of a virtue, after stating that it is concerned with such or such an object-matter, adds that it is, with reference to that object-matter, a habit of mind concordant with right reason; which reason, of course, is only right when (122.) concordant with prudence. Indeed, | all men would seem to have to some extent divined that virtue consists in a certain state of mind concordant with prudence. But yet this definition needs some modification. For virtue is not merely a habit of mind concordant with prudence, but rather a habit of mind in conscious accordance with prudence. And prudence itself is that very right reason with reference to such matters, of which we have been speaking. Now Socrates thought that the virtues were mere processes of reasoning—that they were, in fact, so many distinct sciences—whereas we say that all virtue involves reason. And thus we shall have made it clear that it is impossible to be truly virtuous without prudence, or to be prudent without true virtue. These considerations will serve to solve the arguments sometimes used to prove that the virtues are separable. For, it is alleged, nature does not give to the same man the same inclination toward every virtue; so that it is conceivable that a man should have one moral virtue, and yet not another. This is true enough of our natural instincts towards the various virtues, but entirely untrue of those virtues which give a man a distinctive claim to be called virtuous. For with the simple unity of prudence the collective totality of the various moral virtues is necessarily coexistent. Lastly, it is perfectly clear that, even if prudence were in no way concerned with moral action, man would nevertheless be imperfect without it, in that it is the specific virtue of one of the parts of the soul. And it is also clear that our purpose cannot possibly be right without on the one hand prudence, and on the other moral virtue; the latter giving us the right end, the former the correct means thereunto. Lastly, prudence is in no sense supreme over philosophy, and consequently over the highest part of the soul, any more than medicine is supreme over health. For it does not make use of philosophy as a means to its own ends, but considers the means to philosophy as an end. Its commands are not laid upon philosophy, but are laid down for philosophy. One might as well say that statesmanship is supreme over the Gods, because everything in the state is under its control.

VII.

1. (113.) Having now treated of the virtues, both moral and intellectual, we will commence a fresh subject, and investigate those types of character that ought to be avoided, and which are of three kinds, to wit—vice, incontinence, and brutality. As to the contraries of the first two of these there need be no difficulty; for the contrary of vice we call virtue, and the contrary of incontinence we call self-restraint. But what would seem to be most fittingly opposed to brutality is that virtue which transcends the human, and which is of an heroic or godlike type, such as Priam, in the poems of Homer, ascribes to Hector, when wishing to speak of his great goodness,—

> Not woman-born seemed he, but sprung from Gods.

And so, if it be true, as they say, that men become Gods when they altogether transcend human virtue, it is then clear that the state of character to be opposed to the brutal will be such as we have described. For, exactly as a brute has, properly speaking, neither virtues nor vices, so neither has a God. For the excellence of a God is a something to be held in higher honour than is any human virtue, and the evil nature of a beast is a something specifically distinct from any form of vice. And, exactly as it is a rare thing to find a man of godlike nature,—to use the expression of the Spartans, "a godlike man," which they apply to those whom they excessively admire,—so too brutality is a type of character rarely found among men. It is among savages, indeed, that it is chiefly to be met with, and in some cases it is the result of disease, or of mutilation; and we reserve the term, as one of peculiarly evil import, to be applied to those whose vice is worse than human. About this habit, however, we will hereafter make mention. Vice we have already discussed. And so it only remains to treat of incontinence, and of effeminacy or luxuriousness, and along with them of self-restraint, and endurance; which (124.) habits are not to be supposed to be respectively | identical with virtue and with vice, nor yet to be specifically distinct from them. Our method will be, as elsewhere, to first properly state the facts in question, and to discuss the problems which they involve; and so to establish the validity, if possible, of all the most generally current conceptions respecting the affections of which we treat; but, if not of all, at any rate of the majority of them, and of the most important among them. For the subject will be sufficiently elucidated, if the solution and consequent elimination of difficulties leave a residue of truth confirmed by popular opinion.

Now, self-restraint and endurance are held to be things good and praiseworthy; while incontinence and effeminacy are held to be bad and blameable. And it is further held, that the man of self-restraint is he who holds firmly to his convictions; and that the incontinent man is he who easily abandons his convictions. And it is further held, that the incontinent man knows that his acts are bad, but is led into them by passion; while the man of self-restraint, knowing his desires to be bad, is restrained by reason from the pursuit of them. And it is further held, that the temperate man is one who has self-restraint and endurance; and some make this type of character convertible with temperance—others again do not. And so, too, while some confuse the incontinent man with him who is absolutely intemperate and debauched, others again hold that the two types of character are distinct. And it is further held, that the prudent man cannot possibly be incontinent; while others again hold that it is quite possible to be prudent, or clever, and yet incontinent. And it is further held, that men can be incontinent in respect of anger, and of honour, and of lucre.

Such then are the statements ordinarily made upon the subject; a consideration of which suggests the problem, how it is possible for a man to be incontinent if he have correct moral conceptions. Some, indeed, there are who say that, if a man have true knowledge of what is good, he cannot possibly be such: for that it is, as Socrates used to hold, inconceivable that, when a man has real knowledge of what is for his good, anything else should get the better of him, and should drag him round like a slave to the pursuit of evil. Socrates, indeed, was absolutely opposed to any such view; his own theory being, that what was called incontinence really had no existence; for that no one could have a true conception of the good, and yet act in opposition to it,—all such apparent cases of incontinence being in reality the result of ignorance. The position herein taken up by Socrates is, however, at direct variance with plain and recognised facts, and one ought rather to have enquired with regard to the affection in question, supposing it really to be the result of ignorance, what the nature of that ignorance is; for it is evident that the incontinent man, before he is actually suffering from the affection in question, does not hold the acts which he will shortly commit to be right. And some, again, there are who partly admit, and partly deny this position. For, while they allow that there is nothing which can be of stronger influence than is real knowledge, they yet will not allow that a man can never act in opposition to what he only supposes to be for his good; and hence they say that it is not real knowledge of what is good which the incontinent man possesses when his pleasures master him, but only an opinion. But, if we are to hold that it is only an opinion, and not true knowledge, which the incontinent man possesses, or, in other words, that it is not a strong conviction which opposes itself to his passions, but only a slight one, much as in what is called a case of doubt, then we ought, perhaps, to excuse him for not abiding firmly by his convictions in the teeth of strong bodily desires: whereas vice ought never to be excused, nor indeed ought anything that calls for blame. Are we then to hold that it is prudence in opposition to which the desires of the incontinent man assert themselves,—for prudence has the very

(145.)

strongest influence? Surely this is inconceivable; for it will then follow that the same person can, at the same time, be both incontinent and prudent. And yet no one can say of the prudent man that he voluntarily does the most disgraceful acts. Besides, we have already shown that the essence of prudence is that it disposes us to prudent action. For the prudent man always rightly apprehends the particular circumstances of the moment, and in virtue of his prudence possesses every moral virtue. Moreover, if the man of self-restraint is to be held to be such, in that he has strong and bad desires which he successfully resists, it will follow that self-restraint and temperance are absolutely incompatible; for the desires of the temperate man are neither excessive nor bad. And yet self-restraint cannot but imply desires of such a nature. For, if it be granted that a man's desires are good, and that his character forbids him to follow them, then self-restraint will not in all cases be a good thing: and suppose, again, that a man's desires are weak, and, in addition, are not bad, in such a case self-restraint calls for no admiration; nor, indeed, is self-restraint any great matter, even where our desires are bad, provided that they are also weak. And, again, if we are to assume that self-restraint is such that it makes a man abide by his convictions, entirely irrespectively of their nature, then it may, in some cases, be a bad thing, as when, for example, it makes a man abide by an untrue conviction. And so, too, if incontinence merely consist in abandoning our convictions, be they whatever they may, then, in certain cases, incontinence will be a good thing. Of this Neoptolemus, in the Philoctetes of Sophocles, is a good instance; for he throws up the false part which Ulysses had persuaded him to play, from disgust at the treachery which it involves; and he therein deserves our praises. Moreover, all sophistical paradoxes will, under our present assumption, furnish a moral problem. A man wishes to establish a sophism, that he may, by such success, gain a reputation for cleverness; and so, in the consideration of his demonstration, we (126.) find ourselves involved in | a moral dilemma. Our understanding is, in such a case, entangled. For while, on the one hand, the conclusion at which we have arrived is so unsatisfactory that we cannot acquiesce in it; yet we cannot, on the other hand, continue the discussion, because we cannot solve the difficulty by which we are met. And if, again, our present assumption were true, an argument could be constructed by which to demonstrate that folly, if combined with incontinence, is identical with virtue. For incontinence would lead a man to act in opposition to his convictions, and folly would lead him to suppose that good acts were bad, and ought not to be done; and so the result would be that he would do good acts, and not bad. Lastly, upon the same assumption, he who, from settled conviction, deliberately pursues pleasure in every action, ought to be a better man than is he who acts thus, not from conviction, but from incontinence; for his fault can be more easily cured, all that is wanted being that he should be argued out of his present conviction. Whereas, to the incontinent man the old proverb very aptly applies, "When water chokes us, how are we to wash it down?" For, if he had not been perfectly convinced that what he does is wrong, he might have been argued out of his wrong convictions, and so have abandoned his misdoings; but, as it is, he is convinced that what he does is wrong, and yet he none the less acts in opposition to his convictions. Lastly, if a man may be said to show incontinence, or self-restraint, with respect to all and each of the ordinary objects of desire, what are we to understand by the term "incontinence," when unqualified by any specification? For surely no one suffers from every possible form of incontinence at one and the same time. And yet we say of some people simply that they are "incontinent," without any further qualification of our assertion.

Such, in the main, are the problems which suggest themselves. Among them there are some propositions which must be absolutely refuted, and others which may, after proper explanation, be accepted as true. For, in all cases, the solution of a problem is equivalent to

3. the discovery of a new truth. First, then, we must consider whether the incontinent man can be said to have knowledge, or not; and in what sense it is that he can be said to have knowledge. Secondly, with what it is that we are to hold that incontinence and self-restraint are concerned; whether, that is to say, they are concerned with certain peculiar pleasures and pains alone, or with all pleasures and pains alike. Thirdly, we must enquire whether self-restraint and endurance are identical, or distinct. And, in like manner, all other

questions akin to the present discussion must be
adequately treated. The starting point of our investigation will be, to determine whether the incontinent
man differs from the man of self-restraint, in that he
is concerned with a different class of objects, or in
that he stands in a different relation to the same class
of objects. Is, that is to say, the incontinent man to
be held incontinent, in that he simply has to do with
such and such objects, or rather in virtue of the
peculiar relation in which he stands to them; or are
both these points necessary to constitute incontinence?
And we must then proceed to consider whether incontinence and self-restraint are concerned with every
class of objects indiscriminately, or not. For he who is
simply called "incontinent," without any further qua-
(127.) lification, is not so called with reference to | all objects
indiscriminately, but only with reference to such
objects as the absolutely intemperate and debauched
man pursues; nor does his incontinence merely consist in his pursuit of these objects, in which case it
would be impossible to distinguish between incontinence and intemperance, but in the pursuit of them
under certain definite and peculiar conditions. For,
while the intemperate man deliberately allows pleasure
to influence him, being of opinion that it is always
right to pursue whatever object may be pleasant for
the time being, the incontinent man does not think
such conduct right, but yet none the less pursues
such pleasure. The objection that it is not real
knowledge, but only a true opinion, in defiance of
which the incontinent act, in no way helps the argu-

ment; for, in cases where men have really nothing better than an opinion upon the matter in question, they often manifest no hesitation whatever, and fancy that they have accurate knowledge. And so, if it be held that it is the insufficient nature of their convictions which makes those who have only an opinion more apt to act in opposition to their previous conceptions than are those who have real knowledge, we shall be met by the difficulty that there will, in this respect, be no difference between opinion and real knowledge; for that some men put no less faith in their own uncertified opinions than do others in the verified truths of science; and of this Heraclitus is a good instance. But, inasmuch as there are two distinct senses in which a man may be said to "know" (for he who has knowledge which is not consciously present to his mind is said "to know," equally with him to whose mind such knowledge is consciously present), it follows that there will be a great difference between doing what we know to be wrong, when such knowledge is not consciously present to our mind, and doing what is wrong when we know that it is wrong, and are perfectly conscious of our knowledge. The latter case seems, indeed, inconceivable; which the former, where our knowledge is not consciously present to our mind, does not. And, again, the syllogism, which all action involves and presupposes, has two premisses — a universal major, and a particular minor; so that it becomes perfectly possible for a man to "know" in a certain sense both these premisses, and yet to act in opposition to his knowledge, inasmuch as he consciously recollects the major premiss alone, the minor (although in a certain sense he may be said to "know" it) not being actually present to his mind. For it is the particular or minor term, which is contained in the minor premiss, that in each case constitutes the matter of the action. It must, however, be borne in mind that there are two possible kinds of major premiss to the moral syllogism— one, in which the middle term contains under it the doer of the act in question, the other in which the middle term contains under it the act itself. We may, for example, have, as our major premiss, "all men ought to take dry food," and, as our minor premiss, "I am a man"; or, again, we may have, as our major premiss, "all such or such things are dry"; and in this latter case it is quite possible that a man should either not know the minor premiss, "this particular thing is such or such", or that, even if he know it, it should not be consciously present to his mind. And between the two cases which we have just put, there is the very greatest possible difference—so much so, indeed, that while, in the latter case, it seems in no way strange that a man should know what is right and yet should act against his knowledge, such incontinence would, in the former case, be inconceivable. And, again, men can be said to "know" in yet another sense, different from those just described. For, when we come to consider the possibility of having knowledge of which one makes no conscious use, we recognise yet another meaning that can be given to the phrase "having knowledge," and such that a man can be said to have knowledge, and yet, at the same time, in a certain sense, not to have it—as when, for instance, he is (128.) asleep, or suffering from acute mania, or | intoxicated. And, as a matter of fact, such is very much the condition of those who are under the influence of any very strong emotion. For anger, and sexual desire, and other such things, produce a visible alteration in the body, and are, in some cases, sufficiently strong to bring on an attack of acute mania; and it is evident that incontinence may be compared to cases of this description. Nor is the fact that the incontinent correctly repeat sound moral formularies, any indication of their real state of mind. For even those who are suffering from the violent emotions which we have just mentioned, can go through long demonstrations, and can repeat verse after verse of Empedocles: much as children, who have just begun to learn to speak, string together into a sentence words of the meaning of which they are as yet ignorant; for the right use of language is a thing into which one as it were grows, and which, consequently, requires time for its acquisition. And hence we may suppose that the incontinent talk about their duty in much the same manner as an actor performs his part. And, again, one may consider incontinence from yet another point of view, if one suppose that man is mechanically acted upon by the strongest motive which may, for the time being, be present to his mind. All action presupposes two premisses, one of which, the major, is a universal moral rule, while the other, the minor, specifies the matter with which the particular action in question is concerned; and for its correctness, inasmuch as it is a particular proposition, it is perception that is responsible. When, then, these two premisses have been synthesised into one conclusion, in which the particular action in question is brought under the given moral rule, then, exactly as in intellectual matters the mind cannot but assent to a conclusion legitimately drawn, so, in a practical matter, we are, under our present hypothesis, obliged to carry into effect the conclusion at which we have arrived. Let, for example, the major premiss present to our mind be "all sweet things ought to be tasted", and let the minor premiss be "this is some one among those many particular things which are sweet": then it will of necessity follow that he who is able to do so, by which I mean who is not under actual restraint, will immediately act upon the conclusion which these premisses involve, as soon as he has drawn it. Now let us suppose that there be one universal present to our mind, which asserts that all sweet things are bad for health, and so, by implication, forbids us to take them; and along with it another which asserts that all sweet things are pleasant, and so, by implication, recommends them; and let us also suppose a minor premiss (which of course must be consciously present to our mind), to the effect that this particular thing is sweet; and let us further suppose that the desire for pleasure be so actively present in us as to preponderate over the fear of bad health:—then, while, on the one hand, we have one conclusion which tells us not to taste this particular thing, yet, on the other hand, the strength of our desire leads us to act upon the other and contrary conclusion,—desire being, indeed, often sufficiently strong to actually move each and all of our physical members. And hence it comes to pass that a man acts incontinently, under the sanction, to a certain extent, of reason, that is to say under the sanction of the opinion that this particular sweet thing, being pleasant, ought to be taken: which opinion is not directly opposed to right reason, but only indirectly,—right reason telling us that it ought not to be taken, not because it is sweet and pleasant, but only because it is unwholesome. And so the opposition is rather one between right reason and desire, than between right reason and the wrong opinion under which we act. And hence it is that beasts cannot properly be called incontinent, inasmuch as they have no universal conceptions in which right reason can express itself, but only a sensuous conception and memory of particular facts. To the question how the ignorance of the incontinent man is resolved, and how he again returns to the full possession of his knowledge, the same kind of answer will have to be given as to the question how a drunken man becomes sober, or how a man who is asleep wakes: it is, in

(129.) short, an answer which only a | physiologist proper can give, and will be drawn from topics common to incontinence with many other purely physical phenomena. To conclude,—it is the minor premiss of the moral syllogism upon which our action mainly depends. This minor premiss states an opinion concerning a particular matter of fact, which, as such, is the province of perception, rather than of reason; and it is this minor premiss (and not the major, which, as being universal, is the province of science rather than of perception), which he who acts incontinently either does not know at all, or, if he does know it, knows it much as a drunkard may be said to know the verses of Empedocles which he repeats; he knows it, in other words, rather as a lesson learnt by heart, than as a scientific truth producing inward conviction. And it must also be remembered, that the minor term of the moral syllogism (which is the particular action in question, whatever it may be) is a conception of less universality than is the major term (which is the abstract definition of the good), and, consequently, is not equally with it the object of knowledge,—"knowledge" properly meaning scientific knowledge of universal conceptions. And, from all this, it would seem to result that the conclusion which Socrates sought to establish is correct. For it is not knowledge, strictly and properly so called, that we have when incontinence affects us; nor is it this kind of knowledge which incontinence perverts; but only sensuous knowledge, which is but a quasi-knowledge, given by perception, and not by reason.

4. Thus much, then, is sufficient as to the distinction between real knowledge and quasi-knowledge, and as to the compatibility of incontinence with knowledge. We must now, following the order originally proposed, proceed to enquire whether the term "incontinent" is to be applied to all those alike who pursue any particular desire in opposition to right reason; or whether

it is to be restricted to some one particular class among them; and, if so, with what particular objects it is that incontinence is concerned. Now, it is self-evident that pleasure and pain are the two objects with which, on the one hand, self-restraint and endurance, and, on the other hand, incontinence and effeminacy, are alike concerned. But, among those objects that give pleasure, some may be said to be necessary or inevitable, while others are in themselves, and independently of all other considerations, choiceworthy, although they can be pursued to excess. The term "necessary" must be understood to be restricted to those objects that give bodily pleasure, such as is everything connected with eating, and with the sexual desire, and, indeed, as are all those other bodily objects with which we said that intemperance and temperance were concerned; while the pleasurable objects that are not necessary, but are still choiceworthy for their own sake, are such, for instance, as victory, or honour, or wealth, or any other good and pleasant thing. And so to those who pursue this latter class of objects to excess, in conscious defiance of their better reason, we do not simply apply the term "incontinent," but we call them incontinent in respect of wealth, or of gain, or incontinent of ambition, or of anger, always adding some such further specification, by which to distinguish them from the simply incontinent: just as to "Man"* was added the further specification "who, in such or such a year, was victor at the Olympic Games." For, in his case, his proper name "Man," although it differed

---

* For ἄνθρωπος read 'Ανθρωπος with Aspasius and others.

but slightly from his generic name "man," was yet distinct from it, and so required some such specification by which it might be distinguished. And, in proof of the distinction just laid down, it may be observed that simple incontinence is always blamed, not merely as (130.) being an error, | but as being a definite form of vice, —as being, that is to say, either identical with vice as a whole, or else with some specific and particular form of vice: while none of those are blamed who exhibit any of the specific forms of incontinence above-mentioned. And, again, of those who are concerned with those bodily enjoyments which we stated to be the object-matter of temperance and of intemperance, he who pursues all excessive pleasure, and avoids all excessive pain, whether it come from hunger, or from thirst, or from heat, or from cold, or from any other of the sensations which are transmitted by touch and by taste, and who does not do so with deliberate purpose, but rather against his purpose, that is to say against his better reason,—he is called incontinent; and that not with any further specification, stating him to be incontinent with respect to such or such a thing, as, for instance, with respect to anger, but simply incontinent. And, in illustration of this, it may be remarked that it is with reference to these bodily pleasures and pains alone that men are called intemperate,* and not with reference to any of those pleasures or pains spoken of above, and with reference to which the phrase "incontinence" receives some further specification. And hence it is that simple incontinence

* For παλασσι read ενιασσσα with Zell and others.

and intemperance are roughly classed together, as also are their two contraries, self-restraint and temperance, because they are all to a certain extent concerned with the same kind of pleasures and of pains; while none of the various specific forms of incontinence is ever classed along with intemperance. Intemperance and simple incontinence are indeed concerned with the same pleasures, but involve a different relation towards them; for the intemperate man pursues these pleasures with deliberate purpose, while the incontinent man does not. And hence we should apply the term "intemperate" to him who avoids even ordinary pain and pursues excessive pleasure, being at the time free from desire, or at any rate feeling desire but slightly, rather than to him who acts thus when under the influence of a strong desire. For how would the former act if an overpowering desire were to come upon him, and with it a violent pain caused by the craving for some one of those pleasures which we have elsewhere called necessary? Again, our desires and our pleasures may, exactly as we said before,* be divided into, firstly, those which are essentially good and noble (for some things that yield pleasure are of their own nature choiceworthy), and of this kind are wealth, and gain, and victory, and honour; and, secondly, those which are the exact contraries of these former; and, thirdly, those which stand midway between the two. And with reference to all objects of the first class, and, indeed, of the intermediate class, a man is not blamed for being simply affected by them, that is

* Terminate the parenthesis at κοσμος, as Michelet suggests.

to say for simply desiring them and liking them, but only for carrying such a desire, or such a liking, to excess. And, consequently, we do not hold as depraved those who, in violation of right reason, are so overcome by their desire for some naturally noble and good object, as to pursue it to excess; as when, for instance, a man displays an over excessive zeal in the pursuit of honour, or in his affection for his children and his parents. For, although, on the one hand, all such objects are good in themselves, and although those are to be praised who show a proper zeal about them, yet, on the other hand, it is possible to carry our feel-
(131.) ings | towards them into excess; as, for example, did Niobe, who defied the Gods to produce the equals of her children; or as did Satyrus, who came at last to be known as "the good son," from the absolutely foolish length to which he carried his affection for his father. The fact already stated, that each of these things is in itself, and independently of all other considerations, naturally and essentially choiceworthy, forbids our using the term "vice" with reference to any of them: but still our desire or affection for them can none the less be carried to a bad and blameable excess. And it is for the same reason that, with regard to any of these things, we do not speak of incontinence simply; for simple incontinence is not only a thing to be avoided, but is absolutely blameable and bad. But, because a man can be affected by each one of these objects in much the same way as is the incontinent man by the objects of his desire, we use the term "incontinence" with reference to each one of them, adding

to it, as a further specification, the name of the especial object with which such incontinence is concerned; much as we say of a man that he is a bad doctor or a bad actor, to whom we should never think of applying the simple term "bad" without any such specification. Much then as in the instances just given we do not use the simple term "bad" without any further modification (neither of the two faults in question being a vice, but only resembling vice in so far as ignorance of medicine or of the rules of art may be compared to ignorance of moral principles); so, too, here we must distinctly understand that that alone is properly incontinence, and that that alone is properly self-restraint, which is concerned with the same class of objects as is temperance and as is intemperance; and that to speak of incontinence or of self-restraint with respect to anger, is to extend the terms in question to adjacent and somewhat similar cases. And hence it is that we add to the term "incontinent" a further specification, and say of a man that he is "incontinent of anger," in much the same sense as that in which we use the phrases "incontinent of honour" and "incontinent of gain."

5. Now there are some things that are essentially pleasant of their own nature, and of which some are pleasant absolutely and to all beings alike, while others are pleasant only to certain kinds of animals, and of men, and not to others. And there are other things again that are not really pleasant at all, but that become so from some physical defect, or from long habituation, or from depravity of nature; and

to each of these latter kinds there is a correspondent state or condition of moral depravity. We are speaking here of those states which are commonly called "brutal"; such, for example, as that of the female of whom we are told that she used to rip up those who were with child, and devour the fœtus. Or one might instance the degraded tribes in the neighbourhood of the Pontus, some of whom are said to take pleasure in raw flesh, and others in cannibalism; while of others, again, we are told that each family in its turn provides a child for the common banquet; and then, too, there is the story that is current about Phalaris. The above, then, are fair instances of one class of what may be termed brutal states. In some other cases such brutality is the result of disease, and in others, again, of insanity; such, for instance, as was that of the madman who offered up his mother to the Gods, and partook of the sacrifice; or that of the slave who tore out and devoured his fellow slave's liver. Where brutality is not caused by disease it is sometimes the result of habit, as where people pluck (132.) out and eat their own hair, or | bite their nails, or eat ashes or dirt, or where men desire unnatural intercourse. Such morbid conditions are sometimes the result of a constitution naturally depraved, and sometimes of vicious habits, as in the case of those who have been subjected to unnatural treatment from their youth. In all those cases in which depravity has a physical origin, to speak of it as "incontinence" would be as much a misapplication of terms as it would be to call women incontinent because their desires are those of their own sex; and for the same reason we never speak of "incontinence" in those cases where long habit has brought on chronic disease. And, in fact, the cases of which we have been speaking are all of them, as is simple brutality, a something altogether beyond the pale of vice. And so, too, if a man have such morbid desires, and either conquer them, or be conquered by them, we do not call him, as the case may be, either self-restrained or incontinent, save only in so far as he resembles the self-restrained or the incontinent; exactly as, where a man's angry passions are thus beyond his control, we do not call him simply "incontinent," but "incontinent of anger". For, indeed, whenever folly, or cowardice, or intemperance, or hot temper manifests itself in extravagant excess, it is the result of a nature which was either originally brutal, or which has become such from disease. He, for instance, who is constitutionally such a coward as to be frightened at anything, even at the squeak of a mouse, displays a cowardice such as is that of the lower animals, and which can only be called brutal; and, on the other hand, the case of the man who was "mad when he beheld a cat" was one of disease. Idiots, again, are either by their very nature irrational, and devoid of any higher guide for life than their animal senses, in which case they are called brutal, as are some tribes of remote barbarians; or else they are idiotic from disease, as, for example, epilepsy; or from insanity; in which cases we speak of them as diseased, and not as depraved. In such cases as these a man sometimes suffers from the infirmity, but does not give way to it,—Phalaris, for example, might have restrained his desire to eat children's flesh, and his unnatural sexual appetites,—and sometimes, on the other hand, a man not only suffers from the infirmity, but is also mastered by it. To conclude, then, exactly as there are two kinds of vice, of which one, as being human, is simply called "vice," while the other is further specified as being brutal or morbid; so, too, it is clear that there are two kinds of incontinence, of which the one is either brutal or morbid, while the other is simply called "incontinence," and is co-extensive in its range with ordinary intemperance.

Thus, then, it is clear that the range of incontinence and of self-restraint must be so restricted as to be identical with the range of temperance and of intemperance, and that, where other objects of desire are concerned, there we find another form of incon-
(133.) tinence, [not known as such simply, but in virtue of
6. a transferred application of the term. We will proceed to show that incontinence of anger is less disgraceful than is incontinence of desire. For, in the first place, it would seem that anger may, to some extent, be said to hear the commands of reason, but, at the same time, to mishear them; exactly as do over-ready servants, who rush off before they have heard all that is said, and then mistake their orders; or as do dogs, who bark if they only hear a knock, without waiting to see whether it be made by a friend. And exactly so it would seem that, if a man's nature be hot and hasty, anger catches at the commands of

reason, but hurries to vengeance without waiting to hear them out. Reason, for instance, or, it may be, fancy, tells us that such or such a thing is an insult or a slight, upon which anger, as it were, completes the syllogism by adding, "and all such treatment ought to be resented," and so at once waxes hot against it; whereas desire only requires that the reason, or even the senses, should assert that such or such a particular thing is pleasant, and thereupon at once rushes to the enjoyment of it. And hence anger may, to a certain extent, be said to obey reason, while desire cannot: and hence, too, desire is the more disgraceful of the two. He, indeed, who is incontinent of anger is worsted, not by passion alone, but, to a certain extent, by reason also; whereas he who is incontinent of his desires, is worsted by simple lust alone, without any admixture of reason. And, secondly, it is more excusable in us to follow those impulses that are natural to us, inasmuch as it is more excusable to give way to those desires that are shared by all men alike, provided one give way to them only in so far as they are so shared. Now anger, and with it bitterness of spirit, is much more a part of our nature than are those desires which are excessive and not necessary. This one may illustrate by the well-known story of the defence made by the man who beat his father. "Why," said he, "he used to beat his own father, who had also beaten his father before him. And this rascal here," pointing to his son, "will beat me as soon as he grows man enough. It is a family failing with us." And then there is the story of the man who, when his son was kicking him out of the house, besought him to stop at the door, "for," said he, "that is exactly as far as I kicked your grandfather." Thirdly, the more the craft employed, the greater always is the injustice. Now the passionate man is not crafty, nor does anger dispose us to craft, but rather to open action. But desire is always crafty, as is, men say, the Goddess of desires,—the sea-born

Lady of Cyprus, weaver of deceits,—

of whose embroidered girdle Homer thus speaks,—

Cunning, which robbed the wisest of his wits.

(134.) | And hence it follows that, since incontinence of desire is a more unjust thing than is incontinence of anger, and, consequently, a more disgraceful, it, rather than incontinence of anger, ought to be known by the simple term "incontinence,"—amounting, as it does, almost to a form of vice. Fourthly, no one ever feels pain in the commission of an act of wanton insolence. Now he who acts in a passion always feels pain in the act which he commits; whereas he who acts from wanton insolence feels a pleasure. And so, inasmuch as those acts are the most unjust with which one has most right to be angry, it follows that incontinence of desire is more unjust than is incontinence of anger; for anger, since it has in it no element of wanton insolence, is less unprovoked, and so really less aggressive, than is desire. Thus, then, it is self-evident that incontinence of desire is a more disgraceful thing than is incontinence of anger; and, also, that self-restraint and incontinence, simply so called, are concerned with such desires, that is to say with such pleasures, alone as are strictly bodily. And, consequently, we must distinguish these same bodily pleasures into their various kinds; for, as we said in the beginning, some among them are human and natural, both in their kind and in their extent, while others are brutal, and others, again, are the results of mutilation or of disease. And with this first class of pleasures alone it is that temperance and intemperance are concerned. And hence we never speak of brutes as being either temperate or intemperate, unless it be by a conscious transference of the terms, and an application of them to those cases where some one kind of animal is distinguished from all others by its lasciviousness, or by its destructiveness, or by its voracity. For what are called the "evil" acts of brutes are not done with purpose, and involve no element of reason, but are rather, as is acute mania in man, the result of an abnormal physical condition. And so mere animal brutality is less evil than is vice, although it may none the less be more terrible. It is not that the best principle has been corrupted, as in a depraved man, but that it has no existence. It is almost the same kind of comparison as it would be were we to ask which is worst,—a lifeless thing, or a living? For evil of any kind is always less injurious when it has in it no power of externalising itself, such as is to be found in the reason. One might, indeed, as well ask which is the worst of the two,—injustice, or an unjust man? For, in a certain sense, of course each is worse than the other. It must, however, be remembered, that it is possible for a wicked man to do ten thousand times more evil than can any beast.

7. As regards the pleasures and the pains which come from the senses of touch and of taste, and as regards the desires and the aversions connected with them, with all which it is that intemperance and temperance are, by the definitions of them which have been given before, concerned,—it is possible for our condition to be either such that we yield to things to which most men are superior, or else such that we are superior to (135.) things to which most men yield. If it be pleasure with which we are concerned, we are, in the former case, called incontinent, and, in the latter, self-restrained; while, if it be pain, then we are, in the former case, said to show effeminacy, and, in the latter, endurance. The moral disposition of the majority of mankind may be represented as a balance between these extremes, combined with, it may be, a tendency towards the side of the worst. Now, among our pleasures there are some which may be regarded as necessary, while there are others, again, which are so only when they are pursued to certain lengths and no further,—all excess in them being as unnecessary as perfect abstinence from them is uncalled for; and of our desires and of our pains a similar rule holds good. He then who pursues pleasure in excess, simply because it is in excess, and who purposely chooses such excess for its own sake, and entirely independently of any result, he it is who is intemperate. For it is impossible that such a man should ever

repent; and hence he is hopelessly incurable, for for him who repents not there is no hope of cure. Diametrically opposed to the intemperate man is he whose sense of bodily pleasure is deficient; the temperate man being midway between the two. And what has been just said of intemperance will hold equally good of him who avoids bodily pain, not from physical inability to resist it, but with deliberate purpose. Where a man acts without any such purpose, it may be either because he yields to the attractions of pleasure, or because he cannot withstand the pain which results from an unsatisfied desire; and between these two forms of error there is a wide difference. Every one, however, will admit that he who does a disgraceful act, being at the same time free from desire, or at any rate feeling desire but slightly, is more to be blamed than is he who does such an act under the influence of a strong desire; and that he who, when not in a passion, smites his neighbour, is more to be blamed than is he who does so when in a passion. For how would each of the two have acted had they been under the influence of a strong emotion? And hence it is that the intemperate man is worse than is the incontinent. Now of those whom we described above as acting without deliberate purpose, the one ought properly to be called effeminate, and the other* incontinent. The contradictory of incontinence is self-restraint, and that of effeminacy is endurance: for, to endure implies successful resistance, while to restrain implies mastery; and resistance

---

* For ἀκόλαστος read ἀκρατής with Andronicus and others.

differs from mastery, exactly as the glory of not being
vanquished differs from the glory of victory. And
hence it is that self-restraint is preferable to mere
endurance. He who has too little strength to resist
those pains which most men can and do withstand,—
he it is whom we call effeminate and luxurious.
Indeed, all luxury is a form of effeminacy. Such a
man trails his robe to avoid the fatigue of lifting it,
or feigns infirm health, remaining in happy ignorance
that to counterfeit misery is misery in itself. And,
(136.) with regard to self-restraint and incontinence, the
same rule holds good. For where a man is mastered
by pleasures or by pains, which are violent in kind
and excessive in degree, his case does not call for our
wonder, but rather, if he do his best to withstand
them, for our pity. Such is the case of Philoctetes,
in the play of Theodectes, when he suffers from the
viper's bite; and of Cercyon, in the Alope of Carcinus;
and of those who, in the attempt to restrain their
laughter, give vent to it in one great paroxysm, as
happened to Xenophantus. Our wonder is rather
due where a man is so far mastered by pains or
pleasures against which the majority of men can
successfully hold out, as to be altogether unable to
withstand them,—and that not from disease, or from
any hereditary or natural weakness, as is the case
with the Scythian Kings, with whom effeminacy is
hereditary, or with women, who are constitutionally
weaker than are men. He who is overmuch given
to amusements has sometimes been held to be intemperate, but he is in reality only effeminate; for all

amusement is a species of relaxation, and is consequently intended to act as a relief to the troubles of serious life. But still such relief may be sought to excess, and one form of such excess is an over-fondness for amusements. Of incontinence, again, there are two kinds, the one of which consists in hastiness, and the other in weakness. For, on the one hand, there are some who, after all due deliberation as to the course which they ought to adopt, are weak enough to allow incontinence to force them from the conclusion at which they have arrived; and, on the other hand, there are some who are hurried away by incontinence, because they have never deliberated at all,—I say "some," for of course there are others who act as do children in their play, who, when they have once tickled their fellows, are themselves insensible to tickling, who foresee temptation, and anticipate it, and who so put themselves upon their mettle, and so forearm their reason that, however great may be the pleasure, or however great the pain, they are never mastered by it. That incontinence which takes the form of over-hastiness is chiefly to be found in those whose temperament is either over-passionate, or else atrabilious. For, in the former case, impetuosity, and in the latter a sort of savage violence, leads them to follow the crude conceptions of the imagination, and to abandon the deliberate convictions of reason.

8. When, then, a man is absolutely intemperate and debauched, repentance has, as we have said, no place in him. For he has made evil his good, and by that purpose he abides. But the incontinent man is

always open to repentance. And consequently the conclusion to which our former problems seem to lead is untrue; for, while the intemperate man is incurable, the incontinent man is open to cure. Indeed, intemperance may be fairly likened to such diseases as dropsy and consumption, and incontinence to epilepsy; for the one is a continuous evil, while the (137.) other is | intermittent. And we can further see that incontinence and intemperance are specifically distinct, in that the intemperate man is unconscious that he is acting wrongly, whereas incontinence is always conscious. Of the two forms of incontinence, that in which we are altogether carried away by the violence and the haste of our emotions, is not so bad as is that in which our emotions cause us to abandon a conviction at which we had previously arrived; for, in the latter case, not only is the emotion by which we are mastered less in itself, but it also does not, as in the former, attack us so suddenly as to leave no time for reflection. Indeed, the incontinent man is not unlike those who quickly get drunk, and that with very little wine, or, at any rate, with less than most drinkers. It is clear then, that intemperance and incontinence must not be confounded with one another. But yet they have one point in common. The intemperate man, it is true, acts in pursuit of his purpose, while the incontinent man acts in opposition to his purpose; but still their acts are similar. It is much as Demodocus said of the people of Miletus, —"the Milesians are not fools, but they act like fools." And so the incontinent are not themselves confirmedly bad, but their acts are none the less the acts of bad men. There are, then, as we have said, two types of character, of which the one is such as to lead a man to pursue bodily pleasures which are excessive and opposed to all right reason, not so much because he is convinced that they ought to be pursued, as because he is mastered by them; while the other leads to the deliberate conviction that such pleasures are right, and ought to be pursued. And so, in the former case, a man still remains open to the true conviction, in the latter case he does not. For virtue preserves right principles, vice corrupts them; and the principles which action involves are correct conceptions of the true end of life; much as the principles involved in mathematics are those correct conceptions of the various geometrical figures, which are contained in definitions postulating the existence of their object. And, exactly as in mathematics it is not by deduction that we acquire our first principles, so neither is it here; the true principles of morality being given us by virtue, which is either, as some say, natural to us, or, as we say, acquired by habituation, and which leads us to form right conceptions as to moral principles. He in whom this virtue is to be found—he it is who is the temperate man; he whose character is the very contrary of this, who is intemperate. There is also another type of character, such that a man, in violation of all right reason, is forced by the strength of his passions to abandon his resolutions. Such a man is so far overcome by his passions that he does not act as right reason orders, but still not so far overcome as to deliberately adopt the conviction that all such pleasures ought to be unrestrainedly pursued, and to mould his character in accordance with it. This it is who is the incontinent man, and who is better than is the intemperate, inasmuch as he is not yet absolutely depraved; for the best thing in us—correct moral principle—remains in him intact. Opposed to him is another type of character—that of the man who so abides by his resolutions that no passion ever forces him from them. And enough has now been said to show that this latter is a good state of mind, and that incontinence, as contrasted with it, is bad.

9. (138.) | Are we then to assert that the man of self-restraint is he who abides by his conviction, quite independently of what that conviction may be, and by his purpose, quite independently of what that purpose may be; or is he rather he who abides by his purpose because that purpose is right and good? And so, too, of the incontinent man: is he the man who abandons his purpose, no matter what that purpose be, and his conviction, no matter what that conviction be, or, rather, the man who abandons a conviction which is* true, and a purpose which is right;—to which result the problems previously discussed seem to lead? Or shall we not rather say of self-restraint and of incontinence, that they respectively consist in abiding by and in abandoning a conviction, or, in other words, a

---

* For τῷ ψευδεῖ λόγῳ καὶ τῇ προαιρέσει τῇ μὴ ὀρθῇ read τῷ ἀληθεῖ λόγῳ καὶ τῇ προαιρέσει τῇ ὀρθῇ according to the conjecture of Coraes, or else τῷ μὴ ψευδεῖ λόγῳ καὶ τῇ προαιρέσει τῇ ὀρθῇ.

purpose, which indirectly may be of any kind or sort whatever, but which essentially must be true and right? The distinction between what is essential and what is accidental may be thus illustrated. Where a man chooses or pursues a certain thing as a means to a certain other thing, we say of him, in such a case, that he chooses or pursues the end simply, or directly, or essentially, the means indirectly, or incidentally; so that "simply" and "essentially" must be understood to be convertible terms. And hence, while self-restraint and incontinence may indirectly lead to our either abiding by or abandoning an opinion—that is to say, a purpose—of any kind whatever, yet the essence of self-restraint and of incontinence is that we should either abide by or abandon a true opinion, or, in other words, a good purpose; and this is what is to be understood by the terms "simple self-restraint" and "simple incontinence." There are also certain persons who abide fixedly by their opinions, and who are said to show "strength of character," or "obstinacy," inasmuch as it is difficult to convince them, and still more difficult to reason them out of their previous convictions. This type of character has a certain resemblance to self-restraint (as has prodigality to liberality, and fool-hardiness to courage), but yet differs from it in many important points. For, although the man of self-restraint does not allow passion or desire to move him from his purpose, yet he is none the less open to conviction upon fitting occasions; whereas the obstinate are unaffected by any arguments, although they often conceive strong desires, and are in many cases led by their pleasures. Obstinacy has various forms. Sometimes it shows itself as egotism and opinionativeness, and at times as stolid ignorance, and at times as surly boorishness. Egotism involves certain pleasures and pains of its own; for when the egotistical man remains unconvinced he feels all the pleasure of a victory, and when it has been conclusively shown that he is in the wrong, he is as grieved as if he had sustained a ministerial defeat. And hence it would seem that egotism resembles incontinence rather than self-restraint. There are also, on the other hand, certain persons who abandon their previous convictions from a kind of quasi-incontinence, as does, for instance, Neoptolemus in the Philoctetes of Sophocles. It is a pleasure that forces him from his resolution, but still a noble pleasure. For he gloried in the truth, and Ulysses had persuaded him to lie. And hence we see that it does not follow that, because a man acts under the influence of pleasure, he is on that account intemperate, or depraved, or even incontinent, unless that pleasure be in itself bad.

(139.) | There is, moreover, another type of character, which is such that a man takes less pleasure than he ought in bodily enjoyment, and on this account abandons the right convictions which he has formed. Between this and incontinence, self-restraint stands as it were midway, and so forms the mean. For, while the incontinent man abandons his convictions because he is over-fond of bodily pleasure, he whom we have described abandons them because he is not sufficiently fond of it; whereas the man of self-restraint abides by his convictions, and is not to be moved from them either by over-love of pleasure, or by over-sensibility. Now, inasmuch as self-restraint is a good thing, it follows that the two extreme and mutually contrary habits must be bad; as is indeed clearly the case. But, because the one of the two is to be found in but few cases, and very seldom, it follows that it is self-restraint which is ordinarily opposed to incontinence; exactly as it is temperance which is ordinarily contrasted with intemperance. A name is often transferred from its proper object to others which more or less resemble it; and, by a derivation of this kind, we have become accustomed to speak of the "self-restraint" of the temperate man. For the temperate man and the man of self-restraint resemble each other in that neither is ever induced by bodily pleasure to act in violation of right reason; but they differ from one another in that the latter has bad desires, while the former has not; and also in that the character of the former is such that a pleasure which violates right reason is to him no pleasure at all; while that of the latter is such that, although capable of pleasures of this kind, he yet does not allow them to influence him. Between the incontinent man and the intemperate man there is an analogous relation; for both alike pursue bodily pleasure, but they differ from one another in that the one holds that it is right to pursue such pleasures,

10. and the other does not. It is, moreover, impossible that the same man should be at once prudent and

incontinent; for, as has before been shown, he who is prudent cannot but be morally good. Besides, the essence of prudence is not merely that a man should know what is good, but that he should have that knowledge, and should act up to it; and this the incontinent man can hardly be said to do. But mere cleverness is perfectly compatible with incontinence; and hence it is that men sometimes seem to be prudent, and yet at the same time incontinent:—the true explanation being that cleverness differs from prudence, as has before been pointed out; for it involves a similar element of mere intellectual ability, but not the same soundness of moral purpose. Moreover, the incontinent man sins with knowledge, not in the sense in which he has knowledge who makes conscious use of the knowledge which he possesses, but rather in the sense in which those may be said to have knowledge in whom sleep has produced a temporary oblivion, or intoxication a temporary insanity. And he also acts voluntarily, inasmuch as, in a certain sense, he may be said to know both what it is that he does and why it is that he does it. But yet he must not be set down as absolutely bad and depraved; for the general tenor of his purpose remains, as a whole, good; so (140.) that he is, as it were, only] half depraved. Neither is he unjust; for he plots against no man, inasmuch as he is either too weak to abide by the plans upon which he may have determined, or else of too atrabilious a temperament to form any plans whatever. The incontinent man is not unlike a State which passes every possible measure which may be required, and which has admirable laws, but which never carries its measures into effect, and makes no use of its laws; as runs the pasquinade of Anaxandrides,

> That State hath willed it to which laws are naught.

Whereas the intemperate man is rather to be compared to a State which carries its laws into thorough effect,—only that its laws are bad laws. Moreover, incontinence and self-restraint are each concerned with that which, after its kind, passes the ordinary limits of human action. For the man of self-restraint abides by his resolution more firmly than do the majority of mankind, while the incontinent man abandons his resolutions sooner. Lastly, of the various forms of incontinence, that admits of more hope of a successful cure from which those suffer whose temperament is atrabilious, than does that of those who form elaborate convictions, by which they do not afterwards abide; and that incontinence which is the result of habit is more curable than is that incontinence which originates in physical causes; for habit is more easily to be altered than is nature. Indeed, the very reason why habit is so hard to alter is only because, as Evenus says, it comes at last to resemble nature—

> For use doth breed a habit in a man,
> And perfect habit is a second nature.

Thus, then, we have stated the nature of self-restraint, and of incontinence, and of endurance, and of effeminacy, and also the mutual relations of these various habits to one another; and it now remains

11. to treat of pleasure and of pain. For pleasure and pain are subjects which he ought to consider who would treat of politics philosophically, inasmuch as it is his task to frame that supreme conception of the true end of life, with reference to which it is that we speak of our acts as having an ultimate tendency either for good or for bad. The investigation is, moreover, necessary for several other reasons. We have said that virtue and vice are concerned with pains and with pleasures; and, moreover, most men assert that pleasure is involved in all happiness; and hence it is that they speak of the happy man as being "blessed,"—the word "blessedness" etymologically (141.) signifying | "full of pleasure." Now there are some who hold that no pleasure whatever is either directly or incidentally good,—in fact, that pleasant and good can never be equivalent terms. Others, again, hold that while some pleasures are good, yet the majority of them are bad. And, lastly, there is yet a third view which, while it admits that pleasures may be good as a class, yet denies that the chief good can ever possibly be a pleasure of any kind. In support of the first view, that pleasure is in no sense a good, the following arguments are urged. Firstly, all pleasure whatever is a phenomenon of sense, consisting in a process of alternation between two poles, and resulting in a natural, and consequently perfect, physical condition. But no such process is ever akin to the end in which it results: there is, for example, no affinity between a house and the process of building a house. Secondly, the temperate man avoids pleasures.

Thirdly, that which the prudent man pursues is not so much pleasure as freedom from pain. Fourthly, pleasure of any kind is a direct obstacle to the exercise of reason; and the more intense is the pleasure, the more will this be true. And of this the sexual pleasure is a good instance, for, while it lasts, thought of any kind is impossible. Fifthly, there is no art of pleasure; and yet every good thing has an art by which it is procured. Sixthly, children and beasts pursue pleasures indiscriminately. In proof of the position that all pleasures alike are not good, it is urged that some pleasures are disgraceful, and are held in merited reprobation; and that others are absolutely injurious, for that instances can be given of things which produce pleasure, and which are bad for health. Lastly, to prove that pleasure is not the chief good, it is urged that it is not an absolute end in itself, but only a process of alternation, resulting in such an end.

12. Such, then, or nearly such, are the various arguments that have been brought forward. We will now proceed to show that neither do they prove that pleasure is not in itself a good, nor even that it is not the chief good. In the first place, we can use the term "good" in two distinct senses; for by it we may mean either that which is good absolutely, that is to say for all members alike of such or such a class; or else that which is good relatively, that is to say good for such or such a particular member of a given class, but not for others. In accordance with this distinction, our permanent states, whether natural or acquired, may be spoken of as either absolutely or

relatively good; and hence our processes, whether of continuous development or of alternation, may, even where they seem to be bad, be bad absolutely, or in the abstract, but not relatively, inasmuch as for such or such a person they may be choiceworthy; and others among them, again, may not perhaps always be even relatively good, but may only be good for such or such an individual upon certain particular occasions, and for a short time. These latter are not really pleasures at all, although they seem to be so. They are always accompanied by a pain, and are pursued for the sake of ultimate relief. One may instance the peculiar pleasures sometimes felt by the sick. Secondly, there is yet another division of goods, into good habits, or permanent states, and good energies, or activities, or acts, in and by which these states are manifested. And hence it is clear that those processes which restore us to our natural state are good * indirectly, or in their result, if not good directly, and in themselves. Where we experience a physical desire, which, inasmuch as it is accompanied by a pain, is of course the expression of a defect in some part of our organisation, the pleasure which accompanies the satisfaction of such a desire is the spontaneous expression of those parts of our organisation, whether acquired or primitive, that have all along remained unaffected. And there are, moreover, certain pleasures which are unaccompanied by pain and by physical desire, and which consequently involve no defect in our organisation, — such as are, for instance, the

* For ἡδεῖαι read ἐνεργεῖαι, according to Mr. Chandler's emendation.

(142.) pleasures of | philosophy. In illustration of the distinction just drawn, it may be remarked that the objects which yield us pleasure while our organisation is being perfected, do not yield us pleasure when it is perfect. When our organisation is perfect, then those objects give us pleasure of which we have spoken as directly or absolutely pleasant; but, while it is being restored, we take pleasure in the absolute contraries of these, as, for instance, in vinegar, and in gall, and in other such things, no one of which is pleasant in itself, or absolutely pleasant. And, of course, the pleasures which such objects yield fall under the same rule; for, exactly as the objects that yield us pleasure are related to one another, so, too, are the pleasures which they yield. Neither does it of necessity follow that all pleasure involves a something beyond and better than itself, as those say who assert that all pleasure is a physical process, and is consequently inferior to the end in which it results. For it is not true of all pleasures that they are processes of this kind, or even that they all involve any such process; inasmuch as some of them are the spontaneous expressions of a perfect nature, and are, as such, absolute ends in themselves. Pleasure is not always the result of a physical process towards perfection, inasmuch as it often accompanies the exercise of a perfectly sound faculty. And so it is not true of all pleasures alike that they imply an end beyond themselves, but it is only true of the pleasures which those feel who are moving towards a perfect state of organisation. And hence we can see that pleasure is incorrectly defined as "a phenomenon of sense, consisting in an alternation between two poles, and ultimately resulting in a perfect physical organisation"; but that we ought rather to speak of it as "the spontaneous expression of our natural condition," and to call it "an unhindered activity," instead of "a sensible phenomenon." Nay, more, so far is it from being true that pleasure must be bad because it is a process, that some people actually hold that pleasure cannot but be a process, because it is so distinctively a good. These thinkers, however, confound two things that are really distinct, namely, processes and activities. And, again, to say that all pleasures are bad, because some things that give pleasure are bad for health, is as absurd as to say that all health is bad, because some things that are good for health are bad for making money. Of course, from an indirect point of view such as this, both things pleasant and things healthy may appear to be bad; but it does not follow on this account that they are directly and absolutely bad. Even philosophy may, if pursued under certain conditions, be bad for health. And, again, it is not true that the exercise of prudence, or indeed that of any other similar state or habit, is hindered by its own pleasure, but only that it is hindered by what may be called the alien pleasures which result from the exercise of other states. For the pleasures of contemplation and of investigation only intensify the acts which they accompany. And, again, that there should be no art of pleasure is only what might have been expected; for, indeed, no art ever aims at producing an actual act, but only a capability for such an act.

And yet perfumery and cookery would seem to be arts of pleasure. Lastly, one and the same answer may be given to the arguments, that the temperate man avoids pleasure, that what the prudent man pursues is not so much pleasure as a life free from pain, and that beasts and children pursue pleasure indis-
(143.) criminately. We have already | said in what sense it is that some pleasures are good absolutely, and in what sense it is that some pleasures are good only relatively ; from which, of course, it follows that all pleasures alike are not absolutely good. Now it is this latter class of pleasures—those, namely, that are only relatively good—that beasts and children pursue ; and it is freedom from the pain caused by the desires which these pleasures satisfy that the prudent man pursues : we are speaking here of the pleasures that are preceded by physical desire, and consequently by pain,—or, in other words, of the bodily pleasures, which alone are of this kind,—and not so much of bodily pleasure simply, as of its excess, with which excess it is that intemperance is concerned. These alone are the pleasures which the temperate man avoids, since even temperance has pleasures of its own.

13.   Moreover, it is admitted that pain is an evil, and a thing to be avoided; for some sorts of pain are directly and absolutely bad, others indirectly, in that they in some way impede those energies which are the free expression of our nature. But the opposite of that which ought to be avoided, in so far as it ought to be avoided, and is consequently bad, must itself be good : and therefore pleasure cannot but, from this point of view at

least, be a good. The solution attempted by Speusippus does not really hold,—namely, that pleasure and pain are the contraries of one another, and also of the good, in exactly the same way as the greater is the contrary of the less, while each is the contrary of that which is exactly equal,—for this solution involves what nobody will admit, that all pleasure whatever is the contrary of the good, and consequently a form of evil. Nor does the fact that certain pleasures are bad, in any way render it impossible that some one pleasure should be the chief good; exactly as it is none the less conceivable that some particular science should be the chief good, because certain other kinds of knowledge are bad. And perhaps, too, it necessarily follows, inasmuch as each one of our faculties can only express itself when its activities are unimpeded, that, whether happiness consist in the conjoint activity of all our faculties, or whether in the activity of some particular one amongst them, it must, if it is to be the most choiceworthy of all goods, be unimpeded: and it is in an unimpeded energy of this kind that pleasure, by our very definition, consists. And from this it follows that it is perfectly possible for some one pleasure to be the chief good, although the majority are, very possibly, absolutely bad. And hence it is that all men hold that the happy life has a pleasure of its own, and weave into the chaplet of happiness the blossom of pleasure,—and that too with good reason. For no activity can be perfect if it be impeded, and happiness is a perfect thing. And hence, too, it is that the happy man requires, in addition to his virtue, bodily goods and goods external, or in other words the goods of chance, that the activities in which his happiness consists may be unimpeded. And so those who assert that he who is being tortured upon the wheel, or he who is entangled in sore misfortunes, is none the less happy, provided only that he be good, are, either consciously or unconsciously, indulging in empty talk. And yet happiness must not be identified with mere prosperity, as some have been led to think, from the (144.) fact that good fortune is in it an essential element. |

For even good fortune may become so excessive as to impede our better energies; and it has then perhaps no longer any just claim to be called good fortune, since the limits of good fortune are determined by its influence upon our happiness. And, moreover, the fact that all beings whatever, beasts and men alike, pursue pleasure, is an indication that it is in some sort the highest good.

> When many people lift their voices up,
> Their words fall not in vain.

But still, inasmuch as there is no one natural organisation or acquired condition, which is either best for all beings alike, or held by them to be such, it follows that all beings alike do not pursue the same pleasure, although a pleasure of some kind they all do pursue. Nay, more, perhaps the pleasure which they are each and all pursuing, is not that which they think, or even that which they would avow, but is for all of them alike one and the same; for there is nothing but has in its nature a divine element. The bodily pleasures have entered into the exclusive heritage of the name, because it is to them that men most often give themselves, and because there is no human being incapable of sharing in them: and so, because these are the only pleasures which men know, they think that they are the only pleasures that exist. Lastly, it is clear that, unless pleasure, that is to say the activity which is involved in pleasure, were a good thing, we should not be able to say of the happy man that his life is pleasant. For why should he stand in need of pleasure, if pleasure be not a good thing, and if it be indifferent whether or not life be painful? Indeed, pain could not possibly be an evil (or even a good), unless pleasure were the contrary. And so, why should the happy man avoid pain? Nor, indeed, should we say of the good man that his life is more pleasant than is that of others, were it not that a higher pleasure is involved in his acts.

14. As regards the distinctly bodily pleasures, their nature demands a thorough investigation on the part of those who assert that some pleasures indeed are very choiceworthy, to wit, the nobler pleasures,—but not so the bodily pleasures, which are the objects of intemperance. If this be so, why is it—one may ask—that the bodily pains, which are their opposites, are held to be bad? For the opposite of the bad can only be the good. May not one say that the bodily or necessary pleasures are good, in so far as that is a good which is not bad? Or may not one rather say that they are good, when not pursued beyond a certain point? For those habits or processes which never in themselves exceed the limits of what is good, cannot possibly

involve any over-excess of pleasure,—such excess of pleasure being only possible where the activity in (145.) which it is involved can exceed these limits. | Now in the case of bodily goods this excess is possible, and indeed the intemperate man is such, not merely in that he pursues the bodily or necessary pleasures, but in that he pursues them to excess. (Indeed all men take pleasure to a certain extent in good cookery, and in wine, and in sexual enjoyment, although it is not all men in whom the enjoyment of such pleasures is properly regulated.) But, in his avoidance of pain, the intemperate man is guided by a rule contrary to that which regulates his pursuit of pleasure. For it is not excessive pain alone that he avoids, but pain of any kind. Indeed, it is only the intemperate man, who pursues excessive pleasure as a good, who would think of opposing to such excess all ordinary pain alike as an evil.

We must not, however, confine ourselves to a bare statement of the truth, but must also inquire into the grounds of the ordinary and erroneous view. Such a course will only serve to strengthen our own convictions. For, when we see clearly the grounds that have led to the acceptance of an error, our belief in the truth is all the more strengthened. It remains then that we should state why it is that the bodily pleasures have been held to be more choiceworthy than others. In the first place, they have been held to be such, because they can drive out bodily pain: and it is because bodily pain is often excessive, and bodily pleasure acts as a remedy to it, that men are led to pursue such forms of pleasure as admit of excess, and indeed to pursue bodily pleasure as a whole. Remedies are in their very nature violent; and hence it is that pleasure is sometimes pursued to an almost violent excess, because, from its opposition to the pain which it drives out, and with which it is contrasted, our conception of it becomes intensified. But yet it is on these very grounds that, as has been said before, it has been held that pleasure is not a good,—and that for two reasons. For, firstly, there are certain pleasures which are peculiar to the acts of a nature either naturally depraved, as in a beast, or corrupted by long habit, as in bad men. And, secondly, there are certain others which are of the nature of remedies, and, to feel which, a man must first have a want to be supplied,—and, it may be said, it is better to be sound than to become so. But still such pleasures are the indirect result of a process tending towards our perfection, and so are indirectly good, if not good in themselves. In the second place, bodily pleasure is often pursued, simply because it is intense, by those who are unable to take pleasure in other things: such men resemble those who are in the habit of producing artificial thirst. When their pleasures are harmless, their conduct need not be blamed, but when they are injurious, it becomes distinctly bad. Such men have no other sources of pleasure open to them, and such is the organisation of the majority of mankind that a purely neutral state is to them absolutely painful. There is indeed no living thing for which the process of life does not involve a perpetual travail. To this truth the writings of physiologists bear witness, which tell us that every act of sight and of hearing involves a pain, which, from long custom, has become imperceptible. It is from causes of the same kind that the (146.) stimulus of physical growth acts upon the young as a kind of chronic intoxication, so that youth becomes a thing full of pleasure. And similarly an atrabilious temperament is constantly craving for remedy. For the absence of proper balance in the organisation produces a chronic irritation, and so leads to violent physical cravings. Now a pain can be driven out not only by the pleasure which is its contrary, but indeed by any pleasure whatever of sufficient intensity; and hence it is that men become intemperate and depraved. But those pleasures which are not preceded by bodily desire, and so by pain, cannot possibly be pursued to excess. These are the pleasures given us by those objects that are pleasant naturally and directly, and not indirectly. By indirectly or incidentally pleasant must be understood those objects that are of the nature of remedies; for, when the unsound part of our organisation is cured, the indirect result is an unimpeded energy of that part which has all along remained sound; and hence it is that a pleasure seems to attach itself to all processes of healing. But the term, naturally or directly pleasant, must be restricted to those objects that directly stimulate to activity the sound portion of our organisation. Lastly, the reason why one and the same thing never continuously yields us pleasure, is because our organisation is not simple, consisting, not only of the soul, but also of a second element, the body, which is ours in virtue of our material existence. And hence it often results that the proper activities of the one element do violence to those of the other. But, when the two are in harmonious equilibrium, then the energies of the mind are indifferent to the body, and affect it neither with pain nor with pleasure. And thus we can see that, where the organisation of any being is absolutely simple, the same act will always continuously give a pleasure of the highest kind and of the most intense degree. And hence it is that the pleasure felt by God must be single, continuous, and simple. Such a pleasure God cannot but feel. For activity is not restricted to states of development, in which there is a process from inchoation to perfection, but belongs also to those absolutely perfect states, which are at rest from any such process; and it is in repose, rather than in the struggle of development, that true pleasure is to be found.

Change of all things is sweetest,

as the poet says, because of some defect in our nature. And, exactly as it is the bad man who loves change, so, too, the nature that always craves for change is bad: it is not simple, nor is it good.

Thus, then, we have treated of self-restraint, and of incontinence, and of pleasure, and of pain, and have defined each one of them, and have said how it is that some of them are good and others are evil. It now remains for us to treat of friendship.

VIII.

1. (147.) NEXT in order it follows that we ought to treat of friendship. For friendship, if not in itself a virtue, at least involves and implies virtue; and it is, moreover, an absolute essential for a happy life, since without friends no man would choose to live, although possessed of every other good thing. And, indeed, it is when men are rich, or possessed of high office, or of great hereditary power, that they seem most especially to stand in need of friends. For wherein does such prosperity profit us, if we are deprived of the power of doing good to others, of which power friends are the especial object, and which is most praiseworthy when exercised in their behalf; or how can such prosperity be guarded and preserved without the aid of friends? For the greater it is, the more precarious will it be. In poverty, moreover, and in all other forms of evil fortune, friends are held to be our only refuge. And to the young friendship is of aid in that it keeps them clear of faults, and to the old in that it gives kindly attention, and supplies those deficiencies in action which are always the result of infirmity, and to those who are in their full prime in that it makes noble achievements easier:

The two together stepping,

are the better able both to think and to act. It would

seen, moreover, that it is a law of nature that the offspring should feel a love for its parent, and the parent for its offspring; and that this law holds good not among men alone, but among birds also, and with them almost all other living things; and, indeed, that a mutual affection should exist in all beings of the same kind, and most of all in men; and hence it is that we praise those who love their fellow-men. In travel, too, one can see at once how kindred a thing and how dear is man to man. Friendship would, moreover, seem to form a bond of union which holds together the body politic, and about which legislators busy themselves even more than they do about justice. For unanimity is a thing not unlike friendship, (148.) and the two especial objects of legislators are to create unanimity, and to drive out dissension; which latter is inimical to the well-being of the state. Where, moreover, friendship exists, there we stand in no need of justice; but, where justice exists, there we none the less stand in need of friendship; nay, more, those acts in which justice is most perfectly manifested bear a close resemblance to acts of friendship. Lastly, friendship is not only a necessary thing, but also a noble; for we praise those who love their friends, and to have many friends is held to be a something noble; nay, more, there are some who think that "good man" and "friend" are convertible terms.

Now, concerning friendship not a few controversies have been raised. Some hold that it consists in a species of similarity, and that it is those who resemble one another who become friends: whence come the sayings—"a man is known by his friends," "birds of a feather flock together," and other proverbs to the same effect. And, on the other hand, there are others who assert that all those who are of the same disposition are like the potter in the adage. And there are others again who have investigated this same question yet more deeply, going back to first principles, and to the primary laws of the universe; as does Euripides, when he says,—

> The parched earth yearns for rain. The holy Heaven,
> Laden with showers, yearns to descend in rain
> Upon the earth beneath.

And so, too, Heraclitus tells us that "contradictories are identical," and that "the union of discords is the sweetest concord," and that "strife is the life of all things." Empedocles, again, and others with him, have advanced views diametrically opposed to these, holding it to be a primary law of nature that like should be attracted by like. All those problems, however, in which are involved such primary physical truths as the above, may, with safety, be dismissed, as being alien to our present investigation; and we will confine our attention to those questions alone which have distinct reference to man, and which concern the character and the emotions; as, for example, whether all men alike are capable of friendship, or whether it is impossible for bad men to be friends; and whether there is but one kind of friendship, or more than one. For it would seem that those who hold that there is but one kind of friendship, which, because it varies in degree of intensity, appears to be

distinguishable into more kinds than one, base their
assertion upon insufficient grounds; inasmuch as there
are instances of things which, although distinct from
one another in kind, can yet participate in one and
the same quality in different degrees. Of this question we have treated before.

2. The difficulty as to the various kinds of friendship
will, however, probably find its solution, if we first
determine what it is that is the object of affection.
(149.) For it would seem that affection has its legitimate
objects, and is not exercised indiscriminately; and
that the legitimate object of affection is either that
which is good, or else that which is pleasant, or else
that which is useful. Now that which is useful would
seem to be that by means of which we attain anything
either good or pleasant; so that the three objects of
affection really resolve themselves into two, namely,
the good, and the pleasant, towards which we feel an
affection as towards absolute ends. It remains to
inquire whether the object of our affection is that
which is good really and in the abstract, or that which
is good for our own individual selves; for these two
are not always identical. And with regard to what
is pleasant a similar question can be raised. Now it
would seem that each one of us feels an affection for
that which is good for his own and individual self;
and that, consequently, it is that which is good really
and in the abstract which is really and in the abstract
the object of affection; while that which is good for
the individual will be the object of affection to him
as an individual. It is, then, admitted that the indi-

vidual sets his affections, not so much upon that which
is really and truly good for him, as upon that which
he conceives to be such. But, still, this does not
really affect our position; for we have only to say that
the object upon which the individual sets his affections,
is not so much the true object of affection as
that which appears to him to be such. There are,
then, as we have said, three things that excite our
affection; but, where we are led by any one of these
to feel an affection for a lifeless object, such an affection
is not called a friendship, inasmuch as in it no
reciprocity of affection is involved, nor any wish that
that object may enjoy the highest good of which it
is capable. It is, indeed, almost ridiculous to talk of
wishing wine all the good which it can enjoy, our
highest wish with regard to it being that it may be
preserved in safety for our own enjoyment. But, in
the case of a friend, we say that we ought to wish
him all possible good for his own sake. Those who
wish good to others after this fashion, are said to show
kindly feeling, except in those cases where they meet
with similar good wishes in return,—for a reciprocity
of kindly feeling is commonly held to constitute friendship.
Ought we not, however, to add the further condition
that such reciprocity must be conscious? For
it is quite possible for us to have a kindly feeling
towards those whom we have never seen, but whom
we, nevertheless, suppose to be good men, or useful.
And it is, of course, conceivable that there should be
some among them who are similarly affected towards
ourselves. In such a case there evidently exists

between us a reciprocity of kindly feeling. But still we cannot possibly be called friends, inasmuch as each of us is unconscious of the feeling of the other towards himself. In a word, to constitute friendship it is necessary that men should, for some one of the three reasons above given, have a kindly feeling towards one another, and a mutual desire each for the other's good, and that each should be conscious of this reciprocity of sentiment.

3. The three objects of affection above described differ from one another in kind; and hence it follows that there will also be exactly as many distinct kinds of affection, and, consequently, as many distinct kinds of friendship. There are, indeed, three kinds of friendship, one for each of the three objects of affection; for each of these three objects can give rise to a conscious reciprocity of affection. Now, those who have a friendship for one another, will wish one another good from the point of view of that motive in which their friendship originates. And hence those whose friendship for one another is based upon utility, feel no affection for one another, each for the other's own sake, but only in so far as each derives from the other (150.) some actual benefit. | And so, too, of those whose friendship is based upon pleasure, a similar rule holds good; for we do not feel any affection for a witty man merely in that he is witty, but because his wit gives us pleasure. And hence we can see that the affection of those whose friendship is based upon utility, originates in a sense of their own advantage; and similarly that the affection of those whose friendship

is based upon pleasure, originates in a sense of their own enjoyment; or that, in a word, they do not love their friend for his own sake, and because his character is* what it is, but because he is useful to them, or because he yields them pleasure. These friendships, then, originate incidentally, as an indirect result of self-seeking. For in them our friend is held dear to us, not for his own sake, and because he is of such or such a type of character, but because we derive from him, as the case may be, either pleasure, or else some practical advantage. And hence it is that all such friendships are liable to be quickly broken off, the moment that the friend ceases to be such as he first was; for, when he becomes, as the case may be, either no longer pleasant, or no longer useful, then all affection for him ceases. Now our material interest is by no means a permanent thing, but is, on the contrary, liable to continual change. And so, when that, whatever it may be, upon which the friendship was originally based, comes to an end, then the friendship itself is broken off, since it was never pursued for its own sake, but only with these other ends in view. That form of friendship which is based upon utility, would seem principally to have place among the old (for men of advanced years do not so much pursue what is pleasant as what is useful), or among those who, although still in the prime of life, or, it may be, even young, are nevertheless guided by motives of self-interest. It is but very seldom that friends of this kind pass their lives with one another; at times,

---

* Read with Cardwell μλοέμνος ἐστι, and consult the note of Michelet.

indeed, they do not even derive any pleasure each from the society of the other. Each of them takes pleasure in the company of the other only in so far as he hopes to be benefited by him; and, consequently, when no such benefit accrues, no further need for any such intercourse is felt. It is to this class of friendships that we commonly refer covenants for purposes of mutual hospitality between the inhabitants of different countries. On the other hand, the friendship of the young would seem to be based upon pleasure; for the life of the young is guided by their emotions, and the chief object of their pursuit is that which is pleasant to their own and individual selves, and for the time being. But as age advances our pleasures change. And so the young are quick to form friendships, and quick to break them off; for as their pleasures change the old friendship falls away, and all such pleasure is quick to change. Moreover, the young are apt to form sentimental attachments, for such attachments are, as a rule, a matter of emotion, and have pleasure for their object. And hence the young form strong attachments, and quickly break them off, often not knowing their own mind for a day together. It may be remarked that friends of this kind always desire to pass their time together, and to lead their life in common; for otherwise the essential conditions of their friendship remain unfulfilled.

(151.) | That friendship, however, which obtains between those who are good, and who resemble one another in that they are similarly and equally virtuous, is complete and perfect in itself. For men of this sort will, each of them equally with the other, feel a mutual and reciprocal wish that that may be their lot, which is, from the point of view of their virtue, their highest good; and it must be remembered that their virtue is an essential element in their character, and not an indirect result of it. Now, it is those who wish well to their friend for his own sake who have the highest claim to the title of friend, inasmuch as the friendship of such exists and is felt by them for the sake of their friends alone, and not as an indirect result of any form of self-seeking. And, consequently, the friendship of such men will last as long as they themselves remain virtuous; and virtue is an abiding thing. In a friendship of this kind each of the two friends is good, both in the highest and most abstract sense of being virtuous, and in the lower and particular sense of being serviceable to his friend: for good men are not only good in the abstract sense of the word, but are also of service to one another. And they are also pleasant after the same fashion: for the good are not only pleasant in the highest sense of the word, but are also pleasant in the particular sense of being pleasant to one another. Indeed, each man takes pleasure primarily in his own acts; and, secondarily, in all acts which are of a like nature to his own; and the acts of good men, if not absolutely identical, are at any rate most closely similar. A friendship of this kind is, as might be expected, a lasting thing, inasmuch as in it are united all those requisites which are essential if men are to be really and truly friends. For all friendship is ultimately based, either upon the good or else upon pleasure,—which good or pleasure, if not such really and absolutely, is at least conceived to be such by him who has entered into the friendship,—and involves a certain amount of similarity between the friends. And, in a friendship of this kind, it results directly, and from the very character of the friends, that into it should enter all those essentials which have been enumerated above. For, firstly, all the other forms of friendship are such only in so far as they resemble this; and, secondly, that which is absolutely good will also be pleasant absolutely, and in itself. Now, it is the good and the pleasant that rank the highest among the objects of affection; and, consequently, that love and that friendship which is based upon them has the highest and the best claim to the title. It is only to be expected, however, that such friendships should be rare; for of such men there are but few. And, moreover, such a friendship requires a long time, and a considerable amount of acquaintance. For, as the old aphorism runs, men cannot know one another until they have eaten the proverbial amount of salt in company; nor can they, indeed, each fully admit the other to the position of a friend, until each is fully assured that the other is a worthy object of affection, and has consequently placed in him his fullest confidence. Those who are over quick to treat one another as friends, may indeed wish to be friends, but are not such upon that account alone, unless each of them be also a worthy object of affection, and be assured of the other that he likewise is such. For, although a desire for friendship can be quickly formed, it is not so with friendship itself.

This form of friendship is then complete and perfect in itself, not only as regards the time which it requires for its formation, and the time for which it lasts, but in every other respect as well; and in it there exists upon all points, between the two friends, a reciprocity of mutual good offices, which, if not absolutely identical, are at least so similar as to be equivalent: and thus it is that friends ought to be

4.(152.) affected the one towards the other. [That form of friendship which is based upon pleasure has a certain resemblance to the form just described, in that those who are good are also mutually pleasant to one another. And the same holds good of that form of friendship which is based upon utility; for those who are good derive mutual advantage from the society of one another. These two forms of friendship are most disposed to be permanent, when each of the friends derives from the other a gratification identical with that which he himself yields to him, as, for example, when each of the two yields a pleasure to the other, and derives a pleasure from him. And this still more holds true when the gratification which each derives from the other is not only identical in kind, but also identical in its source; as when the mutual pleasure which two witty persons take in one another becomes the basis of a friendship between them. This last does not hold good in the case of a sentimental friendship between a man and a youth. In such a case, each of the two derives, it is true, a pleasure from the friendship, but each derives that pleasure from a different source—the lover, from the sight of the loved object;

the youth, from the attentions which the lover lavishes upon him. And hence such a friendship often dies out, after that the beauty of youth has passed away; for then the lover loses the old delight of his eyes, and the loved one misses the attentions to which he has been accustomed. Not but that a friendship of this kind is not unfrequently carried on into mature life, in those cases where the two friends are of like disposition, and have learnt from long acquaintance each to love the other's character. Those, on the other hand, who make love a matter of business, and who barter their affections, not for a counter return of pleasure, but for material advantage, have less claim to the title of friend, and their friendship is less abiding. And so, too, those who have become friends from motives of utility, discontinue their friendship as soon as their mutual interests change; for that which each loved all along was, not so much his friend, as his own and individual interest. Hence we can see that that form of friendship which is based upon pleasure, or upon utility, can obtain between two bad men, or between a bad man and a good, or between a man who is neither good nor bad and another like himself, or between a man of this kind and a good man, or, lastly, between a man of this kind and a bad man: whereas that friendship which is based upon the affection which each of the friends feels towards the other for his own sake, can evidently only obtain between the good; for bad men take no pleasure in one another, save only in so far as they derive from one another some

actual benefit. Moreover, the friendship of the good
is the only friendship which slander cannot prejudice.
For it is a very difficult matter to believe a man who
speaks to the prejudice of him whose character we
have thoroughly tested for many years. Friends of
this kind have in one another the most thorough confidence, nor can they conceive it as being, under any
circumstances whatever, possible that either of them
should wrong the other; and their friendship has,
moreover, all those other characteristics which are
essential to constitute a friendship ideally perfect.
But, in other kinds of friendship, it is perfectly possible for the friends to be set at variance by evil
reports of one another. To resume,—inasmuch as men
are in the habit of calling " friends " even those whose
affection is based upon utility,—as is the case in a
friendship between two States (for it would seem that
States enter into alliances with one another from
motives of interest alone),—no less than those whose
affection for one another is based upon pleasure, as is
the affection of children;—it would seem to follow
that we, too, ought to speak of such persons as friends,
(153.) but to do so with the reservation that there are
more kinds of friendship than one; and that that kind
which is primarily and distinctively to be called
friendship, is the friendship which the good feel
towards one another because they are good; while
all other kinds are to be spoken of as friendships
only in virtue of their resemblance to this, inasmuch
as those who enter into them are really friends, only
in so far as they have in their character some

element of good, in virtue of which they resemble
one another—it being remembered that to those who
love pleasure that which is pleasant is a good. Lastly,
it is to be observed, that the two secondary forms of
friendship very seldom coincide, and that it is but
seldom that there exists between the same two people
an affection based upon mutual interest, conjointly
with an affection based upon mutual pleasure. For
things the connection between which is only incidental, are seldom, as a rule, found to coexist.

Friendship is, then, as we have said, divided into
these three kinds: and the friendship of the bad will be
based either upon pleasure, or else upon interest; since
such similarity as there is between them will consist in
one or the other of these two points: while the friendship of the good will be based upon the mutual affection
which they have for one another; their similarity consisting in their virtue. And so the friendship of the
good is absolutely such, and is entered into for its
own sake; while the friendship of the bad is only
incidentally such, for it is an indirect result of self-
seeking, and is only called friendship in virtue of its
5. resemblance to the true. Moreover, exactly as with
regard to the various moral virtues we speak of some
men as being good in that they have a virtuous disposition, and of others in that they do virtuous acts; so,
too, is it in the case of friendship. For there are some
friends whose delight it is to pass their lives together,
and who render one another actual good services;
while there are others again, who may be, perhaps,
asleep, or, it may be, living at a distance from one

another, and who, consequently, do not actually do these friendly acts, but are none the less disposed to do them upon occasion. For separation does not destroy the friendship itself, but only prevents the manifestation of it in friendly acts. But still, where absence has lasted for long, it would seem that it makes men forgetful of their friendship; and hence has come the saying—

> Friendship hath oft been lost for lack of speech.

Moreover, it would seem that neither the aged nor the austere are at all quick to contract friendship; for with them pleasure has but little place; and no man can continuously pass his time with one who is absolutely obnoxious to him, or even with one in whose company he takes no pleasure,—it being, indeed, the primary impulse of our nature to avoid that which gives us pain, and to aim at that which gives us pleasure. Lastly,—those who are mutually satisfied with one another, but who do not pass their lives together, would seem to be kindly disposed towards one another, rather than to be actual friends. There is, indeed, nothing which is so essential to friendship as that friends should pass their lives in the society of one another. For those who are in distress crave assistance; while those whose lot is blessed crave the society of others, inasmuch as they, least of all men, ought to lead a life of isolation. And it is impossible for men to pass their time together, unless they not only are pleasant to one another, but also take pleasure in the same pursuits; and this one

can see in the case of friendships between brothers in
arms.

Thus, then, as has been already stated several times,
the only real friendship is that between the good. For it
would seem that that which is in the abstract the object
of affection, and consequently choiceworthy, is that
which is absolutely and in the abstract either good or
pleasant; and that, to the individual, that is such which
he conceives as being good for or pleasant to himself.
And, from either point of view, the good man must be
to the good man a fit object of affection, and a choiceworthy friend. Now affection resembles a transitory
emotion; friendship a fixed habit, which has become a
part of our character. Indeed, affection may be felt for
a lifeless object; whereas, in the reciprocity of friendship, purpose is involved and implied, and purpose is
always the manifestation and the result of character.
And hence the true friend will wish his friend good
for his own sake, and will do so, not from any sudden
emotion, but because to do so is a part of his own character. And the love which he bears to his friend will,
in reality, be a love for his own good; for, when another
good man contracts a friendship for him, he thereby
becomes to him a good. And hence each friend not
only loves that which is his own good, but also makes a
perfectly equivalent return in the good which he
wishes his friend, and in the pleasure which he yields
him. For, as the old saying runs, "equality makes
friendship." And it is of the friendship of the good

6. that all this is most especially true. Among those
who are austere, or aged, friendship shows itself less;

inasmuch as their disposition is more morose, and they consequently take less pleasure in the society of others. And it is frequent intercourse with others that is not only the best test of friendship, but also its commonest source. And hence it is that the young become friends quickly; while the old do not, inasmuch as men cannot well become friends to those in the society of whom they take no pleasure; and of those, also, who are austere a similar rule holds good. But still such persons may, none the less, be very kindly disposed towards one another. Indeed, they often wish one another all possible good; and are prompt to provide one another with assistance upon occasion of necessity. But still they can scarcely be called friends, inasmuch as they neither pass their time together, nor take any pleasure in the society of one another; and these two conditions are absolutely essential to friendship. One cannot possibly be a friend to many men at once, if the friendship is to be of the highest and perfect kind, any more than one can, at one and the same time, be in love with many different persons. For such a friendship would seem to be a species of excess, and to involve such an intensity of feeling as can only naturally direct itself towards one person. And, besides, it is not an easy matter for many persons, at one and the same time, to give very great pleasure to the same individual; nor, perhaps, for many persons to be, all alike, good men. True friendship, moreover, requires that we should have experience of one another, and that we should be upon terms of close intimacy; and, if our friends are to be many, this is very difficult. But, where our (155.) friendship is based upon interest, or upon pleasure, it is perfectly possible to please many persons at once; for there are many in the world who can contract friendships of this nature, and the services which are entailed require but a short time for their performance. Of all the secondary forms of friendship the one which is most like the true, is that friendship which is based upon pleasure, when in it each of the friends yields the other an identical gratification, and they, consequently, take pleasure, if not each in the other, at any rate in the same pursuits. Of this kind are friendships between youths; for in them liberality of nature is more conspicuous than in others. As for the friendship which is based upon mutual interest, it is principally contracted by the mercenary. Those, moreover, whose lot is blessed, stand in need of friends, not for purposes of interest, but for purposes of pleasure; for they long to have some one with whom to pass their life, and can endure for but a short time anything that gives them pain. Indeed, no man could continuously endure that which gave him pain,—no, not even if it were the chief good. And hence it is that those whose lot is blessed, seek for friends to yield them pleasure. But they ought, perhaps, also to require that the friends whom they seek for this purpose should, in addition, be good men, not only in the highest sense of the word, but also in the particular sense of rendering good services. For so will they have friends in whom are combined the three especial requisites of friendship. Those, on the other hand, who are in authority, would seem to make use of various friends, who are distinct from one another in kind; for some among their intimates are useful to them, and others yield them pleasure, although it is but seldom that, in the same man, these two points are combined. Great men do not look for friends who are to yield them pleasure, and at the same time to be virtuous; nor do they look for men who are serviceable as tools, that they may make use of them to achieve some noble end. They rather seek for friends who are witty, because they crave for amusement; and for others who are cunning and unscrupulous in the execution of any orders that may be given them, because they need such men as instruments; and it is but seldom that these two essentials are combined in the same person. It is true, of course, as has been already said, that the good man is not only a good friend, but also a pleasant, and a useful. But such an one will not become a friend to one who is his superior in worldly position, unless his own superiority in moral worth be also admitted; else he has no equivalent to counterbalance his inferiority in worldly position, and so cannot effect an equal interchange of reciprocal services. It must be noticed, however, that friendships of this kind are exceedingly rare.

The friendships which we have just described, may be called friendships of equality; for, in them, either each friend yields the other the same kind of service, and wishes him the same form of good, or else the services which they render one another are, like goods in barter, equivalent in value, although distinct in kind; as where pleasure is given on the one hand in return for material assistance on the other. We have also observed that they are less permanent than is the true friendship, and that the term "friendship" is not so properly applicable to them. They have, indeed, both a resemblance and a dissimilarity to the same thing; and hence they are held, partly to be friendships, and partly not to be so. They would seem to be friendships, in so far as they resemble that friendship which is based upon virtue; for the one of them involves pleasure, and the other utility, both of which are to be found | in the true friendship. But, on the other hand, their dissimilarity to the true friendship would make it seem that they are not really friendships. For, while the true friendship cannot be disturbed by slanders, or by accusations of any kind, and is of a lasting nature, they are not only liable to sudden ruptures, but also differ from the true friendship in many other important points. There is, also, another class of friendships, comprising what may be called friendships of inequality; such as is, for instance, the friendship of a father for his son, or, indeed, of any older man for a younger; or as is the friendship of a man for his wife, or of one who is in a position of authority of any kind for him who is under authority. These friendships of inequality differ from one another; for the friendship of a parent for his child is one, and that of a ruler for his subjects is another; and that of a father for his son is one, and that of a son for his father is another; and that of a man for his wife is one, and that of a wife for her husband is another. For in each one of these positions is involved a distinct virtue, and a distinct function, and, consequently, a distinct claim upon the affection of others; and hence arise correspondently various forms of affection, and consequently of friendship. In friendships of this nature, neither are the services which the one friend renders to the other identical with those which he receives, nor ought we to expect that they should be such. When, for instance, children render to their parents such services as are due to those who begat them, and parents render to their sons that attention which is due to a child, then the friendship between parents and their children will be a lasting friendship, and a good. Lastly, in all friendships of inequality, the affection between the two friends must be in inverse proportion to the services which are rendered. I mean that the better of the two, for instance, or the one who renders the most advantage to the other, or who is in any other way whatever the superior of his friend, ought to receive a return of affection correspondently greater than is the affection which he bestows. For, when the interchange of affection between two friends is in inverse ratio to the interchange of services, then one may say that equality is the result; and it is equality that is one of the chief characteristics of friendship.

But yet one must, none the less, distinguish between the equality which obtains in justice and the equality which obtains in friendship. In justice, the primary consideration is equality according to proportionate value, to which numerical or quantitative equality is only secondary. But, in friendship, the primary consideration is quantitative equality, and equality according to proportionate value is but of secondary importance. The truth of this rule can be clearly seen whenever virtue, or vice, or wealth, or any other cause, has made any great difference between the relative position of two friends; for, in such a case, not only do they no longer continue to be friends, but they do not even consider any further friendship desirable. In the case of the Gods, the truth of the rule is self-evident; for there is no good thing whatever with respect to which they are not infinitely superior to men. And it is clear, also, in the case of kings; for those who are far their inferiors no more lay claim to friendship with them, than do those who are of no reputation lay claim to (157) friendship with men | of exceeding excellence, or of great wisdom. In all such cases it is, of course, impossible to lay down any abstract rule, as to how great a difference between two friends is compatible with the continuance of their friendship. For while, on the one hand, a man may have much taken from him, and yet none the less continue to be a friend; yet, on the other hand, if it should come to pass that his friend be very widely separated from him—as is God, for instance, from man—he can then no longer continue to be his friend. And hence it is that the problem has arisen, whether friends really wish their friends the greatest possible good, such as, for example, that they should become Gods; for, in such a case, they could not any longer continue to be friends to those who had formed the wish; and, consequently, could no longer continue to be a good to them; for it is only in that* they are friends that friends are a good to one another. If, then, we were right when we said that a friend has the good of his friend in view when he wishes him all possible good, then it will follow that he cannot but wish him to remain such as he now is; and that he will, consequently, wish him, not the absolutely greatest good, but the greatest good of which man is capable. And yet he will not perhaps wish him every possible good: for every man desires his own good rather than the good of another.

8. It may, moreover, be remarked, that the majority of mankind are led by their ambition to prefer to be loved by others, rather than themselves to love others; and that it is on this account that most men are fond of flatterers, inasmuch as the flatterer is a friend who is conscious of his own inferiority, or who pretends to be conscious of it, and, consequently, to love his friend more than he is loved by him. Now love seems to be very closely akin to honour, and it is at honour that most men aim. And yet it would not seem that they choose honour directly, and for its own sake; but rather indirectly, and for the sake of its results. The reason, for instance, why most men rejoice when honour is shown to them by those who are in authority, is because they are led thereby to cherish great hopes. They think that they will obtain from their powerful friends whatever they may want, and they consequently take pleasure in honour, as being a token of prosperity. And, similarly, those who crave to have honour given to them by men of virtue and under-

* We are tempted to read ᾗ γὰρ εἶλοι.

standing, in reality desire to see the opinion which they have formed of their own merit confirmed; and hence what really gives them pleasure is the conviction of their own deserts, to which they are led from their confidence in the opinion of those who enunciate them. But to be loved yields men pleasure, not incidentally, and as a matter of result, but directly and in itself. And hence it is that to be loved is a better thing than it is to be honoured; and that, consequently, true friendship is choiceworthy for its own sake. And it would seem that it is much more essential to true friendship that we should love our friend than that we should be loved by him. This one can see from the affection which mothers delight to lavish upon their children. For they sometimes will even intrust their own offspring to others to be brought up; and, consequently, knowing them to be their own, still continue to love them, but do not seek for any return of affection, if such a mutual attachment is impossible,—it being apparently sufficient for them if they see their (158.) children prosperous. | And so they none the less love their children, even although the children may, from ignorance of their own birth, render them none of those attentions that are a mother's due. And so, since it is more essential to friendship that we should love our friends than that we should be loved by them, and since, consequently, those are praised who love their friends, it follows that the highest virtue of friends, as such, would seem to lie in the love which they bear to one another; and hence, too, it follows that, where there exists between friends a love which is proportioned to their mutual deserts, then they will be firm friends, and their friendship will be a lasting one. And in this way, too, it is possible for those between whom there is the greatest inequality to form a mutual friendship; for, by an unequal return of affection, their present inequality can be equalised. Now, all affection consists in equality and similarity, and most of all in that similarity which exists between the virtuous. For the character of the good man is fixed in itself, and consequently his relations to his friends remain unaltered; and he neither desires that his friend should render him a disgraceful service, nor will he render such to another, but, if anything, will throw obstacles in its way; for the good man will neither do wrong himself, nor allow his friends to do wrong. On the other hand, the wicked have in them nothing lasting; indeed, not even does their wickedness for long preserve the same type. And hence the friendship which they are led to form, from mutual pleasure in the wickedness of one another, endures but for a short time. Those, on the other hand, whose friendship is based upon mutual advantage, or upon mutual pleasure, continue friends for a longer time; for their friendship lasts at least as long as they continue to yield to one another either mutual pleasure or mutual benefit. Lastly, it may be observed, that that form of friendship which is based upon utility, would seem most frequently to originate in a mutual consciousness of contrary necessities; as can be seen in the instance of a friendship between a poor man and a rich, or between an ignorant man and a learned; for each craves for that of which he is conscious that he is deficient, and, in order that he may obtain it, freely offers some other equivalent in exchange. Along with friendships of this kind, one may class the friendship between lover and loved, and between the beautiful and the deformed. And hence it is that the lover often makes himself appear ridiculous, by claiming a return of affection similar to that which he bestows. Such a claim might, of course, fairly be advanced, were the title which the lover has to the affection of the loved similar to that which the loved has to the affection of the lover,—the absurdity only consisting in the entire absence of any such claim. It would, moreover, seem that each thing craves for its contrary, not directly, and for its own sake, but rather indirectly, and because of a longing for that intermediate condition which will result from the union of the two; for this it is that is really good. For that which is dry, for example, it is not a good thing that it should become moist; but, rather, that it should arrive at the mean state. And of that which is hot, and indeed of all other things whatever, a similar rule holds good. We had, however, best perhaps dismiss these purely physical illustrations, inasmuch as they are somewhat alien to a strictly ethical investigation.

9. Now it would seem, as has been already said, that friendship and justice are concerned with the same objects, and have the same field. For there is no known community in which we do not find some form of justice, and along with it some form of friendship;

and it is noticeable that men apply the term "friend" to their fellow-shipmates, and to their fellow-campaigners, and, indeed, to all those who are, in common with themselves, joint members of any community. And, as far as their membership in the community extends, so far also extends their friendship; for so far is it that justice is possible between them. And so the proverb, "true friends have all things in common," was well spoken; for it is community that is the field of friendship. Now, brothers by blood and brothers in arms have all things in common; whereas the members of other communities have, nevertheless, private property of their own, which is in some cases more, and in others less. For friendships can be either more or less perfect. There are, moreover, various forms of justice co-extensive with these various forms of community and of friendship. For that form of justice which is involved in the relation of parents to their children is one, and that which is involved in the mutual relations of brothers to one another is another; and the justice which obtains between brothers in arms is one, and that which obtains among members of the same body politic is another; and of all other forms of friendship whatever the same rule holds good. Similarly, in each one of these several relations, a distinct form of injustice is possible; and such injustice is always worse in proportion as the friendship which it violates ought to have been close. It is, for example, a more grievous wrong to defraud a brother in arms than it is to defraud a fellow-citizen; and it is worse to refuse assistance to a brother than it is to refuse assistance to a foreigner; and it is worse to strike one's father than it is to strike anyone else in the whole world. It would seem, indeed, to follow from the very nature of justice that, as friendship increases, its claims upon us increase along with it; for both justice and friendship have the same field, and have also in that same field an equal range. Now it would seem that all the communities above-mentioned are but members or branches of that one great community which constitutes the body politic; for in them men band together to gain some practical good, and to provide for themselves some one or other of the requisites of material life. And it would seem that it was with the practical interests of mankind in view that the body politic was originally constituted, and has ever since continued to exist; for it is the welfare of mankind that is the aim of the legislator, and the current definition of justice is that it is that which is to the common interest of all men alike. And hence, too, it is that these various subordinate communities aim at man's welfare, not as a whole, but from some particular and special point of view. The object, for instance, of a ship's crew is that they may have a prosperous voyage, and thereby either make a large sum of money, or else achieve some similar result. And so, too, the object of fellow-campaigners is a prosperous war, no matter whether it be booty which they desire, or a victory in the field, or the capture of a besieged city. A similar rule holds good of members of the same clan, and of members of the same local hundred.

(For there are some communities the ultimate object of which would seem to be amusement; as where, for instance, a club is formed that a periodical sacrifice may be regularly held, or a dinner given—the object (160.) of such a club being the solemnisation of a] feast, and the festive gathering which is thereby involved. And all communities of this nature would seem to have as good a claim as have any others to be considered as branches of the one great community of the body politic, inasmuch as the aim of the body politic is not so much our welfare for the time being, as the happiness of our life regarded as an organic whole.) And hence it is that these clan-communities and hundreds solemnise sacrifices, in connection with which they hold large gatherings, and thereby not only pay honour to the Gods, but also provide for themselves holiday and amusement. And it would, indeed, seem that, in old times, such sacrifices and gatherings together of the people were regarded as an offering of the first fruits of the year, and so were held immediately after harvest, at which time they had more leisure than at any other. To conclude, then, it would seem that all communities whatsoever are branches of the body politic, and that consequent upon them are an equal number of forms of friendship—a special form of friendship accompanying each form of community.

10. Now in the body politic there are three possible forms of good government, and along with them three perverted forms, each of which is, as it were, an abnormal condition, or corruption, of one of the good

forms. The good forms of government are monarchy and aristocracy, and, thirdly, a form which ought properly to be called a timocracy, inasmuch as in it the claim to citizenship is determined by a property qualification, but which, however, most men are accustomed to call a mixed government or constitution; and of these three forms monarchy is the best, and timocracy the worst. Tyranny is the perverted form of monarchy. In each there is but one ruler, and he is absolute; but there is, nevertheless, the greatest difference between the two, for the object of the tyrant is his own advantage, while the object of the monarch is the good of his subjects. For no man can possibly be a monarch, unless he be absolutely independent, and enjoy an absolute superfluity of all possible goods. For, as there is nothing of which such a man can possibly stand in need, it follows that he will not consider his own interests, but only the interests of his subjects. And, if there be any monarch who is not such as this, he must be some "Numerical-Majority King," chosen by the irrational award of the ballot, not freely elected on the rational ground of his merits. But tyranny is the exact contradictory of monarchy, inasmuch as the tyrant seeks his own good alone. And so one has only to consider what is the nature of tyranny in itself, to see that it is the worst possible form of government,—the worst, indeed, being here, as elsewhere, that which is the contradictory of the best. Monarchy, then, degenerates into tyranny; for tyranny is the disease of monarchy, and the bad king ultimately passes over into the tyrant.

Similarly, an aristocracy degenerates into an oligarchy, because of the wickedness of its rulers, who administer the affairs of the State in violation of all justice, making over to themselves, at least the largest share, if not the whole of the good things of this life, and contriving that the same persons shall continuously hold office; inasmuch as their only object is the acquisition of private wealth. And thus the government passes into the hands of but a few, and those, too, bad men, and not, as they ought to be, the best. Similarly, a timocracy degenerates into a democracy. The two are indeed very closely allied; for a timocracy resembles a democracy in that it is part of its scheme that the government should be in the hands of a numerical majority, and that all those who satisfy the required assessment should enjoy absolutely equal political privileges. Moreover, democracy is, of all perverted forms of government, the least bad; indeed, its scheme differs but little in its essential features from that of a mixed government, or constitution. Such, then, are the laws to which political changes most frequently conform; for in them is involved the minimum of modification, and, consequently, the easiest conditions of change. The analogue and, indeed, almost the antitype of every form of government, whether good or bad, presents itself to us in the family. The father and his sons constitute a community, the leading conception of which is identical with that of monarchy, inasmuch as the wellbeing of the sons is the one care of their father. And hence it is that Homer calls Zeus "our Father," inasmuch as a monarchy aims at being a paternal government. Among the Persians, however, the relation in which the father stands to his sons is tyrannical, for the Persians treat their sons as if they were slaves. The relation, also, of the master to his slaves is tyrannical, in that it has but one object, to wit, the welfare of the master. And it is clear that the relation in which the master stands to his slaves is right, and that the relation in which the Persian father stands to his sons is wrong. For beings of a different nature require to be governed in different ways. The relation, again, in which a man stands to his wife is aristocratical, for the husband rules in virtue of superior merit, restricting his authority within its proper limits, and making over to the wife all that falls within the legitimate sphere of her duties. Where the husband arrogates to himself the control of everything alike, the marital relation degenerates, and becomes oligarchical; for such supremacy is no longer based upon superior merit, and is, consequently, a contravention of justice. Sometimes, on the other hand, it is the wife who arrogates the rule to herself, on the ground that she is an heiress. Such complete and entire supremacy, whether it be of the husband, whether of the wife, is no longer founded upon merit, but is based upon the undue claims, in the latter case, of superior wealth, and, in the former case, of superior power; upon which false claims it is that the constitution of an oligarchy also depends. Lastly, it would seem that the relation which obtains between brothers is timocratical, for brothers stand on a footing of perfect equality one to another, save only in so far as their respective ages constitute between them a difference in degree. And, consequently, when this difference in age becomes very great, then the friendship that subsists between them is no longer that of brothers.

(162.) Democracy finds its closest parallel in | a family which has lost its head; for in such a one all the members are on a footing of absolute equality; or in which the head is weak and powerless, and each one, consequently, does that which is right in his own eyes.

11. Thus, then, in each form of government is involved an especial form of friendship, the range of which will be determined by the degree to which, in the constitution of the given government, justice manifests itself. The friendship between a monarch and his subjects is based upon the absolute claim which he has upon their gratitude. For the monarch is the benefactor of his people, inasmuch as he devotes his whole talents to their welfare, and tends them as a shepherd does his sheep,—whence it was that Homer called Agamemnon "his people's shepherd." Similar to this is the friendship between a father and his sons, the difference between the two consisting in the greater claim which the father has as a benefactor. For the son owes to his father, not only his very existence, which is, by common consent, the greatest of all goods, but also his nurture and his education. And it may be noticed that we not unfrequently refer these benefits to our ancestors generally. Thus, then, it would seem to be a law of nature, that the father should have rule over his sons, and ancestors over their descen-

dants, and monarchs over their people. And hence,
too, it follows that the forms of friendship involved
in these three relations are friendships of inequality;
and this is the reason why parents are held in honour
by their children. Neither are the claims of justice
in these three relations equally balanced on either
side, but rather, as also is the friendship, proportioned
to the benefits received. The form of friendship
which obtains between man and wife is identical with
that which obtains in an aristocracy. The claim upon
which it is based is that of merit, and the rule by
which it is governed is that to the better should be
assigned the greater good, and to each that which
is appropriate. Identical with this is the rule of
justice between man and wife. Lastly, the friendship of brothers resembles that which obtains between
brothers in arms; for brothers are, upon an average, of
equal merits and of equal age, and ought, consequently,
in most cases, to have the same feelings, and the same
habits. That friendship which binds together the
members of a timocracy is very similar to this. For
the conception of a timocracy is that all the citizens
should enjoy equal political privileges, and should be
of equal merit; and that, consequently, each should
hold office in his turn, and upon the same footing as
his predecessors and successors. Such then are the
rules of friendship in a timocracy. In the perverted
forms of government friendship has as little place as
has justice, and in the worst of the three it has the
least; for of friendship in a tyranny there is little or
none. Where there is no common bond of interest

between ruler and ruled, there there can be no friendship; and there, too, justice is equally impossible. The relation which is involved in such a case is much the same as is that of the craftsman to his tool, or of the soul to the body, or of the owner to the slave; for, in each of these three relations, the owner may be said to confer an absolute benefit upon his property by his use of it. Indeed, towards any lifeless thing, friendship and justice are equally impossible. And this same (163.) rule holds good with regard to a man's | horse, or his ox, or even his slave, if he be considered purely and simply as a slave. For between slave and master there is no one point in common. For a slave is only superior to a tool in that he has the function of animal life, and a tool is only inferior to a slave by the absence of that same function. If, then, a slave be considered as such, friendship between him and his master is impossible; but it becomes possible if he be considered as a fellow human being. For it is agreed that justice is possible wherever one man finds another who is capable of entering into a contract with him, and of regulating his actions by the same common rule of life. And, consequently, friendship is possible between a master and his slave, in so far as the slave is regarded as a human being. Lastly, in tyrannies the range of friendship and of justice is exceedingly restricted, while in democracies it is widest of all; for, where men are perfectly equal to one another, there they will have many things in common.

12.   Thus, then, all friendship is, as has already been said, based upon some form of community. And

hence it is that one must distinguish the friendship of relations and the friendship of brothers in arms from all other kinds. For those forms of friendship which obtain between fellow citizens, or between members of the same clan, or members of the same ship's company, and with them all others of a similar nature, would seem to be more definitely based upon a community than are these, inasmuch as they all evidently involve and presuppose some contract with certain definite stipulations; and along with these one may also class that particular form of friendship which is based upon relations of mutual hospitality and protection between members of different States. Now, of friendship between kinsfolk there are many forms, which can, however, be all shown to be derived from the friendship of the father for his children. For parents love their children, as being a portion of themselves, and children love their parents in that they themselves are a something sprung from them. But parents are much more conscious that their children are sprung from themselves, than are the children that they are sprung from their parents, and the progenitor feels much more vividly his kinship with the offspring, than does the offspring its kinship with its creator. For there is no object whatever but is very closely akin to that from which it springs: even a tooth, for example, is very closely akin to its owner, or a hair, or, indeed, anything whatever. Whereas the source from which any object has sprung need be but very little akin to that object, if, indeed, it be akin at all. And, moreover, length of time makes a very considerable difference. For parents love their children from their birth upward, while children do not begin to love their parents until they are of a considerable age, and have got full possession of their wits and faculties. Hence, too, it is clear why the love of a mother for a child is stronger than is any other. Thus, then, parents love their children as they would love themselves; for a man's own offspring is to him, as it were, a second self, which has, in virtue of its separation, acquired a distinct and individual existence. And children love their parents in that from them they draw their own being. And brothers love one another in that they draw their being from one and the same common source; and hence, inasmuch as they stand in an identical relation to their parents, they, *ipso facto*, stand in an identical relation to one another; and hence, too, have come (164.) the sayings | "blood is thicker than water," "scions of the same root," and others such. Brothers, in a word, combine an identity of nature with a distinct and individual existence. Moreover, community of nurture and equality of age are strong predisposing causes of friendship; for, as the proverb says, "two of an age agree,"— or, again, "fellowship is bred of custom"; and herein lies the similarity between the friendship of brothers by blood and the friendship of brothers in arms. The kinship which subsists between cousins, and between all other kinsfolk, each in their degree, is really to be referred to the kinship between brothers, inasmuch as it depends upon identity of descent from the same pair of ancestors. Indeed, relationship of every degree depends for its closeness or distance upon the closeness or distance of the first founder of the family. The friendship of children for their parents, as also the friendship of man for the Gods, is, as it were, a friendship for a something of exceeding goodness, and far higher than themselves. Our parents are, indeed, our greatest benefactors, for to them we owe, first of all, our very existence and our nurture, and, subsequently, our education. Such a friendship involves more genuine pleasure, and more actual benefit, than does a friendship between strangers, inasmuch as there exists between the friends a much greater community of life. And hence, too, the friendship of brothers by blood involves in it all the points that are essential to the friendship of brothers in arms,—this is true, as a general rule, in virtue of the similarity between brothers, but is all the more true if they be good men and upright,—for brothers by blood are more closely akin to one another than are brothers in arms, and have loved one another from their birth upwards; and there is always a greater community of character between those who are born of the same parents, and who have been reared together, and who have received the same education; and, lastly, the length of their intercourse gives to brothers the most frequent and surest test of their mutual friendship. In all other forms of friendship between kinsfolk the manifestations of affection will be found to vary according to the degree of relationship. Between husband and wife friendship would seem to subsist almost as a law of nature. For man is, of his own nature, more disposed to seek a helpmate, and so to form a pair, than to seek many associates, and so form a State; inasmuch as, in the first place, the family precedes the State, and is more necessary than it; and, in the second place, the desire to procreate their kind is more widely diffused among all living things than is the desire for civil society. And hence, in all other animals, the association between the male and female extends thus far only. Whereas man takes to himself a woman to dwell with him, not only that he may procreate his kind, but also that all the essential requisites of life may be fulfilled. For, from the very first, the functions of the one distinguish themselves from those of the other; so that the employment of the man is one, and the employment of the wife is another; and hence they are of mutual aid and assistance one to another, each adding to the common stock that which belongs to each. And hence, too, it is that this form of friendship seems to involve both mutual benefit and advantage, and mutual pleasure. Nay, more, it is possible for the friendship between husband and wife to be ultimately based upon virtue, if only they both be good and upright. For the husband has a virtue of one kind, and the wife has a virtue of another, and they can consequently feel a mutual | pleasure each in the virtue of the other. Children, moreover, seem to be a great bond of union; and this is the reason why those who are childless are more quickly estranged from one another. For children are to both their parents a common good, and all community of good constitutes a bond of union. Lastly, when we ask by what rule of life a man ought to be guided in his intercourse with his wife, or, more generally, a friend of any kind whatever in his intercourse with his friend, we are only asking what is in each case just. For justice between a man and his friend is one, and justice between a man and a stranger is another; and justice is one between a man and his brother in arms, and another between a man and his fellow-pupil.

13. There are, then, as was said at first, three forms of friendship, each of which may assume the shape either of a friendship of equality or of a friendship of inequality. For a good man can become a friend to one who is his equal in virtue, or can become a friend to his inferior. And of those whose friendship is based upon pleasure, the same rule holds good; as also it does of those whose friendship is based upon utility; inasmuch as the assistance which the one gives to the other can be either equal to that which he receives, or greater than it. And hence we can derive the rule that those whose friendship is one of equality ought each to render to the other an equal return of affection, and with it of all other friendly offices; and that, in the case of those whose friendship is one of inequality, the inferior of the two friends ought so to regulate the return of affection which he makes, that its amount shall be in inverse ratio to the superior claim which his friend has upon his gratitude. It is in that form of friendship which is based upon utility that, as might indeed be expected, disputes and counter-accusations, if not exclusively, at any rate most frequently, arise. For, where a friendship is based upon virtue, there the sole desire of the friends

is to do good to one another; inasmuch as it is in the doing of good that true virtue, and with it true friendship, shows itself. Where friends are engaged in a rivalry of this nature, there dispute and contention have no place. For no man can feel anger against one who loves him, and who confers benefits upon him; but, if he have any proper feeling, will do his best to repay him by similar kindnesses. And he, on the other hand, who has the greater claim upon the affection of the other, inasmuch as he meets with that which he desires, will be the last to dispute the gratitude of his friend. Indeed, the object of each is not his own private advantage, but only that which is really and truly good. Neither do difficulties ever arise in that form of friendship which is based upon pleasure; for in it each of the two obtains exactly that which he desires, inasmuch as what yields them pleasure is that each should pass his life in the society of the other. And, indeed, a man would only appear ridiculous were he to object that the society of his friend no longer yielded him pleasure. For he surely need not pass his time in his company unless he so choose. But, in that form of friendship which is based upon mutual interest, disputes are very apt to arise. For, inasmuch as the only object of a man in such a friendship is to put his friend to the best possible use, it follows that each of the two will always be claiming more than he actually receives, and will always think that he gets less than is his due; and, consequently, each will upbraid the other, on the ground that the claims which he advances are but

fair and reasonable, and that yet they remain unsatisfied. And hence, too, it follows that, in a friendship of this nature, it is impossible to confer benefits suffi-
(166.) ciently great to satisfy the claims of the | recipient. Now it would seem that, exactly as justice is of two kinds—the unwritten law, which is of nature, and the written law, which is of man; so, too, of that friendship which is based upon utility there are two forms, the friendship of confidence, and the friendship of covenant. Thus, then, disputes most commonly arise when men have contracted a relation, on the understanding that their friendship is to be of the first kind, and have then terminated it, as if their friendship were of the second. As for the friendship of covenant, it is always contracted upon certain definite stipulations. There is one form of it which is but little better than a huckster's friendship, and in which none but cash payments are recognised; and there is another form in which, although more liberal credit is allowed, yet the amount due for value received is none the less matter of definite agreement. In this latter case, the fact of the debt is evident, and the plea of not indebted is inadmissible, it being in the postponement of payment that the element of friendship shows itself. And hence it is that, in some States, the law ignores the claims of creditors, and rules that those who have entered into a contract upon terms of good faith must abide by the consequences of their own act. On the other hand, in a friendship of confidence, no express stipulations are involved; but a man makes a gift, or does some similar act of kindness, on the assumption

that it is a friend towards whom he is thus acting. And hence he who has acted thus, holds that he has a moral claim to receive a return of kindness, if not greater than that which he has conferred, yet at least equal to it, on the plea that the benefit which he conferred was not intended as a gift, but rather as a loan made without acknowledgement. And so, if he find that he has contracted the relation in question in a spirit of confidence, and that it is to be concluded in a spirit of strict covenant, he will dispute the conduct of his friend. The reason of this is that most men, if not all, combine an aspiration to seek what is noble with a practical purpose to further their own interests; and while, on the one hand, it is noble to do good without any expectation of a return, it is, on the other hand, to our own interest to receive benefits from others. But still, where it is in a man's power, he ought at once to make a return to the full value of any favour which he may have received; and ought, moreover, to do so freely, and without waiting until he is reminded of the claims upon him. For it is a mistake to run the risk of treating as a true friend one to whom we are under an obligation, when he may not wish to be considered as such. And so the best rule is to act as if we had been mistaken in the commencement, and had received a kindness from one at whose hands it ought not to have been accepted. For,—we ought to say,—he who conferred the benefit in question was not a true friend, nor did he thus act simply for the sake of doing good, and without any hope of reward. And so we ought to conclude the relation in exactly the same way as we should have concluded it had the receipt of the benefit involved definite stipulations as to its repayment. It is clear that he who knowingly receives a benefit conferred in expectation of a return would covenant to make repayment as soon as it should be in his power; and it is equally clear that, were it absolutely out of his power ever to make such a return, he who conferred the benefit would never have consented to confer it. And from this it follows that, where a man is able, he must repay to the full any favour which he may have received. And so one ought, in the beginning, to inquire carefully from whom it is that one is receiving a benefit, and what conditions are implied, in order that one may decide whether the benefit is to be accepted upon such conditions, or not. A further doubt arises whether the measure by which the return of a kindness is to be made is the actual benefit which has been thereby conferred upon the recipient, or rather the good intention of the benefactor. For those who have received a kindness are apt to depreciate it, and to say that what they have received from their benefactor was to him but a little matter, and might with ease have been procured from some one else. And he, on the other hand, who confers a kindness, asserts that (167.) what he gave was his | best, and that it could not have been procured elsewhere, and that it was given under circumstances of great danger, or in some similar crisis. The true solution would seem to be that, where the friendship is based upon utility, the measure to be adopted in the return of a kindness is the amount of the benefit which was actually conferred thereby upon the recipient. For it is in his request that the whole matter originates, and the donor only aids him on the understanding that he himself is to receive the full value of the benefit conferred. The amount, then, of the assistance which has been rendered is exactly equivalent to the actual benefit which has been thereby conferred upon the recipient; and he ought, therefore, to return to the donor as much as he has gained from him; or, perhaps, even more, for the ampler the return the more noble is the act. But, where friendship is based upon the virtue of the friends, there there are no disputes, and the measure to be adopted in the return of a kindness would seem to be the good intention of him by whom it was conferred; for it is in a man's intentions that his virtue, and, indeed, his character as a whole, most distinctively shows itself.

14. In friendships of inequality disputes also arise. For each of the two lays claim to more than he actually receives, and the result of this is that the friendship is broken off. For he whose virtue is superior to that of his friend holds that the larger share is his by right, because "to him that hath shall be given." And so, too, thinks he who confers upon his friend greater benefits than he receives from him. For, as the proverb goes, "he who stands idle must not be paid in full"; and, when the return which is made is not in proportion to the service which has been rendered, then friendship becomes not so much a friendship as a tax. Friendship, indeed, from this point of view, ought to resemble a pecuniary partnership, in which the largest dividend is due to him

who has contributed the largest share to the common
stock. He, on the other hand, who is inferior to his
friend, either in position or in virtue, takes up the
exactly opposite view, and asserts that it is the part
of a good friend to supply his friend's wants; else
what gain were it to be the friend of a good man, or
of a man in authority, if one were to derive no advantage from such a friendship? Now it would seem that
the claims which are advanced on each side are really
just, and that the result of the friendship ought to
be that to each of the two friends should be allotted
the larger share indeed, but still not the larger share
of the same thing. For he who is superior in position
ought to receive the larger share of honour, and he who
stands in need of assistance ought to receive the larger
share of material benefit. For honour is the legitimate reward of virtue and of offices of kindness, and
the assistance which is given to those who are in need
tends naturally to take the shape of material benefit.
And in governments, also, this same rule clearly holds
good; for he who contributes nothing to the common
stock is not held in any honour. That which is the
property of the public is given to him who promotes
the public welfare, and honour is the property of the
public. And it is, consequently, not allowed that a
man should, at one and the same time, receive both
(168.) pay from the public and also honour. | For men
will not submit to a position which is one of inferiority upon every point. And so, to him who
spends his substance upon the State, honour is given,
and, to him who seeks a salary for his services, money;

for, where the return that is made bears a due proportion to the services which have been rendered, there, as has been said before, strict equality is produced, and friendship is kept alive. And, in the intercourse of those whose friendship is one of inequality, a similar rule must be observed; and he who has received pecuniary assistance from his friend, or who is inferior to him in merit, must yield his friend an equivalent return of honour, making return according to his ability. For the return which is required of us in friendship is that which is in our power, rather than that which is due according to the strict letter of justice. Indeed, this latter is not in all cases possible; as, for example, in the case of the due return of honour to be made to the Gods, or to our parents. For no one could ever render them all that honour which is their just due; and, hence, he is held to do his duty towards them who reverences them to the best of his ability. Hence, too, it would seem that, while a son may not renounce his father, a father may renounce his son. The reason of this is, that he who is in debt is always under obligation to make payment. Now nothing that a son can do can ever counterbalance that which his father has done for him, and so a son must always remain in his father's debt. Now, he to whom a debt is due may, if he please, remit it; and, consequently, a father may abnegate his claim upon his son. But yet it would seem that no father would ever sever his connection with his son, unless provoked thereto by a wickedness in him beyond all bounds. For, even if we put out of question the natural affection which a parent has for his child, yet it is hardly in human nature to reject that assistance which a son can render. But, if the son be evil, he will either evade that assistance which it is his duty to render to his father, or will show but scant zeal in the performance of it. For most men desire to have benefits conferred upon themselves, but avoid conferring benefits upon others, as being a profitless task. Thus far, then, we may regard these questions as settled.

IX.

1. Now, in all those friendships in which the two friends have dissimilar objects in view, it is by observation of the rule of exchange according to proportionate values that, as has been said before, real equality is produced, and friendship is kept alive. This we can see in that great community which constitutes the body politic, and in which the cobbler gets, in return for his shoes, an equivalent of proportionate value, as also does the weaver in return for his own wares, and similarly all other craftsmen. Now, in transactions of this nature, a currency has been provided as the one common measure of all (169.) values, to which, as the standard of value, all things whatever are referred, and by which all things are measured. But, in a friendship which is based upon sentimental affection, the lover at times upbraids his friend, and complains that he loves him with a love exceedingly great, and yet receives no love in return; forgetting that he may, very possibly, have nothing in himself to inspire such love. And at times, again, the lover is upbraided by the object of his affection, and is told that in times past he promised everything, and that he now gives nothing. Disputes of this nature occur when the affection of the lover for his friend is based upon the pleasure which he derives

from him, and the affection which he receives in return is based upon the material advantages which the friendship affords; and when each, or either of the two, misses that which he desires. It was upon these objects that the friendship was based; and hence, when the friends no longer get that which is the real object of their affection, then the friendship is broken off. It was not one another that they loved; but, rather, each loved a something which the other had to offer him, and which, whatever it might be, being transitory, the friendship also was such. But that friendship which is founded upon the mutual esteem of the friends each for the character of the other, is entered into for its own sake, and independently of any results; and is, consequently, as has been said before, a permanent thing. Indeed, disputes never arise, unless the practical result of the friendship is other than the friends had expected and wished. For one might as well get nothing as not get that which one actually wants. This may be illustrated by the story of him who promised the harper that the better he sang the more he should receive; but who when, on the morrow, performance of the promise was demanded, said that he had paid for the pleasure of music with the pleasure of hope. This would have been well enough, had it been what each of the two desired; but, when the one desires amusement, and the other payment, and the one gets what he wants, while the other does not, then the transaction is no longer fairly conducted. For a man sets his mind upon that which he happens to want, and for the sake

of that gives his friend whatever it may be that he
gives him. A further question arises, as to whether
it is he who is the first to give who ought to fix the
value of the return that is to be made, or rather he
who is the first to receive. It would seem that the latter
is the true solution; for he who is the first to give,
puts the matter thereby into the hands of the other.
It is upon this rule, it is said, that Protagoras used to
act. For, whenever he taught a subject—no matter
what—he used to bid his pupil to fix the value of the
knowledge which he had acquired, and would be content
to receive so much, and no more. Others, again,
there are who are, in such cases, content to follow the
old rule—"the labourer is worthy of his hire."
Those, however, who exact payment in advance, and
who then can perform none of their promises, simply
because they have held out extravagant expectations,
—these deserve the disputes in which they find themselves
involved, inasmuch as they do not fulfil the
promises which they originally made. The Sophists,
however, are perhaps obliged to act thus, inasmuch
(170.) as, for what they know, no one would be willing to
make any payment. And, consequently, they may
fairly be said to bring upon themselves the disputes
in which they become involved, inasmuch as they do
not discharge those duties, the pay for which they
have taken in advance. Where, on the other hand,
there have been no definite stipulations as to the
terms upon which a service is to be rendered, then
those who, for the sake of the affection which they
bear their friends, are the first to give, are, as has

been said before, exempt from all possible dispute. And such is that friendship which is based upon virtue. As for the return which ought to be made to such friends, the measure by which it is to be estimated is the good intention of their gift. For so he who makes the return acts as a true friend, and as a good man. And it would seem that this same rule ought to be followed by those whose relation is that between the teacher of philosophy and his pupil. For wisdom cannot be bought for gold, nor can it be measured at any price. And hence, perhaps, the best which we have to offer must be held to be enough; as also is the rule of gratitude with reference to the Gods, and to our parents. Where, however, we are not concerned with a free gift, but rather with a gift made upon certain definite stipulations, then the best rule would seem to be that that return should be made, upon which both agree as fair and equitable; and, where this cannot be done, it would seem to be only just that he who was the first to receive should fix the value of the return which is to be made,— even were it not the case that no other mode of settlement is possible. If this rule be followed, then will he who was the first to give, receive from the other, as the fair recompense of his services, either that which was, to that other, the value of the benefit which he received, or else, as the case may be, the price which he would have put upon the pleasure. Such is clearly the general practice of trade; and in some countries, indeed, there is a law to the effect that no suit can be instituted with reference to any voluntary transaction, on the ground that, where a man has placed confidence in another, the transaction ought to be concluded in the same spirit as that in which it was commenced. For the law holds that, where a man has put a matter into the hands of another, it is then only just that he should abide by the decision of him in whom he has thus voluntarily placed confidence. And it is, indeed, to be noticed that the majority of men have one price for that which they possess, and another for that which they wish to get. For every one puts a high value upon that which is his own, and upon that which he has to give to others. The value, however, of the return which is to be made is, in each case, fixed by the judgment of the receiver. Not but that the receiver should be guided in his estimate, not so much by the value to him of the thing in question, now that he actually possesses it, as by the value which he was disposed to set upon it before it became his own.

2. There are, moreover, other questions to be solved, such as are, for example, the following. Ought a man to place his father first in everything, and to obey him upon every point; or ought he rather, when he is sick, to take the advice of his physician; and to record his vote for the office of commander-in-chief in favour of the most experienced officer? And, to take a similar case, ought we to render our services to our friend rather than to a good man; and ought we to return (171.) a kindness to our | benefactor, rather than to make a gift to our brother in arms: it being, of course, assumed in each case that only one of the two alternatives is

possible? May we not say that it is no easy matter to
lay down any one abstract rule, which shall apply, with
equal accuracy, to all such cases alike, inasmuch as they
differ from one another in every variety of circumstance;
—some of them being important, and others trifling;
some, cases where there is the very strongest moral
claim, others, cases of absolute necessity? Thus much,
at any rate, is self-evident, that one must not give
everything that one has to the same person. And
from this it follows, that one ought, as a general rule,
rather to return a benefit which one has actually received, than to confer a gratuitous favour upon a
brother in arms; exactly as one ought rather to repay
a loan to a creditor, than to spend the same sum upon
a present to a friend. And yet it would seem as if
this rule did not always hold good. Ought, for example, a man who has been ransomed from banditti to
pay the ransom of him by whom his own ransom was
formerly paid—and that, too, quite independently of
the question who or what he may be; or to restore to him
the sum which he then paid—supposing him not to be
himself in the hands of banditti, but to simply demand
repayment of the sum then advanced: or ought he rather
to ransom his father, than to do either of these things?
The answer is clear, inasmuch as it is a man's duty to
pay his father's ransom rather even than his own. As
then has been said, it is a paramount rule that a debt
should be repaid. But, if in any given case it be distinctly a more noble thing to make a gift, or if the
necessity for so doing be more urgent, then we must
allow ourselves to deviate from the general rule. At

times, indeed, to repay a previous kindness is not even just; as when, for example, a man has had the foresight to do a good turn to another upon whose integrity he knows that he may depend, and that other has in return to do some good office to a man whom he believes to be a rogue. Nor does it follow that it is always our duty to lend money to those who formerly lent money to us. A man may, for example, have formerly made a loan to another in whose integrity he had confidence, and from whom he consequently expected repayment; but may himself be such a rogue that the other could have no expectation of repayment were he to advance him money in return. Suppose that the case is really such as we have described, then the claims of the two parties cannot be compared. Or suppose that the case be not really one of this kind, but that a man believe it to be such; —he would, even then, do nothing strange in refusing the loan. Indeed, as has been often said before, all general statements concerning the feelings and the actions of men are of necessity subject to the same variation as is the object matter with which they are concerned. It is, however, a self-evident rule that one must not make one and the same return to all those alike who have a claim upon us. And it is also clear that to give to one's father everything which one has to offer, is as uncalled for a thing as it is to sacrifice to Zeus every kind of beast. Now, the return which suits our parents is one, and that which suits our brothers is another; and that which suits our brothers in arms is one, and that which suits our benefactors is another. And one ought, consequently, to render to each man that especial return which is appropriate to him, and suitable to his position. And to these rules the practice of the world would seem to conform. For, when men give a wedding feast, they invite their kinsfolk, to whom equally with themselves belongs the family as a whole, and, consequently, the due performance of all those acts which are especially involved in its existence. And it is for the same reason that men hold it to be the duty of kinsfolk, rather than of others, to make a point (172.) of attending at | a funeral. And it would seem that it is a man's duty to render material assistance to his parents before any one else, looking upon it as a debt which he owes them, and regarding it as more noble to render such assistance to the authors of his existence than to supply his own necessities. And one ought also to render honour to one's parents, exactly as one renders honour to the Gods,—but yet not every kind of honour. For the honour which a man ought to pay to his father is one, and the honour which he ought to pay to his mother is another. Nor ought a man to render to his father that honour which he renders to a philosopher, or to a general, but rather that especial honour which is a father's due; exactly as he ought also to render to his mother that honour which befits her. And, similarly, a man ought to render to everyone who is older than himself that honour which is appropriate to his age, rising up in his presence, and placing him in the highest seat, and showing him similar acts of courtesy. And towards his brothers in arms, and his brothers by blood, he ought to bear himself with openness of speech, and to place all that he possesses at their disposal. And, as regards his kinsfolk, and the members of his clan, and his fellow-citizens, and indeed all those into contact with whom he is thrown, he ought always to endeavour to render to each man that which is not only due to him, but also appropriate to his position, and to carefully estimate and distinguish between the claims which each respectively may have on the ground of relationship, or of merit, or of intimacy. To distinguish between the several claims of those who all stand in the same kind of relation to ourselves is, of course, an easy matter. But, to distinguish between the claims of those, the several relations of whom to ourselves are entirely distinct, and consequently incapable of comparison, is a more difficult task. We ought not, however, on that account, to evade the difficulty, but rather to do the best that is in our power to draw the distinctions in question with all possible accuracy.

3. Another question to be solved is, whether a man ought, or whether he ought not, to break off his friendship with those whose character is no longer such as it was originally. But, may not one answer that, when the friendship was originally based upon utility, or upon pleasure, and the friends no longer fulfil the requisite conditions, then he who breaks off the friendship does nothing strange? For the motive of the friendship was a definite something, the discontinuance of which is a reasonable ground for the cessation of affection. Not but that a man has fair ground for complaint, when another, whose feel-

ings towards himself were grounded simply upon interest, or, it may be, upon pleasure, has pretended to love him for his own sake, and from admiration for his character. For, as indeed we said originally, one of the most frequent causes of disputes between friends is a mutual misconception as to the true nature of their friendship. When, then, a man has been deceived as to the nature of the friendship which another feels for him, and supposes that friendship to be based upon a proper esteem, although his friend has done nothing to give him a reasonable ground for such a misconception, he then has no one to blame but himself. But, when it is the simulation of his pretended friend that has led to the misconception, he then has a just cause for complaint, as much as, if not even more than, he would have had if an attempt had been made to pass counterfeit coin upon him, inasmuch as the wrong which has been done him affects higher and no-
(173.) bler interests. But suppose that a man has formed a friendship for another on the ground of his merits, and that then his friend becomes depraved, and makes no attempt to conceal the alteration in his character. Ought he, in such a case, any longer to feel affection for him? May not one answer, that it is simply impossible for him to do so, inasmuch as the grounds of affection are not indiscriminate—true affection being always based upon a proper esteem? Indeed, not only is it impossible to feel an affection for a bad man, but one ought not even to try to do so. For a man ought neither to make evil his good, nor to liken himself to that which is evil. And, as we have said before, true friendship can only be

felt by like for like. Ought he then, under such circumstances, to break off the friendship immediately? Surely he ought not to do so in all cases alike, but only when his friend has become incurably depraved. Where any hope of amendment still remains, there he ought to do his best to restore his friend to his right mind; and that, too, with even more zeal than that with which he would strive to repair his fortunes— inasmuch as the task is a more noble one, and falls more distinctly within the province of friendship. But, where hope no longer is, then, if he break off the friendship, he does nothing strange. It was not this man that he once loved, but another; and, since he cannot bring him back to his former self, he does well to hold himself aloof. Or, suppose, again, that the one friend remains such as he always was, but that the other becomes so far better a man that the merits of the two can no longer be compared—ought the latter, in such a case, still to treat the former as his friend, or does it become impossible for him to do so? The true answer will be most evident, if we assume that the difference between the friends has come to be very great—as is often the case in friendships that have been contracted in childhood. Suppose, for instance, that the one of the two continues to have only a child's intelligence, while the other so grows in wisdom, and in stature, as to become a perfect man; how can they, in such a case, any longer continue friends, when they no longer take pleasure in the same pursuits, and no longer mutually rejoice and grieve each with the other? In such a case they can no longer feel sympathy for one another. And, without sympathy, it is no longer possible for them to be friends, inasmuch as it is no longer possible for them to pass their lives together. And concerning all this we have already spoken. Ought then a man, in cases of this sort, to behave to his former friend exactly as he would behave to him had they never been friends in times past? Or ought he not rather to bear old acquaintance in mind, and, for the same reason as that for which men hold it right to do a kindness to a friend rather than to a stranger, to let bygone friendship be his excuse for certain small kindnesses to those whom he once loved; unless, indeed, the rupture has been due to a wickedness on their part more than ordinary?

4. Now, the acts by which we manifest our affection for our friends, and by which the nature of our friendship is determined, would seem to originate in the acts by which we manifest our feelings towards ourselves. For the ordinary conception of a friend is that he should be one who wishes his friend that which is good, or that which he holds to be such, for his friend's own sake, and who, as far as he can, carries his wishes into effect; or else that he should be one whose wish it is that his friend should, for his own sake alone, exist and live. It is thus that mothers (147.) feel towards their | children, and true friends, who happen to have fallen out, towards one another. Another conception of friendship is, that friends are those who pass their time together, and who have one common purpose; or that they are those who have

each the same sorrows and the same joys with one another; and this form of sympathy is most especially noticeable in mothers. Such, then, are the ordinarily current definitions of friendship. Now, the good man has each and all of these feelings towards himself. Other men feel thus towards themselves, only in so far as they are convinced of their own goodness. For it would seem, indeed, that, as has been said before, the measure, or standard of reference, in each case, is the highest attainable excellence, or, in other words, the judgment of the good man, to whom such excellence belongs. Now the good man feels thus, inasmuch as he is at unity with himself, and has in his whole soul but one desire. And hence he wishes himself that which is good, or, in other words, that which he conceives to be such, and does his best to carry his wishes into effect,—for the good man will always do his best to realise that which is good. And all this he does for his own sake; inasmuch as he does it for the sake of his reason; and it is in a man's reason that his existence and personality would seem to be centred. And hence he wishes for himself life and safe keeping, and most especially wishes so for that part of himself in which his reason lies: for, to the good and perfect man, existence is of itself a good thing. Thus, then, it is to be observed that each man wishes for himself that which is good from his own point of view. When he has become other than he once was, then no man wishes his new self to have every conceivable kind of good thing,—inasmuch as good cannot be conceived as such, unless it be with reference to that being for whom it is good. The supreme good, for instance, is perpetually enjoyed by God; but this is only because his essence ever remains divine,—let Divinity consist in what it may. And it must also be remembered, that a man's personality is chiefly, if not entirely, centred in his reason. Thus, then, the good man will wish to hold continuous communion with himself, inasmuch as such communion cannot but be pleasant to him. For to him the memories of the past are happy, and the hopes of the future are bright; and memories and hopes of this kind are full of pleasure. He has, moreover, abundant store of thoughts on which to feast his reason; and it is with his own pains, and with his own pleasures, that he most of all feels sympathy. For it is one and the same thing that always gives him pain, and similarly one and the same thing that always gives him pleasure; and not first one thing and then another; for in him, as the saying is, there is no variableness. Now, in that the good man has each and all of these feelings towards himself, and in that he feels towards his friend as he feels towards himself (for a friend is a second self), it follows that true friendship would seem to consist in some one or other of these feelings, and that those alone would seem to be truly friends who entertain these feelings towards one another. As to whether a man can feel a friendship for himself, or whether he can not, it is a question that may for the present be dismissed. Provisionally we may answer that it would seem to be possible, in so far as one or more (175.) of the above-mentioned conditions are satisfied—|and also because, when friendship reaches its extreme limit, it resembles that affection which a man feels for himself. And it would seem that, in the case of most men, these conditions are fulfilled, even although they may be bad men, and wicked. It would appear, however, that they are fulfilled only in so far as men are satisfied with themselves, and believe themselves to be good. For, when a man is absolutely bad, and when his every act is a sin, then he neither has, nor even seems to have, any of these feelings towards himself. One might, indeed, almost say that he cannot possibly have them, if he be bad at all. For the bad are at variance with themselves, so that their desires lead them one way and their better wishes another, as we can see in the case of the incontinent. For, at times, instead of that which they believe to be good, they choose that which is pleasant, although they know it to be bad; and at times, again, cowardice and sloth persuade them to keep aloof even from that which they acknowledge to be the best possible course; and at times, again, when their wickedness has led them into many and great sins, life becomes to them a hateful and a sore burden, and they do away with themselves from off the face of the earth. Thus, then, the wicked seek for companions with whom to pass their days, and shun companionship with themselves; for their memories are many and grievous, and, where hope should be, there fear dwells. And all this they feel when they are alone, but forget when they are with others. And, since they have in them nothing that calls for love, they can feel no affection towards themselves. And, hence, not even in their own joys and sorrows can they have any sympathy with themselves. For their soul is like a city which is at variance with itself, and the one part of it, by reason of their sins, is grieved that it has to abstain from certain things, while the other part is pleased thereat; and the one drags them this way, and the other drags them that, like beasts when they rend a carcase. Since, then, it is impossible that a man should at the same time feel both pain and pleasure in the same thing, but after a little while a man is pained to think that he should have felt such a pleasure, and believes that, could the past be recalled, he would not again wish to take pleasure in such things,— whence it is that the wicked are ever full of repentance,—then from all this it clearly follows that the bad man cannot feel towards himself as towards a friend, since he has nothing in him worthy of affection. And, inasmuch as to be in such a state as this is exceedingly wretched, we must fly from vice with all our strength, and must strive to our utmost to be good; for so shall we feel towards ourselves as towards a friend, and shall become friends to other men.

5. Kindly feeling bears a certain resemblance to friendship, with which, however, it is not on that account (176.) identical. | For kindly feeling is possible towards those with whom we are unacquainted, nor is it necessary that it should be known to its object; but of friendship this is not true. Upon this, indeed, we have remarked before. Neither is kindly feeling to be identified with affection, inasmuch as it is devoid

of that passionate intensity of emotion which is the accompaniment of affection. Affection, moreover, implies length of acquaintance, whereas kindly feeling can arise in a moment. This we can see in the case of competitors at the public games, where a spectator may conceive a kindly feeling towards a particular candidate, and may sympathise with him in his wish for victory, and yet need not on that account feel in any way disposed to render him actual aid in his efforts. For, as we have said before, kindly feeling can arise in a moment, and involves but a superficial liking. It would seem, indeed, as if kindly feeling constituted the commencement of friendship, exactly as it is the pleasure of the eye that is the commencement of love. For no man loves another, unless he has first taken pleasure in the sight of his beauty. But yet this same pleasure does not in itself constitute love, unless the lover also yearn for the loved one in his absence, and long for his return. And, similarly, it is impossible for friendship to exist without kindly feeling, but yet mere kindly feeling does not, on that account, constitute friendship. For all that is essential to kindly feeling is that a man should wish another well; and it is not at all necessary that he should aid him in his efforts, or put himself to any trouble in his behalf. And hence, perhaps, we may be allowed to use a metaphor, and to say of kindly feeling that it is a friendship which has not as yet borne fruit, but which will none the less blossom into full friendship, if it have sufficient time allowed it in which to reach the stage of familiarity. But yet the friendship into which kindly feeling developes, is neither that form of friendship which is based upon utility, nor yet that form of friendship which is based upon pleasure. Indeed, neither utility, nor yet pleasure, ever gives rise to kindly feeling. For, when a man has received a benefit, he makes a return for it in the shape of kindly feeling, and the gratitude which he thus shows is only just. And he, on the other hand, who wishes prosperity to another, only because he hopes ultimately to derive assistance from him, would not seem on that account to have any kindly feeling towards him, but rather, if anything, to have a kindly feeling towards himself; exactly as a man is not held to be a friend to another, if he pays court to him only for the sake of some use to which he means to put him. To conclude, it would seem as if kindly feeling really originated in some kind of virtue or of goodness, and that its commencement is when a man approves himself to another as being noble, or as being brave, or as having some similar claim upon his esteem; exactly as we said was sometimes the case with competitors at the public games.

6. Unanimity, too, clearly has in it an element of friendship. And hence it must not be confounded with mere identity of opinion. For identity of opinion can exist among those who are in absolute ignorance of one another. Neither must the term "unanimity" be applied to those who consciously hold the same view upon any subject whatever; as, for example, to those whose views are identical upon questions of (177.) astronomy. For unanimity | upon matters of this kind has in it no element of friendship. But we say

of a State that it acts with unanimity, when the citizens have but one opinion as to the public weal, and have all but one purpose, and carry out the decrees of the Deliberative as one man. Unanimity, in a word, is concerned, not with matters of speculation, but with matters of action,—and yet not with all even of these, but with such alone as involve great interests, and which equally concern, in the case of individuals, two persons at the least, and, in the case of States, the whole body of the citizens. We speak, for instance, of unanimity in a State, when the citizens are, all to a man, agreed that office should be elective, or that an alliance should be entered into with Lacedæmon, or when they are all agreed that Pittacus should for a period act as dictator, Pittacus himself consenting thereunto. But when, as in the Phœnician Women, each wishes to have the kingdom for himself, then, instead of unanimity, we have faction. For we do not speak of unanimity in those cases where each person has the same view, whatever that view may be; but only where each has the same view, and desires to see it carried out in the same way; as when, for example, both the commons and the upper classes are of opinion that office should be held by those of most ability: for it is under circumstances such as these alone that every man gets that which he desires. Thus then unanimity would appear to be a species of political or public friendship,—which name indeed is often given to it,—for it is concerned with matters which are of public interest, and which have a material bearing upon life. Such unanimity is always to be observed among good men as a class. For good men are of one mind with themselves, and with one another. And so we may say of them that they all, as the proverb goes, "ride at the same moorings," inasmuch as their counsels remain fixed, and do not, like the Euripus, ebb and flow this way and that. For their wish is for what is just, and for what is also at the same time expedient; and to this end they, in common, one and all direct their desires. But among the bad unanimity is as impossible as is friendship, unless it be for but a short time, or in but a small matter. For in all matters where their own interests are concerned they grasp at unfair gain, and in all labour and public duty they make default. Each one of them has his own ends in view, to further which he thwarts his neighbour, and plays the spy upon him. And thus the interests of the State are ruined for want of due attention, and the result is a condition of perpetual party faction, in which, while no man really desires himself to act with justice, yet each forces his neighbour to its observance.

7. It would seem that, as a rule, the benefactor loves him upon whom he has conferred the benefit, more than he who has received a kindness loves him at whose hands he has received it; and this at first appears so strange, that some reasonable explanation of it is required. The generally accepted account is that he upon whom a benefit has been conferred is, *ipso facto*, a debtor, and that the benefactor is his creditor; and that thus,—exactly as in the case of a loan, the debtor (178.) wishes that | his creditor were out of the way, while

the lender will even go so far as to give considerable
attention to the welfare of his debtor,—so too here,
those who have conferred a benefit have an interest in
the existence of its recipient, in that they expect to
reap some benefit in return, whereas the recipient is by
no means anxious to render an equivalent for the kindness which he has received. Now, Epicharmus would
probably say that this explanation takes too low a
view of human nature. But yet it agrees with the
practice of mankind,—the majority of whom have but
short memories, and love to receive rather than to confer a benefit. It would seem, however, that the true
explanation is to be found in one of the most primary
laws of the physical universe, and that there is in
reality no analogy between a benefactor and a creditor. For the creditor feels no affection towards his
debtor, but merely desires his preservation, in order
that payment may be made; whereas those who have
conferred a benefit upon another feel an affection and
love for the recipient of their kindness, and that too
even when he is in no way either useful to them
in the present, or likely ever to be so in the future.
And it would seem that artists feel exactly the same
sort of affection towards their own works. For every
man loves his own work, much more deeply than his
work would ever love him, could it become endowed
with life. And this rule holds perhaps the most true
in the case of poets. For the affection of poets for
their own verses goes to the very greatest lengths,
and they love them exactly as a father loves his child.
Now it would seem that it is upon this analogy that

the affection of benefactors can be best explained, inasmuch as the recipient of a kindness stands in the same relation to the benefactor, as does his own work to an artist. And so the benefactor loves his work more than the work loves its maker. The reason of this is, that their own existence is a thing which all beings alike hold as choice-worthy, and which they, consequently, love; and existence, in its highest sense, consists in the manifestation of our inner self in some external act; as, for example, in the process of life, or in moral action. Now a man's work may in a certain sense be said to be* his own inner self embodied in an external form. And hence it is that a man loves his own work, inasmuch as he holds his own existence dear. And all this is only the result of a primary law of nature. For our work manifests in an actual form that which in our inner self exists only in potentiality. It is also to be observed that, for the benefactor, his act is a noble thing, and that he consequently takes delight in him in whom it is manifested; whereas, for the recipient, there is in the benefactor nothing that is noble, or that reflects honour upon himself, but only a something useful,—and the useful is less pleasant to us than is the noble, and calls forth less affection. Now, of the present, it is the actual and real fact which yields us pleasure, of the future the expectation, and of the past the memory; but, of all things, that is the most pleasant, and, consequently, most of all the object of our affection, which has the most real and actual existence. Now, for the benefactor, his work re-

---

* Read *iori rws*, and consult the note of Michelet.

mains in continual existence, inasmuch as that which is noble, and which reflects honour upon us, is by its very nature durable and lasting; whereas, for the recipient of a kindness, the utility thereof is a perishable thing, and a fleeting. Moreover, the memory of that which reflects honour on us yields us pleasure; while the memory of that which has been useful to us yields us a far less pleasure, if, indeed, it may be said to yield any pleasure at all,—the rule which holds good of the pleasures of memory being exactly the reverse of that which holds good of the pleasures of hope. Moreover, to feel an affection for another involves activity, and, consequently, gives more pleasure than it does to be the object of such an affection; for to be loved involves passivity. And it is he to whom, in any given case, the larger share of a mutual action falls, who will feel the most affection for the other, and who will manifest his affection in the greatest number of ways. Lastly, it may be observed to be a universal rule among men, that they cherish with the greatest affection that which they have acquired with the greatest labour. Those, for instance, who have made their fortune by their own exertions, take far more pleasure in it than do those who have acquired it by inheritance. And it would seem that to receive a kindness involves no labour, whereas to confer a kindness is a matter of trouble. Hence, too, it is that the mother loves her child more than does the father; for to her, more than to him, belongs the labour of its birth, and the sense of right in that which she knows to be her own. And of benefactors, equally with mothers, it would seem that these two points are true.

8. Another problem that suggests itself is whether one ought to give the greatest share of love to one's self, or rather to others. For men censure those who love themselves the most, and, by way of reproach, call them selfish; and the popular conception of a bad man is that in all his actions he has his own interests in view, and that the more wicked he is the more will this be true of him. And so against the bad man the charge is brought that he never acts without an eye to his own welfare. Whereas the good man is guided in all his actions by a sense of honour, and the better man he is the more will this be true of him; and in everything that he does he looks to the interest of his friend, and disregards himself. But with this point of view the facts of life are at variance—as might, indeed, have been expected. For, as the common saying goes, a man ought to give his best love to his best friend; and a man's best friend is he who wishes him well for his own sake, without caring whether others are aware of his affection. But this holds most true of the feelings of a man towards himself; as is, indeed, also, the case with all the other leading characteristics of friendship. For, as has been said before, it is from the attitude of a man towards himself that his attitude towards others is derived. And with this point of view all the popular proverbs agree; such as are, for instance, "one soul in two bodies," "true friends have all things in common," "equality makes friendship," "the knee is nearer than the shin,"—all of which hold most true of the feelings of a man towards himself. For, since the best friend a man

(180.) has is himself,] it follows that he ought to love himself the most. And so it is but reasonable that the problem should suggest itself, which of these two points of view we ought to follow; since each has something to recommend it. And perhaps the best method in such a case is to distinguish between the various meanings of which each statement is susceptible, and so to determine how far it is that each is true, and in what sense. If, then, these two conflicting conceptions of self-love be analysed, the problem will most probably find a solution. Now, those who use the term "selfish" by way of reproach, understand a man to be a lover of himself when he allots to himself the larger share of wealth, or of reputation in the eyes of men, or of bodily pleasure. For it is these things which the majority of men desire, and about which they busy themselves with zeal, as being the greatest of all goods; and hence it is that these things are objects of strife and of contention. Now, those who grasp at the larger share of such goods as these, do so to gratify their lust, and, indeed, their passions as a whole; or, in a word, the irrational part of their soul. Such is the disposition of the majority of mankind, and hence has arisen the bad connotation of the term "self-love,"—inasmuch as the self-love of most men is of this lower form. It is with justice, then, that those are held in bad repute who love themselves after this wise. And it is evident that the term "self-love" must, in its usual acceptation, be understood to apply to those who allot to themselves the larger share of such goods as these. For, where a

man is always busying himself with zeal that his
just acts may outnumber those of any other man,
or where he busies himself thus about temperance, or,
indeed, about any other form of virtue; and where
his conduct, as a whole, is always such as to gain
honour for himself; then no one calls him selfish, or
thinks of blaming him. And yet it would seem that
such a man ought, more than any other, to be said to
show self-love. He certainly allots to himself the
noblest of all goods, and the best; and he gratifies
that part in himself to which supremacy rightfully
belongs, and obeys it in every matter. Now, exactly
as, in the case of a State, we understand by the term
" the State " that part in it to which supremacy belongs; so, too, of every other organised whole the
same rule holds good, and, among others, of the constitution of man. And hence it follows that he, most
of all men, ought to be said to love himself, who
cherishes that part in himself which is supreme, and
in all matters seeks to gratify it. The same thing is
shown by the derivation of the terms " self-restraint "
and " incontinence," which etymologically signify,
the one that reason is supreme in the man, the other
that it is not; and which, consequently, imply that it
is his reason that really constitutes each man's self.
And it is also shown by the fact, that it is when their
acts are reasonable that men most especially hold that
they are their own acts, and that they have been done
voluntarily. It is, then, clear that it is the reason
which, if not entirely, at any rate most especially, constitutes each man's self; and that it is this which the

good man most especially cherishes. And hence it is the good man who, most of all, may be said to love himself; although his self-love is of entirely another kind from that self-love which brings reproach upon (181.) the selfish man, and although he differs from the selfish man as widely as the life of reason differs from the life of passion, and the desire for that which is noble differs from the desire for that by which a man hopes to serve his own private ends. Now, those who most distinguish themselves from others by the zeal with which they pursue noble acts—these all men hold as worthy of esteem and of praise. And, indeed, were men, one and all, to vie with one another in the pursuit of honour, and to strive each to do the noblest acts, then, not only would all the public wants of mankind be fulfilled, but each man would enjoy, as his own especial possession, the greatest of all possible goods,—if, indeed, it be virtue that is such. And hence it follows that the good man ought to be a lover of himself, inasmuch as, if his acts be noble, he will reap good fruit for himself, and will confer great benefit upon others. But, that the bad man should love himself is not well; for he will but injure himself, and with him his neighbours, by following his evil desires. And thus, for the bad man, that which he ought to do is at variance with that which he really does; whereas, for the good man, that which he ought to do is identical with that which he does. For, wherever reason exists, there it chooses that which is best for itself; and the good man, in all things that he does, obeys his reason. It is, moreover, true of

the good man that, for the sake of his friends, and for
the sake of his country, he will do many things; and
that he is ready, if need be, even to die in their behalf.
Money, and honour, and all such other goods as are
objects of strife among mankind, he will regard as
naught, that he may gain for himself the prize of
honour. For he would sooner enjoy an intense pleasure for a moment, than a trifling pleasure for an age;
and he would sooner lead a noble life for a year, than
drag out many ages of insignificant existence; and
his wish will be to do some one act which is great and
noble, rather than many which are trivial and unimportant. And it would seem that, when a man dies
for others, his lot is then such as this. Certain, at
least, it is that he chooses for himself an honour exceedingly great. Such a man will think nothing of
giving up his wealth, that his friends may receive a
larger share; for his friends thereby gain wealth,
while he for himself gains honour; and thus he really
allots to himself the greater good. And, with regard
to honour in the eyes of men, and office in the State,
his conduct will be guided by the same rule; and he
will gladly yield all such distinctions to his friend,
that he may gain for himself that true honour which
alone is worthy of praise. And, hence, with good
reason it is that he is held to be a good man, and an
upright, since he chooses honour rather than all things
else. Nay, more, it is conceivable that at times he
should even yield to his friend an opportunity of
noble action, and that it should reflect greater honour
upon him that the noble act of his friend should be

thus due to his own generosity, than that he should have
(182.) done such an act himself. | Thus, then, it is clear that,
in all those matters wherein praise is really due, the
good man allots to himself the larger share of honour.
And in this sense it is well, as we have said, that a
man should love himself; but that a man should love
himself as do the many, is not well.

9. A further question arises, as to whether the happy
man will want friends, or not. For, it is said, those
stand in no need of friends whose lot is blessed and
all-sufficient, inasmuch as they already enjoy every
possible good. Indeed, the very conception of all-sufficiency is that it is that state in which a man stands
in need of nothing which he has not already got;
whereas a friend is a second self, who provides for us
that which is out of our own power: as, indeed, is to
be understood by the saying—

When Heaven gives happiness, what need of friends?

But yet it seems inconsistent to assign to the happy
man every possible good, and, at the same time, to
deny him the possession of friends, who are held of all
purely external goods to be the greatest. If, moreover, friendship consists rather in the conferring of
kindnesses than in the receiving of them; and if to do
good to others is the characteristic of virtue, and,
consequently, of the good man; and if, too, it be nobler
to do good to our friends than to do good to strangers;
then it will follow that the good man will stand in
need of friends to receive benefits at his hands. And
hence arises the further question, whether it is in

prosperity, or in adversity, that friends are most necessary. For, on the one hand, he who is in misfortune will need friends to aid and assist him; and, on the other, he who is in prosperity will need friends upon whom to confer kindnesses. It would, moreover, seem to be strangely inconsistent to conceive the happy man as leading a life of isolation. No man would choose to be assured in the possession of all possible good at the price of living a solitary life. For man is so constituted by nature as to desire to be a member of a State, and to live in the society of his fellow men. And of the happy man, equally with all others, this holds true; inasmuch as all those goods are his that are part of the scheme of nature. And it is, moreover, clear that it is better for a man to pass his time in the company of friends, and of good men, than in the company of strangers, and of men of no reputation; and that, consequently, the happy man will stand in need of friends. What, then, is the meaning of the statement with the consideration of which we commenced, and in what sense is it true? May we not say that the popular conception of a friend is that he is one who is useful to us; and that the happy man will stand in no need of friends of this sort, inasmuch as he already enjoys all possible goods? And, similarly, he will stand in but little need—if, indeed, in (184.) any—of friends to yield him pleasure. For his | life has in itself a pleasure of its own, and so stands in no need of any alien pleasure from without. And it is because the happy man stands in no need of such friends as these, that it has been held that he does not stand in need of friends at all. But yet it would seem as if the truth herein were something more than overstated. For, as we said in the beginning, all happiness consists in activity. And it is clear that an activity is not to be compared to a piece of property, which its owner possesses once and for all; but that it rather is, as it were, in perpetual play, and recommences its existence at each moment of its continuance. Now, if happiness consists in life, or, in other words, in activity; and if the activities of the good man are not only good in themselves, but also have, as we said in the beginning, a pleasure of their own; and if, moreover, that which is our own, or akin to us, yields us pleasure; and, lastly, if we can contemplate our neighbours better than we can ourselves, and their actions better than we can our own:—then it cannot but be that, for those who are good, the actions of the good, who are their friends, will have a pleasure to yield; inasmuch as in them the two conditions of true and natural pleasure are fulfilled, in that they are not only good in themselves, but also akin to him who contemplates them. And, from all this, it follows that the happy man will stand in need of such friends as these, inasmuch as he will love to contemplate actions which are good in themselves, and akin to his own. And the actions of the good man, who is his friend, will be such. Moreover, men are agreed that the life of the happy man ought to be a pleasant life. Now, for him who leads a life of isolation, life itself is a hard task. For it is no easy matter for a man entirely by himself to maintain a continuous activity; but it becomes more easy, when he is in company with others, and has others than himself whom his activities affect. And thus the activities of the good man, which have, as has been said, a pleasure of their own, become also more continuous. And for perfect happiness such continuity is essential. A pleasure of their own they have, inasmuch as the good man, being good, cannot but take pleasure in acts of virtue, and look with indignation upon acts of vice; exactly as a musician takes pleasure in good music, and is annoyed by bad. It is true, moreover, as Theognis says, that the society of the good is a school in which one cannot but practise virtue. Lastly, if the question be considered from the point of view afforded by the primary laws of nature, it would seem to be a natural ordinance that, for the good man, a good friend should be a choiceworthy thing. For that which has its place in the scheme of nature as a good, is also, as we have elsewhere said, a good thing to the good man, and, moreover, a thing pleasant in itself. Now, in determining the definition of life, we adopt as its criterion, in animals the faculty of perception, and in man the faculties of perception and of thought, always referring to the activity as the evidence of the existence of the faculty. It is, indeed, in the activity that all that is distinctively important in the faculty consists; and hence it would seem that it is the activities of perception and of thought which really constitute the life of man. Now, life is a thing that is in itself, and independently of all results, both good and pleasant; | for in it is to be found that definiteness and harmony which has been held to be the essence of all good. But that which has its place in the scheme of nature as a good, will be a good also to the good man. And this would, perhaps, seem to be the reason why life is a thing which seems sweet to all. But, still, this must not be held to apply to a life which is marred by vice, or by misery, or by pain; for, in such a life, as indeed in all the elements of which it is composed, such traces of harmony as are to be found are dim and broken. As regards pain more especially, we shall hereafter have occasion to set forth this truth more clearly. Thus, then, life is in itself, and independently of all results, both good and pleasant. Of this there is, indeed, sufficient evidence in the fact, that life is, for all men, an object of desire, and most especially so for those who are good and happy; for, for such, their life, in its moral aspect, is most choiceworthy, and their existence is in itself most intrinsically blessed. Now, he who sees is conscious that he sees, and he who hears that he hears, and he who walks that he walks; and, similarly, in the case of all our other faculties, we have in us a something that is conscious of our activities: and we, consequently, perceive that we perceive, and think that we think. And, to be conscious of our own perception, or of our own thought, is, really, to be conscious of our own existence; for it is the activities of perception and of thought which really constitute our existence. But the consciousness of life is a thing that is pleasant in itself; for life is a thing that is by nature good, and to be conscious that we possess in ourselves that which is good, is a pleasant thing. Thus, then, life is a thing that is choiceworthy in itself; and it is such to the good man more than to any other, because, for the good man, existence is a good thing, and a pleasant, in that he takes pleasure in the conscious possession of that which is good absolutely, and in itself. And, exactly as the good man feels towards himself, so, too, does he feel towards his friend, regarding his friend as a second self. And from all this it follows that, exactly as for each man his own existence is a thing choiceworthy and good, so, too, for him, or similarly, the existence of his friend is such. Now, we have said that existence is choiceworthy, because in it is involved the consciousness of the possession of good, which consciousness involves and implies a pleasure of its own. And hence it follows that a man ought to have a sympathetic consciousness of the existence of his friend. And, to acquire this consciousness, friends must live together, or, in other words, each must share in the plans and speculations of the other. For it is this that we understand when we say of men that they live together, and not merely, as of cattle, that they herd in the same haunts. Thus, then, for the happy man, existence is a thing choiceworthy in itself, and independently of all results; being one of those things which, in the scheme of nature as a whole, are good in themselves, and have a pleasure of their own.

(155.) And, similarly, for him the existence of his friend is a good. And thus it follows that a friend is a choiceworthy thing. Now, whensoever any particular thing is choiceworthy for a man, then either he must have that thing, or else, in so far as he has it not, his happiness will be deficient. And thus it conclusively follows, that the happy man will stand in need of good and upright friends.

10. Does it, then, follow that a man cannot have too many friends? Or ought we rather to bear in mind what has so epigrammatically been said as to the relation of mutual hospitality between the inhabitants of different countries—

> Nor many guest-friends may I have, nor none;

and to hold that the most fitting rule for friendship is, neither to be entirely without friends, nor yet to allow the number of our friends to run to excess? Now, as regards that form of friendship which is based upon utility, the rule which we have just given would seem to be especially applicable. For, to make a fitting return to very many persons for the services which they have rendered, is a matter of great difficulty, and for which the ordinary course of life is hardly of sufficient length. And, where the number of our friends is greater than the necessities of our life actually require, then friendship becomes a labour, and a hindrance to noble action. And hence a man stands in no need of many friends of this kind. Similarly, in the case of that friendship which is based upon pleasure, exactly as a little sweetening sweetens the whole mass, so of such friends a few are all that is required. But, in the case of true friends and good, ought it to be our rule to have of such the greatest number possible, or ought there rather to be some limit to the number of our friends, exactly as there is some natural limit to the numbers of a State? For, neither do ten citizens make a State, nor yet ten times ten thousand. But, if it be asked what is, in such cases, the fitting number, the problem is not like a simple equation, which admits of but one solution, but rather like an indeterminate equation, which admits of any solution whatever within certain limits. And hence it follows that the fitting number of friends is a something definite, being, perhaps, the largest number with which it is possible for a man to live. For there is nothing so essential to friendship as that friends should live together; and it is self-evident that, with more than a certain number of persons, it is impossible for a man so to live as to give to each of them any appreciable amount of his time and company. Moreover, a man's friends must also be friends among themselves, or otherwise it will be impossible for them all to associate with one another. And, if their number be large, this will be no easy matter. It is, moreover, a hard task to sympathise in the joys and sorrows of many men, as if they were our own; and we shall probably find ourselves involved in the dilemma of having to sympathise with the joy of that man, and with the sorrow of this, at one and the same time. And so, perhaps, it is a safe rule not to strive to have as many friends as is absolutely (186.) possible, | but rather to be content with such a number that it becomes possible for us to pass our life in their society. And, indeed, it would seem that it is impossible for a man to feel a strong friendship for many friends at once, exactly as it is impossible to feel love for more than one. Love, indeed, may be defined as friendship pushed to its absolute limit, and so can only be felt for one. And, similarly, for friendship to be strong, it must only be felt for a few. To all this it would seem that witness is borne by facts. For it is but seldom that a brotherhood in arms has many members; and, wherever such a friendship has become famous in story, it has always been between two. As for those who are men of many friends, and who are upon intimate terms with all those whom they meet, it would seem that they are not really the friends of any one, except in so far as to move in the same society may be held to constitute friendship. Men of this kind are called over-polite. Not but that it is, of course, quite possible to show all the courtesies of society to any number of persons, and yet, at the same time, not to carry politeness to excess, but to maintain a proper self-respect. But that friendship which is based upon virtue, and in which we love our friend for his own sake, cannot possibly be felt for many. And so, if a man find but a few such friends, he must rest content.

11. It may also be asked, whether it is in prosperity that we most stand in need of friends, or in adversity. It is certain that, in each case alike, men seek for friends. For those who are in adversity stand in need of aid and assistance; and those, on the other hand, whose lot is prosperous, need some one with whom to pass their life, and upon whom to confer benefits; inasmuch as their desire is to make others

also happy. Now, when we are in adversity, then friends become necessary; and, consequently, in such a case we need friends who will be of service to us. But, in prosperity, the possession of friends becomes more noble. And hence the prosperous seek to make friends to themselves of good men, inasmuch as to do good to such, and to pass one's time with them, is the more choiceworthy. When we are in adversity, then the presence of friends is pleasant in itself, and independently of all results. For men feel their sorrow to be lightened when their friends sympathise with them in their distress. And this fact has suggested the further question, whether the assistance which they thus render is mechanical, as when one man aids another in carrying a burden, and so actually relieves him of a portion of the weight; or whether it is rather to be explained upon moral grounds, in that the presence of friends has a pleasure of its own, which, coupled with the consciousness of their sympathy in our sorrow, makes our grief easier to bear. Whether, however, either of these, or whether any other be the true explanation of the relief afforded in misfortune by the presence of friends, we need not now consider; it being sufficient for our present purpose to be assured that the result described does actually take place. But yet their presence is not an entirely unmixed solace. It is, indeed, true, on the one hand, that the very sight of a friend is pleasant, especially when one is in adversity, and that he acts as an ally in our struggle with our sorrows. For, if a friend have tact and

(187.) discernment, he will adopt such a | countenance, and such speech, as shall cheer his friend, knowing, as he does, what is his character, and what are the occasions of his joys and sorrows. But yet, on the other hand, it is a grievous thing for a man to perceive that his own misfortunes give sorrow to his friend. And to bring sorrow upon his friends is a thing which every man does his best to avoid. And hence a man who is of a manly nature will use all caution, lest he should trouble his friends with his own sorrows. Such a man cannot bear to see his friends distressed, unless, indeed, he be of more than ordinary insensibility; nor does he ever welcome demonstrative sympathy, inasmuch as useless lamentation is absolutely alien to his character. But women of the weaker kind, and men of character like to them, are delighted to find others to join in their lamentations; and, when they find such, hold them dear, as being true friends, and showing true sympathy with distress. But the clear rule in this, as in all other cases, is to mould our conduct upon the best model. When, on the other hand, we are in prosperity, then the presence of our friends makes time pass pleasantly, and fills us with the sweet thought that they rejoice with us in our good fortune. And hence it would seem that, when we are in prosperity, we cannot be too ready to summon our friends to share our good fortune—for to confer benefits upon others is a noble thing,—but that we ought to be slow to call upon them to share our misfortunes, inasmuch as we ought to do all that we can to avoid inflicting upon others any portion of our own ills. And hence has come the saying, "one head is enough for trouble." But the most fitting time of all for a man to summon his friends, is when it is in their power to do him a great service with but little trouble to themselves. And so, too, the most fitting time for a man to seek his friends is when they are in distress; and he should seek them with all zeal and willingness, and without waiting to be asked. For friendship shows itself in doing good to others, and especially to those who are in need,—and, above all, in doing good to those who have not claimed such assistance as their right; for this last is not only more noble for both, but also more pleasant. But, when a man's friends are in prosperity, then he ought readily to go to them, if he can in any way aid them in their good fortune— for even in prosperity friends can be of good service; but he should be slow to offer himself to share in their comforts—for to be over eager to receive a benefit is not noble. Not but that we ought to take heed lest, by rejecting favours, we gain a reputation for churlishness: for this not unfrequently happens. Thus, then, it is evident that, under all circumstances alike, the presence of friends is a choiceworthy thing.

12. To conclude; may not one say that, exactly as, for the lover, the most precious of all his pleasures is to look upon the object of his love, and, exactly as he holds the one sense of sight dearer than all the others, because it is by it most of all that Love exists, and in it that he has his birth;—so, too, for

friends, the most choiceworthy of all things is to pass their time together—since the essence of friendship (188.) is | community? Moreover, as a man feels towards himself, so, too, does he feel towards his friend; and, exactly as, in his own case, the consciousness of his own existence is a choiceworthy thing, so, too, is the consciousness of the existence of his friend. And it is when friends pass their lives together that this* consciousness is most vividly realised; and hence, with good reason, to pass their lives together is the object of their desire. And hence, too, in whatever it is that a man conceives existence to be centred, or whatever that be for the sake of which he holds life dear, in the pursuit of that will he wish, in common with his friends, to pass his life. And, for this reason, some drink together, others dice together, others engage together in athletic exercises, others in hunting, and others again in philosophy, passing, in each case, their time in that pursuit which of all things in life they love the best. For, since men desire to pass their lives in the company of their friends, they will do all that, and will share with their friends in all that in which they hold that such community of life most consists. And hence the friendship of the bad itself becomes bad; for, unstable as water, they share in what is evil, and become like unto one another, bad to bad. Whereas the friendship of the good is itself also good, and is intensified by intercourse. Indeed, it would seem that good friends grow in virtue by doing good acts, and by keeping a watch each upon

---

* For αὑτοῖς read αὑτῆς with Zell and Cardwell.

the ways of the other. For with the stamp of his own pleasures each man marks his friend; and this is the meaning of the saying—

> Live with the good, and thou shalt learn their ways.

Here, then, closes our account of friendship. It follows to treat thoroughly of the nature of pleasure.

X.

I. (189.) NEXT, perhaps, it follows to fully treat of pleasure; for it, most of all things, would seem to be part of the very nature of the human race: and hence, too, they train the young, guiding them by the twin rudders of pleasure and of pain. Moreover, the greatest step towards moral virtue would seem to be that we should take pleasure in what we ought, and should loathe what we ought. For pleasure and pain extend throughout the whole course of our life, and have an influence sufficiently critical to turn the scale, either for virtue and happiness, or for the contrary. For all men choose what gives them pleasure, and avoid what gives them pain. And, since the subject is of this nature, it would seem that it, least of all, ought to be passed over, especially since there are upon it many and conflicting views. For some assert that pleasure is the chief good; others, on the contrary, that it is absolutely and altogether bad; the former being, perhaps, convinced of the truth of their statement, while the latter hold that, for the purposes of life, it is best to make out that pleasure is a bad thing, even although it be not such; for that the majority have already quite sufficient inclination towards it, and are, in fact, the slaves of their pleasures; and that so we ought to try to lead them to the exactly contrary course, for that thus they will arrive at the true mean. But in this, perhaps, they are not altogether right. For, in all matters of human feeling and conduct, abstract argument is far less to be relied upon than are facts; and, when it contradicts the results of actual experience, falls into contempt, and involves, with itself, all such truth as it may contain. He who condemns pleasure as a whole, and who has been once observed to aim at pleasure, is held to incline towards it as being, as a whole, choiceworthy. For, in such matters, the many would seem to be incapable of drawing any accurate distinction. And so it would seem that true statements concerning such matters are not only most useful from the scientific point of view, but also from that of their practical bearing upon life. For they are observed to be concordant with facts, and hence they are believed: so that those who understand them are induced to frame their life in accordance (190.) with them. | And, now that we have said enough upon this point, we will turn to a discussion of the various statements that have been made respecting pleasure.

2. Now, Eudoxus conceived pleasure to be the chief good, because he saw that all beings alike, both rational and irrational, make it the aim of their action; and because he held that, in all cases, that which was deemed choiceworthy was good, and that which was deemed most choiceworthy was the highest good. And the fact that all beings were borne towards the same end, was proof that this end was, for all of them,

the best; for everything, said he, naturally discovers its own good, exactly as it also discovers its appropriate food; and that which is good for all things alike, and at which all things alike aim, cannot but be the chief good. His arguments gained strength rather from the excellence of his own character than from any intrinsic worth of their own; for he had, of all men, the highest reputation for temperance, and was, consequently, believed to take up this position, not because he was any friend of pleasure, but because he was convinced of the truth of his assertions. He also held that the argument afforded by the law of contradiction no less proved his point; for that pain, in itself, and independently of its consequences, was a thing which all beings alike did well to shun; and that, consequently, pleasure, its exact contrary, must, for all beings alike, be choiceworthy. And that that, moreover, must be the most choiceworthy of all things, which we do not ever choose from any other inducement than itself, or as a means to anything beyond itself. And that pleasure was confessedly of this nature; for that no one ever proposes to himself the superfluous question, from what motive it is that he feels such or such a pleasure; since all pleasure is choiceworthy in and by itself. Lastly, that pleasure, when added to any other good thing, made it better,—as to justice, for example, and to temperance; and that that by the addition of which a good was made any better, must itself be a good. But, then, this last argument only seems to prove that pleasure is a good of some sort, and not, in any way, that it is more a good than is any

other. For any good whatsoever, if another good be added to it, becomes more choiceworthy than it is if it be taken by itself. Nay, more, it is by much this same argument that Plato shows that it is impossible for pleasure to be the chief good. For, he argues, the life of pleasure is more preferable with the addition of wisdom than it is without it. And so, since the combination of the two is preferable to pleasure alone, and by itself, it follows that it is impossible for pleasure to be the chief good. For it is a criterion of the chief good, that it cannot possibly be made better by any addition. And hence, too, it is clear, not only that the chief good is not pleasure, but also that it is not anything else which, if any other absolute good be added to it, becomes thereby better. What good, then, is there which is both incapable of any addition, and also within our reach? For it is a good of this kind that is the object of our investigations. To resume: those who bring forward
(191.) instances to show that that | at which all beings aim need not on that account be good, would seem to argue to no purpose. For that in which all are agreed, that, we say, is true; and he who denies the sufficiency of such conviction, will hardly himself have better grounds of proof to offer. Had it been brute beasts alone that craved for pleasure, then the point would have deserved consideration. But, since rational beings as well desire it, how can the argument have any weight? And, perhaps, even to the lower animals nature has given a principle of good, higher than themselves, which, in each case, strives to

work out the good of its possessor. Neither does
their answer to the argument drawn from the laws
of contradiction seem satisfactory. For, say they,
it does not follow that, if all pain be evil, all pleasure
is therefore good. For it is possible that an evil may
be the contrary of another evil, and that both a good
and an evil may be the contraries of a something
which is neither. And in this they are not entirely
wrong, although the application of the principle to
the particular case in question is incorrect. For, if
both pleasure and pain were evil, then ought both
equally to have been avoided; if neither evil nor yet
good, then ought each to have been neither pursued
nor avoided,—or, at least, the one ought to have been
either pursued or avoided to exactly the same extent
as the other, and no further. But, as it is, men
clearly do avoid pain as an evil, and pursue pleasure
as a good. And it is, therefore, clear that they are
opposed to one another, as perfect and complete contradictories. Nor does it follow that, because pleasure is not a quality, it therefore is not a good. For
virtuous acts do not answer to the definition of a
quality, nor does even happiness itself. And they
say, moreover, that the good is definite, or absolutely
perfect,—but that pleasure is indefinite, because it
admits of variation in degree. Now, if they are led
to this conclusion because they observe that the
degree to which a man is affected by pleasure may
vary, then the argument which they apply to pleasure will equally disprove the goodness of justice,
and of all the other virtues; with reference to which

we distinctly say that the goodness of different men
is a matter of degree. For, to be just or brave, and
to do just or temperate acts, is a matter of degree.
But, if they mean that pleasure is in itself indefinite,
they most probably miss the right explanation; for
some pleasures are pure, while others have with
them a mixture of pain. And why should it not be
the case that pleasure should be like health, which is
definite in itself, and which yet admits of variation
in degree? For the acmé of healthy temperament
is not identical in all men, nor indeed always identical in the same individual,—but may be relaxed within
certain limits (that is to say, may within certain
limits vary in degree) and yet remain healthy. And
of pleasure, too, a similar rule may possibly hold
(192.) good. And they further say that the good | is com-
plete in itself, while processes of development or of
alternation are incomplete, and presuppose an end
beyond themselves. And they then attempt to show
that all pleasure is a process of development or of
alternation. But their arguments do not seem con-
clusive, nor does it even seem true that pleasure is a
process of development. For every such process must,
of its very nature, proceed either quickly or slowly.
And this quickness or slowness, if it be not absolute,
as it is in the development of the universe as a whole,
must at least be relative, as it is in the development
of its various parts. But of pleasure neither quickness nor slowness, whether absolute or relative, is
possibly predicable. One can, indeed, *become pleased*
quickly, exactly as one can become angry quickly;

but one cannot *be pleased* quickly,—not even as compared with another man,—although, as compared with another man, it is possible to walk quickly, and to grow quickly, and so forth. In a word, the transition into a state of pleasure may take place either quickly or slowly, but the actual feeling of pleasure, I mean the being pleased, cannot possibly be either quick or slow. And in what sense can pleasure possibly be a process of alternation? For it is held that the poles of such a process are not arbitrary, but that each pole is resolved back again into that out of which it was originally generated; and that pain is the process by which is destroyed that state or condition, in the production of which pleasure consists. And, more definitely, we are told that pain involves and consists in a defect in our natural condition, and that pleasure is the counter process of restoration. But all this is merely true of the bodily affections. If pleasure be, in truth, such a process of restoration, then that in which this process goes on ought to feel the pleasure, and pleasure ought therefore to be felt exclusively by the body—which does not, however, appear to be the case. Pleasure, therefore, is not in itself a process of restoration; although, while such a process is going on, a man may feel a pleasure, much as, while undergoing an amputation, he may feel a pain. Indeed, this opinion would seem to have arisen from too exclusive a consideration of those pleasures and pains which are involved in eating and drinking. For herein it really does seem that we are conscious of a bodily deficiency, and that we consequently commence by feeling a pain, and that we then feel a pleasure when that deficiency is supplied. But then this is by no means true of all the pleasures. The pleasures of learning, for instance, are not preceded by any pain; and, among the pleasures of sense, the same is true of the pleasures of smell, as it is also of many sounds, and sights, and memories, and hopes. What is there, then, of which these can possibly be the processes of production? For, in none of them is there involved any previous deficiency to be supplied. In answer to those who allege the disgraceful pleasures as a proof that all pleasures are bad, one may answer that such things do not really give any pleasure at all. For it does not follow that, because a thing is pleasant to those (193.) who are in bad health, | it is therefore to be held to be pleasant to any save these; exactly as that is not of necessity to be held healthy, or sweet, or bitter, which may seem such to the sick; nor is that to be held white which may look such to those who suffer from ophthalmia. And may not one also reply, that the pleasures in question are in themselves choiceworthy, although not such when viewed with reference to the source from which they are derived; much as wealth is choiceworthy, although not when it has been gained by treason,—and health, although not if it be viewed as the result of eating a something peculiarly nauseous? And may not one also say that pleasures differ from one another in kind? For the pleasures which are derived from noble sources are of one kind, and the pleasures which are derived from disgraceful sources

are of another; and one cannot feel the pleasure of
the just man, unless one be just; nor the pleasure
of the musician, unless one be a musician; and of all
other pleasures a similar rule holds good. Moreover,
the distinction which we draw between the friend and
the sycophant would seem clearly to show that pleasure and the good are not identical, or, at all events,
that pleasures differ in kind. For the object of the
intercourse of the friend is the good, while that of the
intercourse of the sycophant is pleasure; and, while
the latter meets with reproach, the former meets with
praise, since the objects of their intercourse differ.
Moreover, no one would choose to live through his
whole life with only a child's understanding, although
taking the keenest possible pleasure in childish objects;
or to purchase pleasure as the reward of some most
disgraceful act, even if assured that he would never
feel a moment's pain. Lastly, there are many things
about which we should busy ourselves with zeal, even
if they brought no pleasure with them; such as are,
for instance, sight, memory, knowledge, and the
possession of virtue. And, even although such things
are of necessity accompanied by a pleasure of their
own, yet this really makes no difference; for we should
none the less choose each one of them, even if no
pleasure whatever resulted from it. It would seem,
then, to be clear that neither is pleasure, as a whole,
identical with the good, nor is all pleasure choiceworthy; and, also, that there are certain pleasures that
are choiceworthy in and by themselves, and which
differ from all other pleasures in kind, or in their

source. And this may be held to be a sufficient account of the current opinions concerning pleasure and pain.

4. What is the genus, and what the essence of pleasure, will become more evident if we entirely recommence the subject. It would seem that the act of sight is, at any moment whatever of its continuance, absolutely perfect and complete in itself; for it stands in need of nothing beyond itself, by the subsequent addition of which it will be made perfect in its kind. And pleasure, too, would seem to be of a similar nature; for it is in itself a complete whole,—by which I mean, that we can fix upon no moment in the continuance of a (194) pleasure at which a longer | continuance will be necessary to make it perfect in its kind. And hence it is untrue that pleasure is a process of development. For every such process requires time in which to take place, and presupposes some end beyond itself at which it aims. The process, for instance, of building a temple can only properly be called complete when it has succeeded in producing that at which it aims, that is to say, the temple; and, consequently, can only become complete in the whole time which it takes to build that temple, or in the last indivisible moment of that time. But, in the various portions of that time as a whole, the various processes that take place are all incomplete in themselves, and differ in kind from the entire process as a whole, and from one another. For the process of fitting together the blocks is distinct in kind from that of the erection of the row of columns, and both these are distinct in kind from that of the building of the temple as a whole. Now, the process of building

the temple as a whole is (when once the temple has been built) complete; for there is nothing which is wanted to complete the carrying out of the plan. But the process of laying the stylobate, and that of adding the triglyph, are (even when each is finished) incomplete in themselves, since the result of each is only a part of the proposed plan as a whole. They, therefore, differ in kind from the entire process; and hence, also, it is that one cannot say of a process that it is perfect in kind at any moment of its continuance, but can only say so of it, with truth, when the whole time which it requires has actually elapsed. And of walking, and indeed of all other processes, the same rule holds good. Locomotion, for instance, may be defined as a process commencing in a place whence, and terminating in a place whither. And of locomotion there are several distinct kinds; as are flying, walking, leaping, and so forth. And not only is this true of locomotion as a whole, but, even of walking, the same rule is true. For the space between the whence and the whither is not identical in the stadium as a whole, and in a portion of the stadium, nor in one portion, and in another. Nor is it the same thing to cross this particular line as to cross that; for it is not a line in the abstract which we have to cross, but a line in a definite locality; and one line is in a different locality from another. We have elsewhere given an exact and abstract account of the nature of processes, from which it would seem that no process can properly be called complete at any moment of its continuance; but that the majority are incomplete in themselves, and that they also differ from one another in kind, since their determinants in each case are the whence and the whither. But pleasure is, at any moment of its continuance, perfect in kind. And hence it is clear that pleasure is altogether distinct from any kind of process, being a complete whole, and absolutely perfect in itself. And the same thing would seem to follow from the fact that we cannot go through any process, except it be in time; but that we can feel pleasure altogether irrespectively of time; for that only is an absolute whole which is complete in itself at the present indivisible moment. And from all this it is clear that it is incorrect to say that pleasure is, in any sense, a process of development, or of alternation. It is not all things indiscriminately that can be said to be the results of such a process, but only those things that are divisible into parts, and so are not absolute wholes. No process of alternate perfection and imperfection is involved in the act of sight, or in a mathematical point, or in the unit; nor are any of these things in any way concerned with any process (195.) of development, | or of alternation: nor yet is pleasure; for pleasure is, like them, an absolute whole. Now, all sense requires a sensible object upon which to act, and acts perfectly only when it is in good condition, and acting upon its best object: it would, indeed, seem to be essential to a perfect act, that it should be of this kind, and that these conditions should be fulfilled; nor need it matter whether we say that it is the sense which acts, or the organ in which it resides. And hence it follows, that the act will, in each case, be best when the sense is in the best possible condition, and is acting

upon its best object. And such an act will not only
be most perfect in itself, but will also give the highest
pleasure. For, in every act of sense a pleasure is
involved; as also in every act of reason, whether
discursive or contemplative;—and the most perfect
act will give the highest pleasure;—and the most perfect act is that in which the faculty is in good condition,
and is acting upon its best and highest object. But
the excellence of the pleasure, and the excellence
of the object, and the excellence of the faculty, do
not all three perfect the act in the same way; as
neither is health the cause of our being healthy in
the same sense as is the physician. That each of the
senses has a pleasure of its own is self-evident, for we
say of sights and of sounds that they are pleasant.
And it is also evident that such a pleasure is then
most especially involved, when the sense is at its
best, and is acting upon an object similarly excellent.
When, then, the sensible object and the sentient
subject are in this condition, a pleasure will always
continue to be the result, as long as neither the active
nor the passive factor be withdrawn. The pleasure,
then, in each case perfects the act, not as might some
definite quality continuously existing in its object,
but rather as an additional flush of perfection, such
as is the bloom of those who are in their prime. As
long, then, as the object of thought, or the object of
sense be such as it ought, and that which perceives,
or that which thinks be also such, the act, whether it
be of perception or of thought, will always involve a
pleasure. For, in those cases where there is a similar

passive and a similar active factor, between which a similar relation is involved, in the very nature of things a similar result must follow. How, then, is it that no one ever feels pleasure continuously? Is it not because one flags? For no human activity can possibly be continuous. And, consequently, a continuous pleasure is an impossibility; for all pleasure is the result of activity. For this same reason it is that some things gratify us as long as they are new to us, but, when the novelty of them has once worn off, no longer yield us the same pleasure as at first. For, at first the understanding is stimulated, and (196.) occupies itself upon its | object with its full energy, as does one who looks you full in the face; but afterwards the act is no longer such, but becomes negligent, like a careless glance, and, consequently, the pleasure fades. There is good reason to suppose that all men desire pleasure, since * all men crave for the consciousness of active life. Life consists in activity, and each man's activities show themselves in and with those things which he most loves; as, for instance, the activities of the musician manifest themselves with his hearing in the matter of music, and those of the philosopher with his understanding in the matter of speculation, and so forth in all other cases. Now, since pleasure perfects all our activities, it follows that it also perfects that activity of life as a whole, which is the object of every man's desire. With good reason, then, is it that men make pleasure

---

* "Ὄτι pro ὅτι Bekkerus solus;—nescio an vitio typothetæ."—*Michelet.*

their aim. For pleasure perfects for each one of us that active exercise of life which all hold choiceworthy. But, whether we pursue life for the sake of the pleasure which it yields, or pleasure for the sake of the life which it perfects, is a problem which may for the present be dismissed. It is evident that the two are, in actual fact, so closely connected as to be inseparable. For without activity there can be no pleasure, and without pleasure no activity can be per-

5. fect. And hence it would seem that pleasures differ in kind. For, things that are distinct from one another in kind, can only be perfected by things that are also distinct from one another in kind. This rule evidently holds good of all products of nature and of art, as of animals, for instance, and of trees, and of pictures, and of statues, and of houses, and of furniture; and, similarly, it is clear that activities which differ in kind can only be perfected by things which also differ in kind. Now, the activities of the intellect differ in kind from those of the senses, and those of the senses differ from one another in kind; and, consequently, the pleasures by which they are perfected will also differ from one another in kind. And we shall clearly be led to the same conclusion, if we reflect upon the close affinity which exists between the pleasure which perfects each particular act and the act itself. Each act is intensified by its appropriate pleasure; and it is those who take a pleasure in the act who, in each case, form the most accurate judgment, or produce the most perfect result. Those, for instance, who take pleasure in the solution of a

geometrical problem, make better geometricians than do other men, and perceive a mathematical truth with greater ease and quickness. And of those who take pleasure in singing, and of those who take pleasure in architecture, the same rule holds good;—it being, indeed, universally true that those who take pleasure in the performance of their peculiar function improve their aptitude for, and their skill in, its performance. It follows, therefore, that pleasure intensifies the act which it accompanies; and that which intensifies anything else cannot but have an affinity with it. But, (197.) where things | differ from one another in kind, then other things that are severally akin to them will also differ in kind. Our conclusion is yet further established by the fact, that every act is impeded by the pleasure of any other act whatever. Those, for instance, who are fond of the flute, are unable to give any attention to an argument, should they chance to overhear a flute-player; inasmuch as the pleasure which they take in flute-playing is greater than is that which they take in the act in which they are at the time engaged; and so the pleasure of flute-playing destroys the act of philosophic discussion. And, in all other cases where a man is occupied upon two objects at once, the same result follows. For the more pleasant of the two acts overpowers the other. As the difference between the two, in respect of the pleasure which they give, increases, the effect becomes yet more marked, and at last, indeed, becomes so great that the less pleasant of the two acts is altogether discontinued. And hence

it is, that, when we take a very great pleasure in any
one thing, we find ourselves entirely unable to do
anything else at the same time with it; and that,
whenever we do do two things at once, it is because
we take but little pleasure in either. Those, for
instance, who eat nuts and biscuits at the theatre, do
so with most assiduity when the acting is bad. And
thus, since its appropriate pleasure adds definiteness
to each act, and so makes it better, and more continuous, while an alien pleasure of any kind mars and
destroys it, it is clear that pleasures must differ very
widely from one another. Indeed, an alien pleasure
produces upon any act much the same effect as does
its special and appropriate pain. For it is by its own
special and appropriate pain that every act is destroyed.
If, for example, a man ceases to take pleasure in
writing, or in casting up accounts, and begins to feel
pain in doing so, he then ceases, as the case may be,
either to write or to cast up his accounts, inasmuch
as the act has become painful to him. In a word, its
own special pleasure produces upon each act a result
exactly contrary to that which is produced by its
special pain. (By "special," or "appropriate," are,
of course, to be understood those pleasures and pains
which not only accompany the act, but are directly
and essentially its effect.) Whereas, any alien pleasure produces, as we have said, exactly the same
result as does the special pain; for, like the special
pain, it destroys the act, although it does not destroy
it in the same way. Now, inasmuch as our acts differ
from one another, some of them being good, others

bad, some of them choiceworthy, others to be shunned, and yet others again indifferent,—it results that our pleasures will follow a similar rule, since each act has a special pleasure of its own. Thus, then, the pleasure which follows upon, and which is appropriate to a good act, will itself be good, while that which follows upon a disgraceful act will be bad; exactly as desire for a noble object is praiseworthy,
(198.) | while desire for a disgraceful object is culpable. Moreover, there is more affinity between the act and the pleasure which is bound up with it, than there is between the act and the impulse from which it results. Impulse is distinct from action in two ways : in time it is antecedent to it; in its nature it is less perfect and final. But the pleasure is in time coincident with the act, and in its own nature is so incapable of any distinction from it, as to render it open to question whether pleasure and action ought not to be identified. We must not, however, upon this account, identify pleasure with thought or with perception. For this we have no warrant. It is only because the two are, as a matter of fact, inseparable, that they have been held by some to be absolutely identical. Thus, then, exactly as our acts can be distinguished from one another, so too can our pleasures. Now, sight can be distinguished from touch by its purity, as also can hearing and smell from taste. And, similarly, the pleasures which are consequent upon our acts can be distinguished from one another;—the pleasures, that is to say, of the intellect can be distinguished from these, the pleasures of sense; and in each of these

two classes, again, the particular pleasures can be distinguished from one another. And, again, exactly as each living thing has its own peculiar vital functions, so, too, it has its own peculiar pleasure, which accompanies their manifestation. A consideration of particular instances will make this evident; for the pleasure of a horse is one, and that of a hound is another, and that of a man is yet another ; for, as says Heraclitus, "an ass will sooner a bottle of hay than all your gold ;" for asses take more pleasure in provender than in gold. Thus, then, where beings are distinct from one another in kind, their pleasures will also be distinct in kind. And, from this it ought to follow, that the various pleasures of the same being ought not to differ from one another. But yet, in the case of men at any rate, there is no small difference between the various pleasures. For the same thing will gratify some men, and will annoy others ; and will to some be grievous and hateful, and to others pleasant and dear. Of things sweet, for instance, this rule clearly holds good ; for that which seems sweet to him who is in a fever, will no more seem sweet to him who is in health, than will that which seems warm to him who has lost his strength, seem such to him who is in sound condition; and of many other things a similar rule holds good. And hence it follows that, in all such cases, the standard of reference must be that judgment at which he arrives whose condition, whether of mind or of body, is sound. If, then, this be true, as it is held to be,—if, that is to say, the standard in each case be the highest possible excellence or virtue, or, in other words, that judgment which the good man, as such, forms,—then it will follow that those alone will be pleasures which the good man holds to be such, and those things alone will be pleasant in which he takes delight. Nor need we wonder that those things which he scorns may yet seem to others to be pleasant; for many are the ways in which human nature can be ruined and marred. Such things, then, as these are not really pleasant, but only seem to be such to men who are of this kind, (199.) and in [this condition. And, hence it is clear that such pleasures as are confessedly disgraceful must not be allowed to be pleasures at all, except in the judgment of those whose nature is thus depraved. And so, among those pleasures that are held to be good, what or which are we to say is peculiarly the pleasure of man? Evidently man's acts must be our criterion, for it is upon his acts that his pleasures are consequent. Whether, then, human perfection and blessedness manifest itself in some one energy, or whether it manifest itself in more than one, those pleasures alone which perfect the acts in which it manifests itself, have any claim to the distinctive title of the pleasure of man; while all other pleasures, exactly as the acts upon which they follow, have to this title but a secondary and, indeed, almost fractional claim.

6. We have now treated of the various forms of virtue, and of the different kinds of friendship, and of pleasure; and it only remains that we should give a sketch of happiness, inasmuch as we make it the end and consummation of all things human. A recapitulation of our previous statements will serve to abbreviate our discussion. That happiness is something more than a mere permanent state or condition of the mind, we have already said; for, in that case, a man might possess it who passed his existence in a perpetual sleep, and whose life did not rise above that of plants; or he might possess it who suffered the heaviest possible misfortunes. Since, then, we cannot admit this supposition, and must, consequently, hold that happiness, as has been said before, essentially consists in some form of activity; and since some among our activities are said to be "necessary," inasmuch as they are choiceworthy for the sake of something beyond themselves, while others are absolutely good and choiceworthy for their own sakes; it evidently follows that happiness must be placed in the class of acts which are good in themselves, and not in the class of acts which are only good as leading to something else. For happiness stands in need of nothing to complete its perfection, but is in itself absolutely all-sufficient. Now, an act is choiceworthy in itself when, beyond the action itself, nothing is looked for from the doing of it. And to this definition it would seem that all virtuous acts correspond; for, to do what is noble and good is a thing which is choiceworthy in and by itself. And the same holds good of all those recreations from which pleasure is derived, and which cannot possibly be pursued for the sake of their results, inasmuch as the pursuit of them leads a man to neglect his person and his property, and so really does him more harm than good. It is to pursuits of this latter kind that the majority of those who are reputed happy betake themselves; and hence it is that those who have a pleasant adroitness in such amusements are held in high favour at the courts of tyrants; for they lay themselves out to yield pleasure to their lord after his (200.) heart's desire, and a tyrant needs courtiers | of this kind. Thus, then, these things are fancied to be constituents of happiness, because those who are in high power spend their leisure in them. But, it would seem that we must not argue from the example of such men. For it is virtue and reason from which good acts proceed, and it is not high power that constitutes virtue and reason. Nor does it follow that, because those who have never tasted pure pleasure, such as becomes a free man, betake themselves to the pleasures of the body, we are on that account to hold that these latter are the more choiceworthy. For, even children believe that those things which are held in honour by themselves are the noblest of all goods. It is, indeed, but reasonable to believe that, exactly as that which is held in honour by a child is one, and that which is held in honour by a man is another, so, too, that which is held in honour by the bad is one, and that which is held in honour by the good is another. We must remember, also, what has so often been said before, that that which is really precious and pleasant is that which approves itself as such to the good man. And from all this it follows, that to each man those acts will be most choiceworthy which follow from, and correspond with his character; and to the good man, consequently, acts of virtue. And, hence it follows, that happiness does not consist in mere amusement. For, it is inconceivable that amusement should be the end and consummation of everything, and that a man should endure a lifetime of labour and suffering, with nothing higher than amusement in view. And this would be the case, were happiness identical with mere amusement. For there is, indeed, nothing whatever upon earth which we do not choose for the sake of something else beyond itself, with the one exception of happiness—happiness being the one end of all things else. Now, that all earnestness and toil should tend to no higher end than mere amusement, is a view of life which is worse than childish, and fit only for a fool. But the saying of Anacharsis, "play makes us fit for work," would seem to be well spoken; for it would seem that amusement is a species of rest, and that men stand in need of rest, inasmuch as continuous exertion is impossible. And, hence, rest cannot be an end in itself, inasmuch as it is only sought with a view to subsequent action. Now, the life of happiness is a life of virtue, and is, consequently, an earnest life, consisting in something more than mere amusement. We are agreed that earnestness is better than is merriment and amusement; and that, the better be the faculty, and the better the man, the more earnest always, and the more upright will be the acts. And, the better be the man, the higher will be his acts, and, consequently, the happier. Of mere bodily pleasure there is no one but can take his fill, the slave equally with the best of men. But, that a slave has any portion in happiness, no one grants, any more than that he enjoys the life of a freeman and a citizen. It is not in pursuits of this kind that happiness consists, but, as (201.) has been said before, | in acts of virtue.

7. Since, then, happiness consists in an activity wherein virtue is consciously manifested, it follows, as a matter of course, that the virtue thus manifested will be the highest which we possess; or that, in other words, it will constitute the highest excellence of the noblest of our faculties. Whether, then, this be our reason, or whether it be a something else, which, in the course of nature, seems to rule in us, and to take the lead, and to occupy itself with the consideration of what is noble and divine, either as being a something absolutely divine in itself, or as being the most divine element in man; the activity in which this part of ourselves so manifests itself that the essential conditions of its own special excellence are fulfilled, will constitute finally perfect happiness. That this activity will consist in the contemplation of abstract truth, we have already said; and it would seem that our statement is consistent with what we said before, and also with the truth. For, in the first place, this activity will be the highest which is possible; inasmuch as reason is the highest of our faculties, and the objects upon which reason exercises itself are the highest of all objects of thought. And, in the second place, it is the most continuous; inasmuch as, of all our acts, the exercise of the pure reason can be the most continuously carried on. We are, moreover, agreed that in all happiness pleasure is an essential element; and,

of all those acts in which any human excellence whatsoever is manifested, philosophic speculation upon abstract truth is confessedly the most pleasant. Clear it certainly is that philosophy possesses pleasures of its own, wonderful for their purity and for their certainty; and it is but reasonable to suppose that, for those who are already possessed of the truth, the pursuit of speculation has greater pleasures than it has for those who are still inquirers. Fourthly, it is to the act of philosophic speculation that what is called "all-sufficiency" most especially belongs. As regards the bare necessaries of life, of these the philosopher and the just man, and all others, stand in equal need. But, after that life has been adequately equipped with all that is absolutely necessary, the just man still stands in further need of persons towards whom, and in conjunction with whom, he can act justly; and of the temperate man, and of the brave man, and indeed of all those in whom any moral virtue manifests itself, a similar rule holds good. Whereas the philosopher can exercise himself in speculation, even although absolutely secluded from the society of others; and, indeed, the wiser he is the more easy for him will this be. For, although, perhaps, he may be the better for having fellow-workers in his speculations, yet none the less he, of all men, is absolutely in himself the most all-sufficient. Fifthly, it would seem that, of all our acts, philosophic speculation is the only one which is loved absolutely for itself, and quite independently of its results. For the contemplation of abstract truth yields no result whatever beyond and besides itself; whereas every moral action yields a something, either more or less, over and above the mere act. Then, again, it would seem that happiness is the very antithesis of a busy life, in that it is compatible with perfect leisure. And it is with such (202.) | leisure in view that a busy life is always led, exactly as war is only waged for the sake of ultimate peace. Now, the virtues of practical life manifest themselves in the field of politics or of war, and the acts which they involve are incompatible with perfect leisure. Of war, indeed, this holds absolutely true; for no one ever chooses war for its own sake, or for its own sake prepares a war. A man would, indeed, seem to have an absolute thirst for blood, if he were to make enemies of his friends, that battle and bloodshed might ensue. Equally incompatible with leisure are the pursuits of the politician, their object being something more than the mere pleasure of an active political life, regarded as an end in itself. The ultimate object of the politician is to secure for himself and for his fellow-citizens power and honour, or, in a word, happiness; and, that happiness is not to be identified with an active political life, we have shown by the fact, that in our search for each we invariably regard it as a something distinct from the other. Thus, then, of all virtuous action, that which has political life or war for its field is foremost in beauty and in dignity, but still is none the less incompatible with perfect leisure, in that it has a further end beyond itself at which it aims, and is not choiceworthy for its own sake. Whereas the activity of the intellect, manifesting itself in pure speculation, is in itself preeminently earnest and good, and has no further end beyond itself at which to aim. It has, moreover, a pleasure of its own, and that, too, a pleasure by which it is itself intensified. And, in a word, in this activity alone is to be found absolute all-sufficiency, and, along with it, the possibility of perfect leisure, and an entire absence of care, in so far as is compatible with the conditions of human life, and, indeed, each and all of the essentials of perfect blessedness. And hence it follows, that it is in this activity that perfectly final human happiness consists, if only the one condition be fulfilled, of a sufficient length of life; for, in happiness there must be nothing insufficient. Moreover, a life thus passed will be higher than human; for it will not be in so far as he is human that a man will lead it, but in so far as he has in him a divine element. And, by as much as this is higher than is that compound part of our organisation into which material factors enter, by so much is that activity in which it is manifested higher than is that of any other virtue whatsoever. Since, in other words, the reason is a divine thing if contrasted with human nature as a whole, the life of reason will also be divine, as contrasted with the ordinary and human life. Nor ought we to follow the advice of the old saw, "let not man meddle with great matters which are too high for him," but rather, as far as in us lies, to act as if immortality were our share, by seeking in (203.) everything that we | do to lead a life in conformity with that element in ourselves which is highest and best. For, although physically it may be insignificant, it is none the less far more powerful and far more precious than is any other part of our nature. In this part, moreover, it is that the true self of each one of us would seem to have its place, since a man's self is identical with that which is supreme in him, and most precious. Strange, indeed, would it be, were a man to choose, not the life which is peculiarly his own, but the life of some other kind of being. And here, again, we may apply what we have said before. For that is, for each being, best and most pleasant, in which its nature finds for itself a fit expression. Sweetest, then, and best of all things for man is the life of reason; since reason it is that constitutes the essence of humanity. And thus the happiest of all lives is the life philosophic.

8. Happy in but a secondary sense is that life in which all other virtue finds its manifestation; inasmuch as its activities are, at the best, but human. For justice, and bravery, and all other virtue, finds its field in the mutual relations of man with man,—in contract, that is to say, and in matters of business, and in the various other actions which life involves, and also in the regulation of the emotions,—in each and all of which our conduct has to be carefully modified, as circumstances demand. Now, all such matters as these are in their very nature clearly human. In some cases, indeed, we are concerned with a material result of our physical organisation; and it would seem that moral virtue is very closely akin to the purely physical emotions. Now, between prudence and moral virtue

there is a reciprocal connection; for the principles
which prudence involves must be in concordance with
moral virtue, and the standard of moral virtue must be
determined by prudence. The moral virtues, inasmuch
as between them and the physical emotions there is
an inseparable connection, find their field in the
composite part of our nature; and any excellence of
which this part may be capable never rises above a
human standard. And hence it follows, that the life
in which such virtue finds its expression, and the
happiness which is its result, will not transcend the
ordinary limits of humanity. But that happiness
which results from the exercise of the reason, stands
absolutely isolated from all human matters. We
make this statement provisionally, inasmuch as an exact
definition of our conception would entail greater
labour than is practically necessary for our present
purpose. Of all external equipment such happiness
stands but little in need, or certainly less than does
that happiness which is the result of moral virtue. As
for the absolute necessaries of life, we may grant that
these are, in either case, equally indispensable, notwithstanding
that the statesman does, as a matter of fact,
busy himself about his bodily welfare, and about all
such other matters, more than does the philosopher.
Herein, however, the difference will be but unimportant.
But, when we come to contrast the distinctive
activities of moral with those of intellectual virtue,
we shall find between them a wide difference. For, if
the liberal man is to do liberal acts, he will stand in
(304.) need of money; | and the just man will stand in the

same need, if he is to return the full value of that which he has received. For, our intentions, however good, are known to ourselves alone, and even the unjust make a pretence of wishing to act fairly. And, similarly, the brave man requires a crisis which only physical force can settle, if he is to display his bravery in action in its full beauty. And the temperate man, too, requires opportunity for licence. For how can temperance, or, indeed, any other moral virtue, show itself, unless fitting opportunity be given? It has, indeed, been disputed whether it is in our purpose, or whether it is rather in our actions, that virtue most distinctively manifests itself; for, as a matter of fact, it shows itself in each. It is, of course, self-evident that perfect virtue implies both a perfect purpose, and also perfect acts. Now, if our acts are to be perfect, many purely external conditions must be fulfilled; and these will be all the more numerous in proportion as our acts are grander and fairer. Whereas, not only does the philosopher stand in no need of any such conditions for the perfect exercise of speculation, but rather, if anything, finds all external circumstances a hindrance to thought. In so far, however, as he is a man, and is consequently obliged to live in the society of his fellows, acts of moral virtue are his only choice. And, consequently, for his life as man, these external conditions of which we have spoken are essential. There is, moreover, yet a further proof that the perfection of happiness consists in the exercise of philosophic thought. Our conception of the Gods is, that they lead a blessed and a happy life; and,

this being so, what sort of moral action is it fitting to
ascribe to them? Are their acts those of justice?
Surely it is absurd to conceive the Gods as making
bargains, or restoring deposits, or engaging in any
other form of contract. Are their acts, then, those of
bravery, and do they withstand that which is terrible,
and engage in great risks, because it is noble to do so?
Or, do they delight in liberal acts? And, if so, whom
have they to whom to give? And how absurd it is
to conceive a currency, or any similar medium of exchange, as in use among them. And, as for temperance, what meaning can possibly be attached to the
conception of divine temperance? The grossness of
such praise is evident, when we remember that a God
cannot have evil passions. In short, were the enu-
meration to be completed, it would be evident that
every form of moral virtue is, for the Gods, a something contemptible and insignificant. But yet, we all
hold that they enjoy a life of some sort, and, consequently, that they have activities of their own.
For it cannot be supposed that the divine existence
consists, like that of Endymion, in a perpetual sleep.
And, where moral action, and with it, *a fortiori*,
artistic production is impossible, the only possible
conception of life is that it should consist in philosophic thought. And, hence it follows, that the divine
life, in all its exceeding blessedness, will consist in the
exercise of philosophic thought. And, of all human
activities whatsoever, that will be the happiest which
(205.) is | most akin to the divine. In illustration of this,
it may be observed that no other living thing, save

man alone, has any share in happiness such as this; inasmuch as there is no living thing, save man, to whom all participation in any activity of this kind has not been absolutely denied. And so, for the Gods, their whole life is blessed: for man, his life is blessed only in so far as it approximates to the perpetual activity of the divine thought. But, of brute beasts, no one is happy, since there is no one which in any way participates in philosophic thought. Thus, then, as far as philosophic thought enters into our life, so far also does happiness, and the more we think the happier we shall be,—and that, not because thinking indirectly leads to happiness, but rather because the two are essentially convertible. Indeed, the act of thought is, like happiness, a something that, in itself, and of its own nature, calls for honour. And, from all this it follows, that happiness will consist in some form of philosophic thought.

But nevertheless, in so far as he is man, the happy man will need external prosperity. Human nature is not in itself sufficient for the continuous exercise of philosophic speculation, unless, in addition, we enjoy perfect bodily health, and have sufficient means for actual maintenance, and, indeed, for all the other requisites of our material welfare. And yet, we must not hold, that,—because it is impossible to be blessed without a certain amount of external prosperity,—therefore he who is to be happy will stand in need of much good fortune, and of great. It is not superfluity such as this that constitutes all-sufficiency, nor is such superfluity necessary for moral action. One need not be "lord of both land and sea," to achieve noble deeds,—nay, more, for virtuous action, but moderate good fortune is all that is required. And, to this plain witness is borne by facts; for it would seem that, for private persons, just and fair dealing is fully as easy a task as it is for rulers, if not perhaps even an easier. Such moderate good fortune is, then, all that is required; inasmuch as his life will be happy whose acts are those of virtue. Nor was the definition of happiness which Solon gave inapt, when he said that the happy man was "he whose equipment of external goods was moderate, and whose actions were"—so, at least, he held—"the noblest possible, and whose life had been temperately ordered:" for those whose possessions are moderate can, no less than others, act as is right. It would seem, moreover, that the conception which Anaxagoras formed of the happy man did not imply the possession of wealth, or of great political power. For he said that he should not wonder were the many to regard his conception of happiness as fantastic and untenable, inasmuch as they are entirely led by external circumstances, which are, indeed, the only things that attract their notice. And, hence we can see that, with our own definition of happiness, (206.) the | opinions of the wise agree. Such confirmation has, of course, a weight of its own. But still, in all questions that have any practical import, the test of truth is to be found in facts, or, in other words, in the lives of men,—the appeal to which is ultimate and final. And so we must consider all that we have said, testing it by facts, and by the actual practice of human life,—with which, if our speculations agree, they may be accepted as true;—if they disagree, they must be held to be mere empty theories. Lastly, he who exercises his reason, and who tends it with all care, and who is of sound mind and healthy judgment,—he would seem of all men to be dearest to the Gods. For, if the Gods in any way concern themselves with human affairs, as is, indeed, held to be the case, it is but reasonable to suppose that they should take pleasure in that which is of all things the highest and the most akin to the divine nature,— that is to say, the reason,—and that, to those who give all their love to this, and who hold it in the highest honour, they should make some return of kindness; on the ground that such men bestow their care upon that which they themselves hold dear, and that they act rightly herein, and nobly. Now, that it is of the philosopher that all this most especially holds true, is almost self-evident. And, therefore, the philosopher is, of all men, the dearest to the Gods. And, hence it is but reasonable to hold that he is, of all men, the happiest. So that, even from this point of view, the philosopher has, of all men, the best claim to be considered happy.

9. Thus, then, we have given an adequate sketch of happiness, and of the various virtues, and of friendship, and of pleasure. But yet, we must not, on this account, hold that our original purpose is fulfilled; but rather that, as we have said all along, the real end of all speculation upon human action is not so much that we should have a theoretic acquaintance with,

and knowledge of moral rules, as that we should
actually carry them into effect. It is not enough, in
other words, that we should be students of moral philosophy, and should know in what it is that virtue really
consists; but we must, further, endeavour to acquire for
ourselves a habit of virtue, either by the practice of
virtuous acts, or else by use of other means—if such
there be—by which to become virtuous. Now, if
mere moral precepts were, in themselves, sufficient to
make men good, then "many," as Theognis says,
"and great would their guerdons justly have been,"
and our only task would be to provide them in sufficient store. But, as a matter of fact, it is evident
that such maxims have indeed sufficient strength to
encourage and stimulate to the practice of virtue such
among the young as are already liberally-minded; and
that, if a man's nature be from the first well-bred and
full of a true love for honour, they can render it
amenable to the influence of virtue. But, for most
men, mere precept is powerless to dispose them to
noble conduct. For their nature is such, that they are
not ruled by a proper sense of shame, but only by
(107.) fear, and do not abstain from vice because of the disgrace which attaches to it, but because of the punish-
ments which its practice involves. For their life is
ruled by the passion of the moment, and their
practice is to pursue their own peculiar pleasures,
and the means thereunto, and to avoid those pains
that are the contraries thereof; while, of what
is truly noble, and really pleasant, they have no
thought, nor have they ever tasted its sweetness.

And, what precepts can possibly reharmonise the discord of such a life as this? If not absolutely impossible, it is certainly more than difficult, for any mere arguments to efface old and deeply ingrained stains of character. Nay, we ought, perhaps, to be well content if, even when possessed of all the means which are ordinarily held to lead to an upright life, some share of virtue may be our lot. Now, about the formation of virtue, there are three distinct opinions. For some hold that it comes by nature; others, that it is the result of habituation and practice; and others, again, that it can be taught, in the same way as can any purely intellectual matter. Now, that which comes by nature is clearly not in our own power, but rather comes by some divine dispensation, as a free gift to those who are fortunate in the highest sense of the word. And, on the other hand, it would seem as if mere precept and instruction were not of equal efficacy in all cases alike, but only in those where the soul of the listener has been so trained by habituation in the practice of good acts, as to take pleasure in what is noble, and to loathe what is wrong,—exactly as the earth must be broken up before it can give nourishment to the seed. For he whose life is ruled by the passion of the moment, would neither listen to precepts exhorting him to abstain from vice, nor, if he listened, would he understand. And, when a man's state is such as this, how can any arguments work a change in him? It would, indeed, seem as if passion were deaf to precept, and yielded to nothing but to force alone. Thus, then, we can see that moral teaching presupposes a character in the pupil already so far akin to virtue as to love what is noble, and to resent that which brings disgrace. Now, for a man to meet with a right guidance towards virtue from his youth up, is no easy matter, unless his education be guided by laws which have this same virtue for their type. For, to lead a life of temperance and of endurance is for most men no pleasant task, and least of all is it so for the young. And, hence we can see, that the mode of nurture for the young, and the pursuits which they are to practice, ought to be regulated by law; for nothing will ever be grievous which custom has made familiar. Nor is it, perhaps, sufficient that, when young, we should meet with fit nurture and right care. For, when we have reached man's estate, we must still practise the lessons of our childhood, and accustom ourselves to the same pursuits; and we shall, consequently, still need laws to regulate these matters, and, indeed, to prescribe the entire course of our life as a whole. For the nature of most men is such that they obey restraint rather than reason, and do not so much love honour as stand in fear of punishment. And hence it is that some have (208.) held it to be the duty of the legislator to exhort men to the practice of virtue, and to preach to them the pursuit of what is noble for its own sake. For, it is said, those who have been previously trained in right and good habits will then be obedient to such instruction. But that, when men are stiff-necked and of evil nature, then the legislator must lay upon them pains and penalties; and, if there be anyone past all hope of redemption, must put away such an

one from out of the State. For he who is of upright
nature, and whose life is ruled by the standard of
what is noble, will be obedient to the wisdom of
his teachers; but the wicked, who is ever craving for
pleasure, must suffer punishment and pain, exactly
as we hold in a beast of burden which has no understanding. And hence, too, it is said that punishment ought to consist of those particular forms of
pain that are the contraries of the pleasures which
the wicked love. It would seem, then, that, as has
been already said, he who is to be a good man must
first receive proper nurture, and be trained in good
habits; and must then, in accordance with this previous training, lead a life devoted to the practice of
virtue, and must not, either against his will, or with
his will, ever do any disgraceful act: and that all this
is only possible for those whose life is ordered by
some rational system, and organised in accordance
with a perfect moral code, enforced by a sanction of
sufficient strength. But, to secure this, the paren-
tal rule has not sufficient strength, and power of compulsion,—nor, indeed, is the authority of any one
man whatever sufficient for such a purpose, unless
he be an absolute monarch, or possess some such
irresistible power. Whereas, the commands of law
carry with them a compulsory sanction of their own,
being, as it were, the dictates in which abstract prudence and reason are embodied. And, moreover, where
our fellow-man thwarts our impulses, we none the less
conceive a hatred for him, even although he do so with
right and justice upon his side; whereas, when the law

enjoins what is right, it addresses itself to us in abstract commands, which consequently incur no odium. Lacedæmon, however, and one or two other States, are the only instances in which the legislator appears to have concerned himself about the nurture of the young, and the mode of life of the citizens. For, in far the greatest number of States at present existing, all these matters have been overlooked, and each man lives as is right in his own eyes, exercising over "children and spouse" a primitive and "patriarchal sway," like the one-eyed giant in Homer. Now, of course, by far the best method of education is that there should be a public system of training, conducted in accordance with moral principles, and that we should be able to carry it into full effect. But, inasmuch as education is neglected by the State, it becomes the duty of the individual to aid his own children and friends in the pursuit of virtue, or, at least, to endeavour to do so with the strongest purpose. And it would seem, from what we have said, that the easiest mode for a man to effect this result is that he should make himself master of the general theory of legislation. For (209.) every system of State education is controlled | by a code of laws, and, where the education in question is good, the code is approximately perfect. Whether such a code be written or unwritten, and whether it be adapted to the training of a single individual or of many, would seem to be indifferent; as is also the case in music, and in gymnastics, and, indeed, in all the other practical branches of education. Thus then, exactly as in a State law and custom are supreme,

similarly in the family we find paternal precept and
the force of habit: and these are rendered all the more
efficacious by the claims of relationship and of gratitude for past services, the minds of children being from
the very first naturally affectionate and submissive.
There is, moreover, a difference between private and
public education, which may be illustrated by the
analogy of the practice of medicine. As a general
rule, a fever must be treated by repose and low diet,
but still to this rule there may none the less be individual exceptions. And, similarly, a professor of
boxing does not teach all his pupils to fight in
one and the same style. Thus, then, it would
seem that, to secure individual perfection, private
attention is necessary; for, by it, the individual
pupil will find his peculiar necessities met with
greater certainty. But yet, he who is to be successful in his treatment of individual cases,—whether
he be a physician, or whether a trainer, or whatever
it be that he professes,—must none the less have a
thorough acquaintance with those general principles,
the formula for which is, "in all cases whatsoever,"
or, more definitely, "in all cases whatsoever of such,
or of such a nature." For the ordinary conception
of science is, that it is concerned with general laws,
and the ordinary conception herein is also the correct.
Not but that a man may, perhaps, occasionally be
successful in his treatment of a particular case,
even although he be absolutely ignorant of scientific
rules, provided that he have an accurate, although
empiric knowledge of what will be the effect of each

of his specifics; exactly as we often see persons who can treat their own ailments with the most perfect success, although absolutely unable to prescribe for others. But, in spite of all this, he who really wishes to be a master of his own especial craft, and to grasp it in its entirety, must work his way to the highest general conceptions, and, in so far as they admit of determinate knowledge, must make himself master of them. For it is with general conceptions, as we have already said, that science is concerned. If, then, we are to hold that good laws make good men, it will follow that he who desires to improve others, whether many or few, by his own personal supervision, must do his best to make himself a master of the general theory of legislation. For, to take the first person who may offer himself, or be offered by others, as a pupil, and to mould him to virtue, is a task by no means in the power of the first comer, but rather of him alone who has perfect knowledge;—as holds good, also, in the case of medicine, and, indeed, of everything (110.) | else which requires for its successful performance attention and prudence. And, from this it follows, that our next inquiry must be, from whom can the theory of legislation be learnt, and in what manner. And, to this the right answer would seem to be, that we must study it exactly as we study anything else—or, in other words, that we must learn it from politicians. To teach it ought certainly to be their task, if we were right when we said that the theory of legislation was one of the four subdivisions of political science. But then, we must remember that there is a clear difference between political science and all other sciences and arts whatsoever. For, in all the other sciences, as in medicine, for instance, and in painting, we find that the same persons both teach the general theory of the science, and also practise it as a profession. But, in the case of political science, although the Sophists profess to teach it in theory, yet no one of them is actually engaged in its practice, politics, as a profession, being in the hands of statesmen. And it would seem that statesmen are not guided in their practice by any knowledge of scientific principles, but rather that they have some special aptitude for the subject, combined with a knowledge of certain empiric rules. We certainly never find a statesman writing a treatise upon political philosophy, or delivering lectures upon his special subject, although it would seem that either of these were a nobler task than to compose harangues by which to convince a jury, or to persuade a public meeting. Nor is there any instance on record of a statesman having, by his instruction, made a statesman of his own son, or of any of his friends. And yet it is but reasonable to suppose that they would have done so, had it been in their power; for there is no nobler legacy which they could have bequeathed to their State, nor is there any heirloom which they would have preferred to the possession of political power, either for themselves, or for those whom they held most dear. And yet it must none the less be admitted that politics has in it a large empirical element. Were not this the case, familiarity

with office would not make men statesmen. And
hence it would seem that those who desire a thorough
knowledge of political philosophy need some acquaintance with the actual practice of States. As for
those among the Sophists who profess political philosophy, the last thing that one would say of them
would be that they teach that which they profess.
As a matter of fact, they have not the least knowledge, either as to what the science is, or with what
it is concerned. Else they would never have iden-
tified it with rhetoric, or have degraded it by
subordinating it to rhetoric; nor would they have
held that legislation is an easy task, if one first
make a collection of the most famous laws; for that,
out of such a collection, one can, of course, select
the best;—as if such a selection did not imply
considerable power of appreciation, and as if a
correct judgment in such matters were not, as is
a correct judgment in music, the most difficult
of tasks. For, in each and all of the arts, it is those
alone who have adequate experience, who can form a
correct judgment upon the special merits of any particular piece of work, or who can properly understand
by what means and how it is produced, and what com-
(211.) binations of details are | harmonious, and so allowable.
Whereas, those who are devoid of such experience
must rest content, if they have sufficient power of
appreciation to keep them from overlooking the merits,
or, as the case may be, the demerits of the work as a
whole. All this one can see clearly in the case of
painting. Now, laws stand in the same relation to

political science, as do the products of art to art itself. How, then, is it possible, by the mere inspection of various laws, for a man to acquire a competent knowledge of the theory of legislation, or a power of discerning which laws are the best? No man ever yet became a competent physician by the study of medical treatises. And yet, those who write upon medicine do not confine themselves to giving a list of the drugs employed, but, in addition, make some attempt to classify the various diseases, and to assign to each its specific remedy, and to give rules by which it may be treated with success. And all this is, of course, very useful to those who already possess some knowledge of medicine, but is absolutely useless for those who have no such knowledge. And hence it would seem that, for those who can come to an opinion of their own, and who can judge what has been well ruled, and what has not, and what is consistent, and what is inconsistent, it is a very useful thing to study such collections of laws and of constitutions; but that, if a man apply himself to such a study with his mind unprepared by any previous training, it will be impossible for him to form a correct judgment upon that which he reads, unless it be by haphazard,—the most that he can hope to acquire being a certain increased power of appreciation.

Since, then, the subject of legislation is one which previous writers have omitted to sufficiently investigate, it were best, perhaps, that we should enter upon the consideration of it ourselves, and that, along with it, we should discuss the general theory of government; and so, as far as in us lies, complete that branch of philosophy the object of which is man. And, consequently, we will first attempt to examine in detail all such particular statements of our predecessors as may commend themselves. And we will then proceed to frame a collection of constitutions, and to derive therefrom certain general rules as to what are the causes by which a State is preserved, and what are the causes by which it is destroyed; and, further, to determine what modification must be made in these general rules, so that they may be applicable to each particular form of constitution. And we will then, further, proceed to consider for what reasons it is that some governments are successful, and others are not. For, after such an investigation, we shall be in a better position to determine, not only what is the absolutely best form of government, but also how each particular form of government must be ordered, and of what laws and of what customs it must make use. Here, then, we abandon Ethics, and commence the consideration of Politics.

www.ingramcontent.com/pod-product-compliance
Lightning Source LLC
Chambersburg PA
CBHW022333230426
43664CB00040B/417